Transforming Communications – Studies in Cross-Media Research

Series Editors
Uwe Hasebrink
Hans Bredow Institute for Media Research
University of Hamburg
Hamburg, Germany

Andreas Hepp
ZeMKI
University of Bremen
Bremen, Germany

We live in times that are characterised by a multiplicity of media: Traditional media like television, radio and newspapers remain important, but have all undergone fundamental change in the wake of digitalization.

New media have been emerging with an increasing speed: Internet platforms, mobile media and the many different software-based communication media we are recently confronted with as 'apps'. This process is experiencing yet another boost from the ongoing and increasingly fast sequence of technological media innovations. In our modern social world, communication processes take place across a variety of media. As a consequence, we can no longer explain the influences of media by focusing on any one single medium, its content and possible effects. In order to explain how media changes are related to transformations in culture and society we have to take into account the cross-media character of communications.

In view of this, the book series 'Transforming Communications' is dedicated to cross-media communication research. It aims to support all kinds of research that are interested in processes of communication taking place across different kinds of media and that subsequently make media's transformative potential accessible. With this profile, the series addresses a wide range of different areas of study: media production, representation and appropriation as well as media technologies and their use, all from a current as well as a a historical perspective. The series 'Transforming Communications' lends itself to different kinds of publication within a wide range of theoretical and methodological backgrounds. The idea is to stimulate academic engagement in cross-media issues by supporting the publication of rigorous scholarly work, text books, and thematically-focused volumes, whether theoretically or empirically oriented.

Editorial Board
Nick Couldry, LSE, UK
Kim Christian Schrøder, University of Roskilde, Denmark
Maren Hartmann, University of Arts Berlin, Germany
Knut Lundby, University of Oslo, Norway
Klaus Bruhn Jensen, University of Copenhagen, Denmark
Peter Lunt, University of Leicester, United Kingdom
Mirca Madianou, Goldsmiths College, University of London, United Kingdom
Silvio Waisbord, George Washington University, Washington, DC, USA

More information about this series at
http://www.palgrave.com/gp/series/15351

Ingrid Paus-Hasebrink · Jasmin Kulterer ·
Philip Sinner

Social Inequality, Childhood and the Media

A Longitudinal Study of the Mediatization of Socialisation

Ingrid Paus-Hasebrink
University of Salzburg
Salzburg, Austria

Jasmin Kulterer
University of Klagenfurt
Klagenfurt, Austria

Philip Sinner
University of Salzburg
Salzburg, Austria

Transforming Communications – Studies in Cross-Media Research
ISBN 978-3-030-02652-3   ISBN 978-3-030-02653-0   (eBook)
https://doi.org/10.1007/978-3-030-02653-0

Library of Congress Control Number: 2018962859

© The Editor(s) (if applicable) and The Author(s) 2019. This book is an open access publication.

Open Access This book is licensed under the terms of the Creative Commons Attribution 4.0 International License (http://creativecommons.org/licenses/by/4.0/), which permits use, sharing, adaptation, distribution and reproduction in any medium or format, as long as you give appropriate credit to the original author(s) and the source, provide a link to the Creative Commons licence and indicate if changes were made.

The images or other third party material in this book are included in the book's Creative Commons licence, unless indicated otherwise in a credit line to the material. If material is not included in the book's Creative Commons licence and your intended use is not permitted by statutory regulation or exceeds the permitted use, you will need to obtain permission directly from the copyright holder.

The use of general descriptive names, registered names, trademarks, service marks, etc. in this publication does not imply, even in the absence of a specific statement, that such names are exempt from the relevant protective laws and regulations and therefore free for general use.
The publisher, the authors, and the editors are safe to assume that the advice and information in this book are believed to be true and accurate at the date of publication. Neither the publisher nor the authors or the editors give a warranty, express or implied, with respect to the material contained herein or for any errors or omissions that may have been made. The publisher remains neutral with regard to jurisdictional claims in published maps and institutional affiliations.

Cover design by Aikihiro Nakayama

This Palgrave Macmillan imprint is published by the registered company Springer Nature Switzerland AG
The registered company address is: Gewerbestrasse 11, 6330 Cham, Switzerland

Dedicated To Our Families.

Preface

This book, *Social Inequality, Childhood and the Media: A Longitudinal Study of the Mediatization of Socialisation*, is based on an investigation of the role of media within the socialisation of socially disadvantaged children and their families in Austria. It was initiated by Ingrid Paus-Hasebrink in 2005 and subsequently extended to cover adolescents. Our study, therefore, aligns with three German books (Paus-Hasebrink & Bichler, 2008; Paus-Hasebrink & Kulterer, 2014; Paus-Hasebrink (Ed.), 2017) and many articles in journals and chapters in edited volumes. It provides insight into over twelve years of research in a challenging field and tackles issues in developing theory and those of methodology. In doing so, we pay special attention to the last six years, when our children passed through their late childhood or adolescence, respectively.

Such a long-term project may be considered something akin to a *gold standard* in order to research not only in the short-term but also cater for development. The project was underpinned by the firm belief that socially disadvantaged people, and children in particular, deserve the support of the whole society, of which academia is no less a part. Therefore, the book follows the premise behind Norbert Elias' idea of research, namely that it is obligated to serve humanity (Elias, 1987); this means its goal is both academic and social. On the one hand, it provides evidence-based research on the role media plays at various stages in the lives of the children in our panel. On the other, it advocates developing concepts to enable different stakeholders to provide individualised support for children and their families. This book intends to draw attention to, and raise awareness of, the situation of socially disadvantaged children, their needs and rights.

However, we have to emphasise that it would have been impossible to realise such a long-term project alone without support from a wide range of people. We, therefore, wish to thank all those who have supported us. Firstly, we want to thank all 20 (later on 18) families who invited us to their homes over and over again, although they were simultaneously coping with everyday demands and challenges. Secondly, a project like this needs a reliable partner keeping faith with us. In this respect, we would like to thank The Anniversary Fund of the Oesterreichische Nationalbank (OeNB) for financing the whole study in three separate peer-reviewed projects from 2005 to 2017. We felt particularly honoured when the project was invited to the 50th anniversary of the fund and named a *unique flagship project*. Our thanks also go to Salzburg University Library for supporting an open-access publication such as this. Without money nothing is possible, of course, yet money is not everything. This saying is even more true of people. Our thanks go to our great team: our project's researchers, Michelle Bichler, Anna Bramböck, Andreas Oberlinner, Fabian Prochazka, Daniel von Reinersdorff and Sebastian Reeh, and our secretary, Monika Hoppenthaler. Furthermore, we want to thank Uwe Hasebrink for his critical reading of an earlier version of the manuscript and Hans-Ulrich Sinner for his support in reviewing the citation and the references of this book. Finally, we want to thank Uwe Hasebrink and Andreas Hepp; we are glad that our book is part of their series, *Transforming Communications – Studies in Cross-Media Research*.

The German author, Thomas Mann, once said: *To think and to thank are related terms … (Denken und danken sind verwandte Wörter…).* With this in mind, we hope that this book will be a fruitful contribution to the community at large. More specifically, we hope that it will serve as a springboard for further research on socially disadvantaged children, adolescents, families and the media.

Salzburg, Austria	Ingrid Paus-Hasebrink
Klagenfurt, Austria	Jasmin Kulterer
Salzburg, Austria	Philip Sinner

REFERENCES

Elias, N. (1987). *Engagement und Distanzierung. Arbeiten zur Wissenssoziologie I* [Engagement and dissociation: Academic works on the sociology of knowledge I]. Frankfurt am Main, Germany: Suhrkamp.

Paus-Hasebrink, I. (Ed.). (2017). *Langzeitstudie zur Rolle von Medien in der Sozialisation sozial benachteiligter Heranwachsender. Lebensphase Jugend* [Longitudinal study on the role of media within socialisation of socially disadvantaged adolescents: Phase of adolescence]. Baden-Baden, Germany: Nomos.

Paus-Hasebrink, I., & Bichler, M. (2008). *Mediensozialisationsforschung. Theoretische Fundierung und Fallbeispiel sozial benachteiligte Kinder* [Media socialisation research—Theoretical foundation and a case study on socially disadvantaged children]. Assisted by C. Wijnen. Innsbruck, Austria: Studienverlag.

Paus-Hasebrink, I., & Kulterer, J. (2014). *Praxeologische Mediensozialisationsforschung. Langzeitstudie zu sozial benachteiligten Heranwachsenden* [Praxeological media socialisation research: A longitudinal study regarding socially disadvantaged adolescents]. Assisted by P. Sinner. Baden-Baden, Germany: Nomos.

Contents

1 **Framing the Study** 1
   1.1 *The Concept of This Book* 2
   1.2 *An Overview of This Book* 3
   References 8

2 **Social Inequality, Childhood and the Media** 11
   2.1 *Introduction* 11
   2.2 *National Contexts of Inequality* 11
       2.2.1 *Social Disadvantage in Rich Western Societies* 11
       2.2.2 *The Case of Austria and Germany* 14
       2.2.3 *The Inequality Gap in Western Societies, and in Austria and in Germany* 16
   2.3 *Inequality and Mediatization* 19
       2.3.1 *The Concept of Mediatization* 19
       2.3.2 *Mediatization and Its Consequences for Socially Disadvantaged Young People* 22
       2.3.3 *Social Disadvantages and Media Experiences* 26
   2.4 *Conclusion* 31
   References 33

3 **The Role of Media Within Young People's Socialisation: A Theoretical Approach** 45
   3.1 *Introduction* 45

	3.2	Socialisation from Different Disciplinary Perspectives	46
		3.2.1 Socialisation from a Psychological Perspective	47
		3.2.2 Socialisation from a Sociological Perspective	48
		3.2.3 Perspectives on the Process of Socialisation in Media and Communications Research	49
	3.3	On the Role of Developmental Tasks in the Framework of Socialisation Processes	51
		3.3.1 Childhood and Adolescence—More Than Age-Based Phases	52
		3.3.2 Adolescence—A Phase of Transition	54
		3.3.3 "Meta-Developmental Tasks"	55
		3.3.4 Developmental Tasks and Media Contexts	56
	3.4	The Family Context in Socialisation	57
		3.4.1 On the Relevance of the Parent–Child Relationship	57
		3.4.2 On the Relevance of Doing Family	58
	3.5	A Praxeological Approach to Researching Children's Socialisation	59
		3.5.1 The Lifeworld and Related Contexts	60
		3.5.2 Three Analytic Concepts: Options, Outlines and Competences for Action	63
	3.6	Conclusion	65
	References		66
4	**The Methodological Approach of the Long-Term Study**		**77**
	4.1	Introduction	77
	4.2	Recruitment of the Families	79
	4.3	The Challenges of Managing a Long-Term Study	82
	4.4	Data Collection	83
		4.4.1 Standardised Questionnaire	86
		4.4.2 Guided In-Depth Interview with the Parents	86
		4.4.3 Guided In-Depth Interview with the Children and Adolescents	88
		4.4.4 Observation Protocol	90
		4.4.5 Complementary Methods for Adolescents: Thinking Aloud, Network Maps, Photos	90
		4.4.6 Final Call-Back Interview	93
	4.5	Data Processing and Data Analysis	94

4.6	Ethical Challenges	97
4.7	Conclusion	98
References		100

5 Family Descriptions 107
5.1 Introduction 107
5.2 The Families of the Panel 107
    5.2.1 The Aufbauer Family with Their Daughter, Amelie 107
    5.2.2 The Boll Family with Their Son, Gregor 108
    5.2.3 The Dornbacher Family with Their Daughter, Gudrun 109
    5.2.4 The Ebner Family with Their Daughter, Elisabeth 109
    5.2.5 The Fein Family with Their Daughter, Olivia 110
    5.2.6 The Grubert Family with Their Son, Erich 110
    5.2.7 The Hirtner Family with Their Son, Mario 111
    5.2.8 The Holzner Family with Their Son, Benedikt 112
    5.2.9 The Kaiser Family with Their Son, Torsten 112
    5.2.10 The Landinger Family with Their Son, Timo 113
    5.2.11 The Oblinger Family with Their Son, Manfred 113
    5.2.12 The Öllinger Family with Their Daughter, Viktoria 114
    5.2.13 The Pfortner Family with Their Son, Helmut 115
    5.2.14 The Rohringer Family with Their Daughter, Isabelle 115
    5.2.15 The Scheib Family with Their Daughter, Susanne 116
    5.2.16 The Stab Family with Their Daughter, Simone 116
    5.2.17 The Weiss Family with Their Son, Alfons 117
    5.2.18 The Zarbl Family with Their Son, Norbert 117
5.3 Conclusion 118

6 Socialisation in Different Socialisation Contexts 121
6.1 Introduction 121
6.2 Media as a Context for Socialisation 123
    6.2.1 The Role of Media, Extending Over Preschool and Elementary School into Mid-Childhood 123
    6.2.2 The Role of Media in the Phase of Adolescence 127
    6.2.3 Conclusion 133

6.3	The Family as Socialisation Context	134
6.4	Extra-Familial Socialisation Contexts	138
	6.4.1 Relatives and Friends of the Family	138
	6.4.2 Peers, Friends and Romantic Relationships	139
	6.4.3 Kindergarten, School and Apprenticeship	142
	6.4.4 Assisted Living Communities and Apprenticeship Hostels	144
	6.4.5 (Sports)Clubs	144
	6.4.6 Politics and Society	146
6.5	Conclusion	148
	References	150

7 The Interplay Between Family and Media as Socialisation Contexts: Parents' Mediation Practices — 157

7.1	Introduction	157
7.2	On the Role of Mediation Practices Amid Social Inequality	158
7.3	Selected Findings from the Longitudinal Study: From Kindergarten to Youth	159
7.4	Practices of Parental Mediation	161
	7.4.1 Laissez-faire	162
	7.4.2 Unmethodical Restriction	164
	7.4.3 Arbitrary Control or Exploitation of Dominance	164
	7.4.4 Amicability	166
	7.4.5 Child-Centred Mediation Practices	166
7.5	Conclusion	167
	References	168

8 The Typology of Socially Disadvantaged Families — 171

8.1	Introduction	171
8.2	The Families of Type 1	174
	8.2.1 The Case of Timo Landinger and His Family	175
	8.2.2 Other Families of Type 1	181
	8.2.3 The Fein Family	184
8.3	The Families of Type 2	187
	8.3.1 The Case of Benedikt Holzner and His Family	188
	8.3.2 Other Families of Type 2	194

	8.4	The Families of Type 3	198
	8.4.1	The Case of Simone Stab and Her Family	199
	8.4.2	The Other Families of Type 3	205
	8.5	The Families of Type 4	211
	8.5.1	The Case of Erich Grubert and His Family	212
	8.5.2	The Other Families of Type 4	218
	8.6	Conclusion	224
	References		229
9	**Discussion and Conclusion**	231
	9.1	The Objectives of This Longitudinal Study	231
	9.2	The Theoretical Framework	234
	9.3	On the Longitudinal Study and Its Process	236
	9.4	The Scope of This Study	240
	9.5	The Particular Challenges of a Longitudinal Study	241
	9.6	The Media and Socio-Pedagogical and Political Consequences	243
	References		248
Appendix			255
Index			303

List of Figures

Fig. 1.1	The waves of research at a glance	6
Fig. 2.1	Children (6–13 years) in Germany who use the internet (at least occasionally) (percentages; $n=1200$) (*Source* KIM 2006–2016; www.mpfs.de)	22
Fig. 2.2	Cell phone and smartphone ownership among adolescents (12–19 years) in Germany (percentages) (*Source* JIM 1998–2017; http://www.mpfs.de)	23
Fig. 4.1	Relevant contextual factors for children's socialisation	78
Fig. 4.2	Methods of data collection in the different waves of research at a glance	83
Fig. 4.3	Methods of data collection	84
Fig. 4.4	Overview of data processing and data analysis	94
Fig. 8.1	First typology 2014 and revised typology 2016	172
Fig. 8.2	Four family types—typology 2016	173
Fig. 8.3	Network map by Timo Landinger in 2016 (Tracing based on the original, translated and anonymised by the authors)	178
Fig. 8.4	Network map by Benedikt Holzner in 2016 (Tracing based on the original, translated and anonymised by the authors)	190
Fig. 8.5	Network map by Simone Stab in 2016 (Tracing based on the original, translated and anonymised by the authors)	204
Fig. 8.6	Network map by Gregor Boll in 2016 (Tracing based on the original, translated and anonymised by the authors)	208
Fig. 8.7	Network map by Erich Grubert in 2016 (Tracing based on the original, translated and anonymised by the authors)	213
Fig. 8.8	Network map by Gudrun Dornbacher in 2014 (Tracing based on the original, translated and anonymised by the authors)	223

List of Tables

Table 2.1	Risk of poverty or being marginalised in different groups in Austria 2016	17
Table 3.1	Options for action, outlines for action and competences for action	65
Table 4.1	The families—An overview	80

CHAPTER 1

Framing the Study

Poverty is not only a severe problem in so-called poor countries. The rich countries of the Western society are also having to face rising figures of poor people or people at risk of poverty or marginalisation. This development goes hand-in-hand with a widening inequality gap in most of the OECD countries (UNICEF, 2016, p. 2). People nowadays often feel bewildered and insecure and many of them are afraid of being pushed to the margins of society. Unfortunately, for younger people poverty or the risk of poverty or being marginalised is an increasing problem (UNICEF, 2016, p. 2). At the same time, we witness far-reaching societal and medial transformation processes, which we discuss as aspects of the "*meta process*" (Krotz, 2014, p. 137, emphasis in original) of mediatization. However, it should be emphasised that social disadvantage in rich countries is strongly connected to a lack of participation opportunities, which, in turn, are quite often linked with communication and media. It is against the backdrop of these developments that we have formulated the central research question of our project: How do socially disadvantaged life circumstances affect adolescents, their socialisation and their opportunities to participate in society, and what is the role of media in this context?

1.1   The Concept of This Book

Our study, "*Social inequality, childhood and the media: A longitudinal study of the mediatization of socialisation*", focuses on precisely these questions to deal with adolescents growing up in socially disadvantaged families. Such adolescents are at risk of lacking social opportunities and may well not be able to perceive and profit from the possibilities of the social space in which they grow up. Here it is important to note that it is scarcely enough only to think about the adolescents' social rights. Rather more, being able to benefit from these rights is what counts. In this context we must recognise that the term "socially disadvantaged circumstances" does not only concern the material level of living in everyday life, but also includes individual living conditions as a whole (see Rosenmayr & Majce, 1978). So, we are setting out to observe the "'cumulative disadvantage', in the sense of a reciprocal reinforcement of poverty, illness and social isolation" (Hörl, 1999, p. 172, translated by the authors). The concept of social disadvantage clearly indicates the contrast with adolescents in better circumstances (see Hörl, 1999 as well as Fehr, 2017) and points to inequality. The term social inequality connotes the imperative (see Hörl, 1999, p. 172; see as well Fehr, 2017) to remove disadvantage.

This particular understanding, coupled with the object of serving society forms one of the starting points of the longitudinal study we present here. Following Norbert Elias (1987), we offer "dedicated social research" (for details see Paus-Hasebrink & Bichler, 2008; Paus-Hasebrink & Kulterer, 2014) with not only a scientific outcome but also a social one. Our initial impulse derives from different analyses that focused on an emerging gap in society's socio-economic structure. Today, society is a consumer society, but, of course, not everyone is able to participate equally in its prosperity. Several scientific studies suggest a growing socio-economic gap in society and warn about further and increasing discrepancies between "winners" and "losers" during the process of growing up (see Rauschenbach, 2011, p. 5). It is likely that socially disadvantaged children, even in rich countries like Austria (see Chapter 2), will be pushed towards the edge of society. This prejudices their socialisation and their opportunities for participation in society. Finally, there is a close connection between family and social structure[1]: The allocation of core resources, like income, formal education and the profession of the wage earner(s) in a family, is highly unequal. In this context, the media are important since they are an integral part of everyday life. It stands to reason that the resources of social participation via media are unequally distributed, as are the social and cultural resources of different social groups (see Niesyto, 2009). With developing mediatization, manifested in the convergence of old and new media as well as with the temporal and spatial dissolution of boundaries of media contents and services, media are becoming increasingly important for society as a whole, as well as for the everyday life of every individual in it (see Krotz, 2013).

The media determine many of our everyday practices and, therefore, produce new communicative practices as they shape everyday life. This raises the questions: How does this manifest itself in the everyday life of socially disadvantaged children and adolescents? How is their everyday life shaped?

This study specifically asks how socially disadvantaged adolescents use media, which practices they develop to cope with their everyday life and how they integrate media contents and services meaningfully into it, against the background of their current lifeworld situation. How does the socialisation (see Chapter 3) of adolescents within socially disadvantaged conditions proceed, and how are the media relevant during their socialisation? The important issues are, hence, the construction of an individual identity, the structure of knowledge, the perception of ways to participate in society and the mediation of values in and through the media, as well as the socio-economic and socio-emotional changes in core relationship groups. Against this background, it is crucial to consider the *double, interweaving dynamic* of the ongoing media-technological changes in media contents and services, on the one hand, and the dynamic governing the development of children in their socialisation their specific social situation, on the other. Socialisation today is mediatised socialisation (see Couldry & Hepp, 2017, p. 151).

1.2 An Overview of This Book

Chapter 2 of this book is devoted to outlining the connections between social inequality, childhood and media. The first part is dedicated to national contexts of social inequality. It provides a discussion of social disadvantage in rich Western societies, with the specific examples of Austria and Germany, in order to better understand the specific circumstances that socially disadvantaged families encounter in the national context. The second part deals with the connection between inequality and mediatization, and what implications emerge for children affected by an unequal distribution of resources and opportunities as they grow up. One central argument is that a disadvantageous position in a mediatised society often leads to a lack of participation in society (education, job perspectives and so on). In our mediatised Western societies, participation is closely connected to (digital) media, so that socialisation often becomes media socialisation. Following, we will preface a survey of relevant trends in global mediatization with a literature review covering the evidence of the links between social disadvantages and media experiences. To conclude, we will discuss the consequences of mediatization for academic research on young people's growing up in general and for our study on media socialisation among socially disadvantaged adolescents in particular.

Chapter 3 introduces the theoretical framework that underlies this study. It presents a praxeological research perspective on the processes of the media socialisation of children and adolescents. One of the main arguments is that socialisation has to be contextualised in a dynamic and interlinked process, that is connected to both the individual child and the relevant social contexts like family, peers, institutional contexts such as kindergarten and school, and non-institutional recreational contexts. The interactions of these contexts have to be systematically analysed, in order to understand how children make sense of their life and, in this context, of the media within their everyday lives. The chapter starts out by providing an overview of how socialisation is theorised in different disciplines, such as psychology and sociology, and then moves on to the perspective of media and communications, where we look at the rich empirical evidence on young people's use of media devices and products. By introducing the theoretical concept of developmental tasks (Havighurst, 1972), the chapter explores a way of theoretically grasping the interface between the individual, subjective level and the level of society and of objective factors in the process of growing up. At this point, definitions of childhood-specific and adolescence-specific developmental tasks are discussed as well. Subsequently, we look at the relevance of different socialisation contexts in a child's life and in a child's attempt to come to terms with its developmental tasks; the concept of *doing family* gains particular relevance in this discussion. Finally, based on the assumption that the conduct of everyday life is manifested in social milieus where individuals attempt to realise their specific goals in life, including their own particular plans and wishes, the authors introduce the three analytical concepts: *options, outlines* and *competences for action*, that allow a theoretical and empirical understanding of the connection between a social milieu, and the subjective structure of making sense of one's life. It is argued that, based on these three analytical concepts, the role of the media becomes understandable and comprehensible as it relates to the interlinkage of subjective perception, action-driven orientations, and everyday life practices against the backdrop of sociostructural conditions.

Chapter 4 outlines how the theoretical foundation of the study (Chapter 3) calls for a specific methodological concept. This chapter focuses on the ways in which the methodological approach was designed in order to grasp the complexity of the topic and later on revised in order to grasp new challenges caused by the longitudinal character of the project. In order to understand the processes of socialisation, this study has been designed as a qualitative panel study on a selected sample of 20 (later 18) children who were five to six years old when the research started in 2005 and who were 17–18 years old when it was ended. At the core of the chapter, we deal with the questions how to collect, to process and analyse data from a qualitative longitudinal study over the 12 years from 2005 to 2017 (Fig. 1.1).

Following the logic of triangulation (Denzin & Lincoln, 2011, p. 2), we discuss the development of a rich design where all the components draw on, complement, and control each other in the processes of data collection and analysis; that way, we will argue, research becomes transparent and comprehensible in terms of intersubjectivity. The whole process of developing and using the methodological design is covered in much detail to allow for a deeper understanding of the logic behind, the purpose and the demands of a qualitative longitudinal study. The chapter covers all the relevant steps from the recruitment of the families, the ethical challenges and the actual data collection to the methods that were used. At the core of the methods to be presented and discussed are the guided in-depth interviews with children and parents over six waves of research (from 2005 until end of 2016), moving on to additional methods like observations protocols, a short standardised questionnaire for the parent(s) concerning income, formal education, and other topics, and finally later additions to the design—the adolescents were asked to draw network maps concerning important persons and media and to demonstrate their most favourite social media application, using the method of thinking aloud, and to take photos of their favourite spots in their rooms—are explained. Furthermore, after the sixth wave of research, we conducted telephone interviews with the adolescents in our panel and their parents, in order to get a final update on their personal situation. The chapter also addresses how the collected data was processed and prepared for analysis, including transcription and thorough anonymisation of the sensitive data and how the actual analysis was conducted. This part of the chapter is especially important and innovative from a methodological perspective, as in existing literature this issue is rarely discussed extensively with regard to longitudinal research.

Chapter 5 consists of brief descriptions of the 18 families that were still part of the sample by the time the study came to an end. The chapter consists of a short summary of each family's situation as it developed over the years. With regard to the relevant selection criteria (see Chapter 4) at the beginning of the project, the focus is on the socio-economic situation of each family, with particular attention being paid to income, job situation, housing situation, formal education (of parents), family constellation (nuclear family, patchwork family, single-parent households, extended families, migration background and so on). The summaries give an idea of the dynamic that each family experienced throughout the years, especially with regard to their socio-economic and socio-emotional development.

Chapter 6 provides a perspective on the dynamic media environment and patterns of socialisation within the panel over nearly twelve years of research. This chapter focuses on the core aspects that are the heart of the study: the dynamic development of the children and their media repertoires (Hasebrink & Popp, 2006), on the one hand, and, on the other,

	W1	W2		W3	W4	W5	W6	
Other contexts								
Media context								
Family context								
Age of child	5	6	7	8	9	10	11	12	13	14	15	16	17
Year	2005	2006	2007	2008	2009	2010	2011	2012	2013	2014	2015	2016	2017

Fig. 1.1 The waves of research at a glance

the role of different contexts of socialisation as they affect the children in different ways at various stages of their personal development throughout the years. Twelve years is a long time, during which the children in the panel not only get older, but also a lot can change as far as the situation of the family in general is concerned. The chapter unravels what happened between the time when the study began in 2005, when the children were between four and six years old, when their lives were mainly framed by their experiences at home or in kindergarten, and then later, when other contexts such as schools and friends became more relevant, so that by the time it ended in spring 2017, they were teenagers about to make important life decisions. This chapter highlights how the children's media usage and especially their motives for using certain types of media content changed in this context. We argue in this chapter that, at the same time, technology is progressing and it leads to transformations on the level of media products and media use. Among them are the processes of digitalisation and convergence that have greatly affected and altered the media's role in society and in individual lifeworlds. Against this background, the chapter sheds light on the variety of manners in which the children incorporate media (classic as well as "new" media) into their everyday lives, how they form media repertoires and how media are part of a complex array of socialisation contexts with varying functions and purposes.

Chapter 7 has a stronger focus on the interplay between family and media as socialisation contexts in the sample where it looks at ways in which parents approach parenting and the mediation of media literacy. As a first step, the chapter introduces insights from relevant studies and theoretical concepts. Secondly, it focuses on parents' mediation practices and how they changed over time with respect to both the children's age and the changing media over nearly twelve years of research. Against this background, the following different practices of parents' mediation practices that were uncovered in the panel will be discussed: *laissez-faire*, *unmethodical restriction*, *arbitrary control and exploitation of dominance*, *amicability* and *child-centred* and how they are related to *options for action, outlines for action and competences for action*.

Chapter 8 presents a typology of the families in the sample of the study at hand. We explain how the discovery of similarities and differences of living as a family were the starting point for developing a typology in which the main dimensions for characterising the families were the socio-economic situation, the socio-emotional climate and the identifiable coping strategies. The four types of families we discovered are explained in detail, and each family in the sample is portrayed and discussed with regard to their allocation to the specific type. The typology focuses on the most recent data but also takes the development of the families over the years into account. The arguments in the chapter are amplified through selected cases that delve deeper into the individual lifeworlds of the children and their families. This chapter helps to understand how many of the researched families are often overtaxed in multiple ways and experience different forms of deprivation on many levels.

Finally, Chapter 9 discusses the scope of the approach as presented, its limitations and benefits and its potential. Based on the results of the longitudinal study, it discusses how the complex interplay of factors that were shown to shape the lives of children as they grew up can help policymakers and stakeholders to develop more individualised approaches for the support and encouragement of children and their families. While the empirical work of this study has been done in Austria, the theoretical framework and the methodological approach have a general scope, since they can be applied in any country. Furthermore, we wish to emphasise that the findings do not reflect particularities of the Austrian context. Within the theoretical framework they will be interpreted as empirical evidence showing how contextual conditions, patterns of *doing family*, and individual factors shape socialisation processes; this interaction between the different contexts and individual factors is not a regional particularity but a general pattern that is relevant for understanding socialisation within mediatised worlds in general.

NOTE

1. Following the poverty report of the Bertelsmann Stiftung (2016), the growing up of children in poverty-vulnerable families is often shaped by a package of problems. In addition to chronic financial issues, there are factors like illnesses, the divorce of the parents, cramped housing and unsafe routes to school (Laubstein, Holz, & Seddig, 2016, pp. 12–15, 51, 55).

References

Bertelsmann Stiftung. (2016). *Kinderarmut. Kinder im SGB-II-Bezug in Deutschland* [Child poverty in Germany]. Gütersloh, Germany: Bertelsmann Stiftung. Retrieved from https://www.bertelsmann-stiftung.de/de/themen/aktuelle-meldungen/2016/september/kinderarmut-in-deutschland-waechst-weiter-mit-folgen-fuers-ganze-leben/.

Couldry, N., & Hepp, A. (2017). *The mediated construction of reality*. Cambridge, UK: Polity Press.
Denzin, N. K., & Lincoln, Y. S. (2011). Introduction. In N. K. Denzin & Y. S. Lincoln (Eds.), *The SAGE handbook of qualitative research* (pp. 1–20). Los Angeles, CA, London, UK, and New Dehli, India: Sage.
Elias, N. (1987). *Engagement und Distanzierung. Arbeiten zur Wissenssoziologie I* [Engagement and dissociation: Academic works on the sociology of knowledge I]. Frankfurt am Main, Germany: Suhrkamp.
Fehr, S. (2017). *Familien in der Falle: Dynamik familialer Armut in der individualisierten Erwerbsgesellschaft* [Families in a trap: Dynamics of familial poverty in the individualised employment society]. Weinheim, Germany: Beltz.
Hasebrink, U., & Popp, J. (2006). Media repertoires as a result of selective media use: A conceptual approach to the analysis of patterns of exposure. *Communications, 31*(2), 369–387.
Havighurst, R. J. (1972). *Developmental tasks and education* (3rd ed.). New York, NY: McKay.
Hörl, J. (1999). Die Wahrnehmung sozialer Benachteiligung in Österreich – Konsens und Polarisierung [The perception of social disadvantage in Austria—Consensus and polarisation]. *SWS-Rundschau, 2*, 171–188.
Krotz, F. (2013). Aufwachsen in mediatisierten Welten [Growing up in mediatised worlds]. In C. Wijnen, S. Trültzsch & C. Ortner (Eds.), *Medienwelten im Wandel. Kommunikationswissenschaftliche Positionen, Perspektiven und Konsequenzen* [Media worlds in transition: Scientific positions, perspectives and consequences in communications] (pp. 39–53). Wiesbaden: VS Verlag. S. 39–53.
Krotz, F. (2014). Mediatization as a mover in modernity: Social and cultural change in the context of media change. In K. Lundby (Ed.), *Mediatization of communication: Handbook of communication science* (pp. 131–162). Berlin, Germany: de Gruyter.
Laubstein, C., Holz, G., & Seddig, N. (2016). *Armutsfolgen für arme Kinder und Jugendliche. Erkenntnisse aus empirischen Studien in Deutschland* [Consequences of poverty for children and adolescents: Empirical evidence from research in Germany]. Gütersloh, Germany: Bertelsmann Stiftung. Retrieved from https://www.bertelsmann-stiftung.de/fileadmin/files/BSt/Publikationen/GrauePublikationen/Studie_WB_Armutsfolgen_fuer_Kinder_und_Jugendliche_2016.pdf.
Niesyto, H. (2009). Digitale Medien, soziale Benachteiligung und soziale Distinktion [Digital media, social disadvantage and social distinction]. *Medienpädagogik. Zeitschrift für Theorie und Praxis der Medienbildung. Themenheft Nr., 17*, 1–19. Retrieved from http://www.medienpaed.com/article/view/115/115.

Paus-Hasebrink, I., & Bichler, M. (2008). *Mediensozialisationsforschung. Theoretische Fundierung und Fallbeispiel sozial benachteiligte Kinder* [Media socialisation research—Theoretical foundation and a case study on socially disadvantaged children]. Assisted by C. Wijnen. Innsbruck, Austria: Studienverlag.

Paus-Hasebrink, I., & Kulterer, J. (2014). *Praxeologische Mediensozialisationsforschung. Langzeitstudie zu sozial benachteiligten Heranwachsenden* [Praxeological media socialisation research: A longitudinal study regarding socially disadvantaged adolescents]. Assisted by P. Sinner. Baden-Baden, Germany: Nomos.

Rauschenbach, T. (2011). Aufwachsen unter neuen Vorzeichen [Growing up under new conditions]. *DJI Impulse, 1,* 4–7.

Rosenmayr, L., & Majce, G. (1978). Die soziale Benachteiligung [Social disadvantage]. In L. Rosenmayr & H. Rosenmayr (Eds.), *Der alte Mensch in der Gesellschaft* [The elderly in the society] (pp. 231–260). Reinbek bei Hamburg, Germany: Rowohlt.

UNICEF. (2016). *Fairness for children: A league table of inequality in child well-being in rich countries.* Innocenti Report Card 13. Children in the Developed World. Florence, Italy: UNICEF Office of Research—Innocenti. Retrieved from https://www.unicef-irc.org/publications/pdf/RC13_eng.pdf.

Open Access This chapter is licensed under the terms of the Creative Commons Attribution 4.0 International License (http://creativecommons.org/licenses/by/4.0/), which permits use, sharing, adaptation, distribution and reproduction in any medium or format, as long as you give appropriate credit to the original author(s) and the source, provide a link to the Creative Commons licence and indicate if changes were made.

The images or other third party material in this chapter are included in the chapter's Creative Commons licence, unless indicated otherwise in a credit line to the material. If material is not included in the chapter's Creative Commons licence and your intended use is not permitted by statutory regulation or exceeds the permitted use, you will need to obtain permission directly from the copyright holder.

CHAPTER 2

Social Inequality, Childhood and the Media

2.1 Introduction

Our study deals with socially disadvantaged children and adolescents in Austria. Hence, we discuss their life circumstances, their opportunities to participate in society, the process of their socialisation and, in this context, the role of media. To better understand the specific challenges facing them as they grow up in a rich country like Austria, we will initially examine the framing conditions in Austria and in other countries, as well as the relevant analytical concepts. Our topics are the national contexts of inequality, the particular nature of being socially disadvantaged in a rich Western society (particularly the examples of Austria and Germany) and, as a consequence, the inequality gap. We then go on to connect these findings with the concept of mediatization and to outline what our findings mean for academia. In conclusion, we offer an insight into the state of research and will, against this backdrop, set out the concrete aim of our longitudinal study.

2.2 National Contexts of Inequality

2.2.1 Social Disadvantage in Rich Western Societies

In rich countries, social disadvantage is normally not synonymous with severe poverty or material deprivation on an existential level. But poor people, or people at risk of poverty or of being marginalised, run the risk of being further pushed to the margins of society due to a lack of opportunities and possibilities for participation. It is children and adolescents who are particularly at risk: in many rich countries, where the percentage of younger people who are poor or at risk of poverty or marginalisation is higher than that in the population at large. However, there are examples, like Austria and Germany, which demonstrate the opposite case, because this relationship is reversed in these two countries (see, for example, Guio, Gordon, & Marlier, 2017, p. 217; UNICEF, 2016, p. 2). Nevertheless, even in our specific examples, young people are especially at risk where they are affected by the conditions of their families. Poverty or social disadvantage do not mean material deprivation alone. A lack of financial resources also has a major impact on educational achievement, and thus children's life prospects (for example, access to the labour market). In addition, leisure opportunities, social participation, physical health and well-being are also affected. And in consequence, children from lower-income households tend to be sick more often, not only when they are young but also as adults. This results in a poorer state of health than that displayed by the population at large (cf. SOS Kinderdorf, 2017). These recent findings are specific to Austria and fit in with recent research on social disadvantage (cf. Berka & Trappel, 2017, pp. 122–124; Bertelsmann Stiftung, 2016; Einböck, Proyer, & Fenninger, 2015, pp. 14–16; Laubstein, Holz, & Seddig, 2016, pp. 12–16 and 18–24; Paus-Hasebrink, 2017, pp. 15–17; Paus-Hasebrink & Bichler, 2008, pp. 17–23; Paus-Hasebrink & Kulterer, 2014a, pp. 18–24; UNICEF, 2016, p. 2). Further aspects of disadvantage are higher rates of obesity, addiction developing at a younger age, underachievement in education, fewer friends and peers outside the family and smaller personal networks, limited access to cultural events and sports communities, as well as inability to participate in public discourse and problematic patterns of media usage. In more general terms, these facets and categories of social disadvantage can be subsumed under the headings: "Income", "Education", "Health" and "Life satisfaction" (UNICEF, 2016, p. 12). In particular, living a satisfactory life is closely linked to current living conditions, future prospects and opportunities to participate.

There are numerous differing approaches to defining social disadvantage. They include simpler ones only based on formal education and family income, but also the more complex, taking into account additional factors. In the last analysis, the design of a particular project will be aligned with research questions and the resources available. However, as far as social disadvantage goes, the national contexts are of prime importance, because specific living conditions have to be seen comparatively across an entire country. In this respect, it is also important to note that poverty or social disadvantage in some regions of Asia, Africa, South America, or even in some countries of Southern and Eastern Europe, is not comparable to being poor or socially disadvantaged in rich Western societies, like Austria or Germany, with their well-developed welfare states. In such countries, social disadvantage is closely linked to a lack of opportunities for participation in society (cf. Berka & Trappel, 2017, pp. 66–68, 122–124; Paus-Hasebrink, Sinner, & Prochazka, 2014, p. 2; van Dijk, 2013, p. 35). People risk a sense of being left behind, with children and single parents being particularly vulnerable. Guio et al. (2017, p. 213) have compiled a list of 18 items in order to build a material deprivation "indicator related to the children (aged 1–15 years) population". This list of items is closely linked with the 2009 EU-SILC (EU Survey on Income and Living Conditions) data on material deprivation related to child deprivation (Guio et al., 2017, p. 210). Beside obvious material items, such as food, clothing and shoes, house heating or the ownership of a car, it includes also farther-reaching needs, such as access to suitable books, a personal place to do homework, leisure activities, opportunities to celebrate and to invite friends and to participate in school activities or trips. Unfortunately, we have to state that, in rich countries too, there is a remarkable percentage (3–18%) of deprived "children lacking at least 3 out of 18 items". The value for Austria is 12% and for Germany 15% (Guio et al., 2017, p. 217, quotation is bold in original). The percentage of such deprived children is very low for non-poor children in rich countries, but it rockets upward when it comes to poor children: "even the best performing countries (with the exception of Sweden) do not manage to protect income-poor children from material deprivation" (Guio et al., 2017, p. 218). It should be noted that. alongside Belgium and France, Austria is one of the countries facing the most serious inequality between poor and non-poor children, indicating the impact that poverty has on Austrian children's lives.

Based on several studies of childhood, adolescence, poverty and social disadvantage in Germany (AWO-ISS, 2012, 2013; Bertelsmann Stiftung, 2016; Palentien, 2003) and Austria (Einböck et al., 2015), but also considering more detailed studies of selected regions (for example, Caritas, 2016), we have to state that poverty and social disadvantage, with their concomitant consequences for the everyday life and the future prospects of the persons concerned, are serious problems in rich countries. Even though there is a positive development (Guio et al., 2017, p. 217), and the poverty rates of children in Austria or Germany are lower than in many other countries, there are some countries doing still better. Norway, for example, is rich, whereas the Czech Republic is less so, yet both countries display a poverty rate among children significantly lower than in Germany and Austria (cf. UNICEF, 2016, p. 4). However, (national) efforts to lower the proportion of young people at risk of poverty or being marginalised are laudable, given that the United Nations Convention on the Rights of the Child stipulates that the goal should be a reduction to 0.0%. In accordance with this, new Sustainable Development Goals (SDGs) for 2030 were adopted by the United Nations in 2015 in order to replace the Millennium Development Goals: Goal 1 is named "*End poverty in all its forms everywhere*", this includes topic 1.1 "by 2030, eradicate extreme poverty for all people" and topic 1.2 "by 2030, reduce at least by half the proportion of men, women and children of all ages living in poverty in all its dimensions according to national definitions", while goal 10 represents the aim to "*reduce inequality within and among countries*" (Atkinson, Guio, & Marlier, 2017, pp. 44–45, emphasis in original). The SDGs are more ambitious than the social inclusion target of the European Union for 2020. But "halving poverty by 2030 should not be beyond the resources of a rich continent" (Atkinson et al., 2017, p. 47).

2.2.2 The Case of Austria and Germany

Austria and Germany certainly belong to the wealthiest countries in the European Union and the world at large. We highlight the example of Austria because it is the source of the study presented here. But in addition, we also focus on Germany for several reasons. To begin with, two families moved to different parts of Germany during the study, and one girl was attending school on the other side of the border—the State of Salzburg shares a common EuRegio with parts of the State of Bavaria. But even more important is the fact that Austria and Germany are closely interlinked in many ways, although their national contexts do differ: firstly, they share a common language area (but also with parts of

Belgium, Denmark, Luxembourg, Italy and Switzerland), which means that their national media systems are interwoven; secondly, they share a long and eventful history; thirdly, they share common cultural values and traditions; fourthly, the scientific communities of both countries are closely linked as well, and research findings concerning Germany are often utilised by Austrian authorities too, because of their lack of national data.

Based on a comparison of the gross domestic product (GDP), Austria is the fourth richest country in the European Union, while Germany is the seventh. However, the individual consumption expenditure of households (goods and services, adjusted for purchasing power) ranks Germany second and Austria third. Unchallenged leader in both rankings is Luxembourg (ORF/APA, 2017). Germany, in particular, is currently characterised by stable growth, high tax revenues and the lowest unemployment rates since 1989 (cf. Eurostat, 2017c, pp. 30–31). That said, the reforms of the German welfare state and labour market, the so-called "Gesetze für moderne Dienstleistungen am Arbeitsmarkt" (Four Laws for Modern Services on the Labour Market), have resulted in a rising number of so-called "working poor" (AWO-ISS, 2012, pp. 6–7) and a growth of inequality. Compared to Germany, economic development in Austria has been lagging behind in recent years (cf. Eurostat, 2017c, pp. 60–61). But the Austrian state's social welfare system is somewhat more comprehensive than that in Germany. Austria has higher pensions, higher unemployment benefits over a longer period, study grants, social housing and family allowances (Statistik Austria, 2017a, pp. 4–6). Such transfer payments reduce the income inequality gap by 39.2% in Austria, but only by 31.5% in Germany. By contrast however, the reduction is even greater in the UK, at 48.4% (UNICEF, 2016, p. 16).

What has come to be called the *refugee crisis* is another important aspect of the situation in Austria and Germany (see Chapter 6 on socialisation in different contexts). Together with Sweden, Italy, Spain, and Greece, in recent years Germany and Austria have had the greatest problems in dealing with very high numbers of refugees. In addition, both countries are preferred destinations for people called *economic migrants* and for poor people from South-Eastern countries of the European Union. This situation was one reason behind the favourable electoral results for right-wing parties like the *FPÖ* in Austria and the *AfD* in Germany, both of which have tried to capitalise on people's fear of being left behind. Difficult times (see Lange & Xyländer, 2011), as exemplified by the *refugee crisis*, are challenges for the state and society in general, because people who are already socially disadvantaged are afraid of becoming further marginalised and alienated from the rest of society. But despite the increase in social inequality and the national and regional disparities in the European Union, being poor is not a one-way street in Germany (AWO-ISS, 2013, p. 19). Social advancement or a sustainable improvement of your socio-economic situation are possible. Social disadvantage is often closely linked to a migration background. However, a relevant aspect here is the way poor migrant adolescents tend to deal better with economic problems than poor German non-migrant teenagers, in part because the former are supported by stronger social networks through strong family structures (AWO-ISS, 2012, p. 2). Therefore, it is important to keep in mind that a migration background is not, per se, a reason for social disadvantage. It is much rather the case that relevant contexts have to be taken into account, and a migration background should not be advanced as a simple explanation for lacking participation opportunities or lower formal education.

2.2.3 *The Inequality Gap in Western Societies, and in Austria and in Germany*

Although some findings on Austria and Germany generate a positive image, we should nevertheless remember that all that glitters is not gold. "The gap between rich and poor [is] at its highest level for some three decades in most OECD countries" and all "across the OECD, the risks of poverty have been shifting from the elderly towards youth since the 1980s" (UNICEF, 2016, p. 2). In contrast to the current positive situation, these developments apply to the European Union as a whole, as well as Austria and Germany. We have seen increasing rates of poverty and social exclusion since the mid-1980s in Europe, due to rising unemployment rates, changing ways of living together and reductions in social benefits (Bertelsmann Stiftung, 2016; Palentien, 2003). The unequal distribution of resources and opportunities affects family life (Jokinen & Kuronen, 2011, p. 45). Socially disadvantaged families have to face and to cope with particular challenges, such as unemployment, often interlinked with health problems, and critical socio-emotional problems (Paus-Hasebrink & Kulterer, 2014b). However, socially disadvantaged people need and merit the support of society, and children and adolescents particularly so, because they are not responsible for the economic circumstances they are facing. "In addition, few dispute that childhood experiences have a profound effect not only on children's current lives, but also on their future opportunities and prospects. Likewise, social and economic disadvantages in early life increase the risk of having lower earnings, lower standards of health and lower skills in adulthood. This in turn can perpetuate disadvantage across generations" (UNICEF, 2016, p. 2).

Today, the child poverty rate (measured as 50% of the national median household income) is 7.2% in Germany and 9.6% Austria. On this measure, Finland (3.7%), Norway (4.5%) and Denmark (4.8%) (UNICEF, 2016, p. 4) are the leading countries. In contrast to the UNICEF data, it is more common in the European Union to make use of the indicator, "risk of poverty or marginalisation". This includes those people exhibiting at least one of the following three criteria (see Statistik Austria, 2017b, pp. 80–81): (a) living in a household with a household income of less than 60% of the national median (2016: 14% of the population); (b) significant material deprivation (2016: 3% of the population); (c) people under 60 unemployed or with very low earnings (2016: 8%). According to this, the proportion of people at risk of poverty or of being marginalised in Austria decreased from 20.6% in 2008 to 18% in 2016 (Statistik Austria, 2017a, p. 2; see Eurostat, 2017a, pp. 30–31, for a comparison between EU-28, Euro-area 19, EFTA and EU candidates). Compared to this percentage for the whole population, the respective percentage for young people up to 19 was 20.0% in 2016 (see Table 2.1). While these figures, taken in isolation, do not indicate a particular risk of poverty threatening children and adolescents, the results become more problematic if we take a closer look at family structures. The risk of poverty or being marginalised is considerably higher for single-parent families: 38%. In addition, the number

Table 2.1 Risk of poverty or being marginalised in different groups in Austria 2016

Total population	18%
Children (up to 19 years)	20%
Single parent families	38%
Multiperson households + 1 child	12%
Multiperson households + 2 children	13%
Multiperson households + 3 or more children	31%

Statistik Austria (2017b, pp. 80–81)

of children in a family is also linked with a higher risk of poverty or being marginalised: for multiperson households with at least three children, the risk of poverty or being marginalised is 31% (Statistik Austria, 2017b, pp. 80–81). Furthermore, long-term unemployment and low formal education are relevant factors behind poverty in Austria.

Across the whole population in Germany, the proportion of people at risk of poverty or being marginalised turns out to be a bit higher than in Austria, at 20%. The risk for younger people (under 18 in Germany) is slightly lower than in Austria (19%) (Statistisches Bundesamt, 2017a). It is worth noting that the situation is not uniform throughout Germany; there are notable differences between the German Länder (Federal States) and in particular between Eastern and Western areas of the country (see Statistisches Bundesamt, 2017b). In addition, single-parent households are particularly at risk in Germany: the quota of such families at risk of poverty or being marginalised was 40% in 2014 (Statistisches Bundesamt, 2016, pp. 173 and 176). And just as in Austria, people unemployed long-term and people with a low level of education are also particularly at risk.

These figures are in line with the results of the UNICEF report on inequality in children's well-being in rich countries. Austria and Germany both belong to a group of countries in which the relative gap of income inequality remained more or less stable in the period of 2008–2013: Austria reports a reduction of the relative gap in income inequality by 0.8%, while Germany reports a small increase of 0.5% (UNICEF, 2016, p. 15). Having this in mind, we should nevertheless emphasise: "Income gaps have widened in the majority of rich countries" (UNICEF, 2016, p. 14; quotation is bold in original). However, developments in Austria and Germany actually appear more favourable if we look back to the middle of the first decade of the twenty-first century, when the long-term study on which this book is based started (see also Eurostat, 2017b, p. 2). The groups of people who are especially at risk were the same as today, but the proportion of people at risk of poverty or being marginalised was, according to the data of Statistik Austria and AWO-ISS, significantly higher. 27% of adolescents under 20 years old in Austria were at risk of poverty (see Paus-Hasebrink & Bichler, 2008, pp. 18–19). A broad overview of the development of "persistent poverty rates" between 2008 and 2011 is provided by Jenkins and Van Kerm (2017, p. 401).

2.3 Inequality and Mediatization

The above findings on social disadvantage, inequality, and child poverty in rich countries become particularly important when we think of our rapidly changing world. We describe it by popularly using terms such as globalisation, individualisation, digitalisation or information society (see Castells, 2011; van Dijk, 2012).

2.3.1 The Concept of Mediatization

All these concepts are based on knowledge, communication, exchange and participation, and they refer to a transformation process where technological innovations, changing lifestyles, new work and life patterns, as well as emerging needs, are inextricably linked (Carpentier, Schrøder, & Hallett, 2014). In communication and media studies, this fundamental change is primarily discussed as the "*meta process*" of mediatization (Krotz, 2014, p. 137, emphasis in original), which is itself "a concept with which to grasp media and societal change" (Krotz, 2009, p. 21). Mediatization refers "to the meta process by which everyday practices and social relations are increasingly shaped by mediating technologies and media organizations" (Livingstone, 2009, p. 3). Even beyond ongoing discussions regarding the *correct* term, "mediatization or mediation" (Couldry, 2008, p. 373), or "*Mediatisierung* (mediatization) and *Medialisierung* (medialisation)" (Livingstone, 2009, p. 3; see also Couldry & Hepp, 2013), the concept of mediatization itself, its outreach and its relevance to the field are matter of debate (Lunt & Livingstone, 2016, p. 462). The discussion is moving between two antipodes: For one thing, Deacon and Stanyer (2014, p. 1032) argue that mediatization is at risk to become a "concept of no difference". Furthermore, they (Deacon & Stanyer, 2015, p. 655) voice their criticisms, because they see "the rise of a concept that claims to provide 'holistic' theoretical framework for explaining and analysing such processes" as the fundamental change of media, institutions, technologies and society. Otherwise, Hepp, Hjarvard, and Lundby (2015, p. 314) highlight "how mediatization research engages with the complex relationship between changes in media and communication, on the one hand, and changes in various fields of culture and society on the other". Hence, they see "the concept of mediatization" as a "part of a paradigmatic shift within media and communication research" (Hepp et al., 2015, p. 314).

Regardless of the discussion about the term and critical voices, the concept of mediatization is widely accepted and within the past ten years, the observable phenomena that are interpreted as indicators of mediatization have become more intense and ubiquitous and have gained speed (see Hepp & Hasebrink, 2018, p. 17). It has become increasingly difficult in our society to preserve media-free times and places, locations Hepp and Hasebrink (2018, p. 18) term "temporary oases of de-mediatization".

What does this intensified process of mediatization mean to children and young people? How do they make use of the abundance of media? In this respect, we can identify some global trends (see Hasebrink & Paus-Hasebrink, 2013), which are shaped by the changing media environment. Empirical evidence regarding these trends is provided by national studies on children's and adolescents' media use in different countries—for example, the Ofcom Children and Parents Report in the United Kingdom (Ofcom, 2017) or several studies from the United States (Common Sense Media, 2015, 2016, 2017; Rideout, Foehr, & Roberts, 2010). Similarly, for Upper Austria we can refer to a series of annual surveys on children's and adolescents' media usage (most recently, Education Group, 2016, 2017). The main studies for Germany are JIM (Youth, Information and [Multi-]Media) and KIM (Childhood, Internet, Media) (most recently, MPFS, 2016, 2017). In what follows we will outline some of the most important global trends. After that, we will illustrate recent developments through selected statistics for Austria or Germany. We take the data from these two countries as illustrating the general media-related context, in which the socially disadvantaged children and adolescents of our study grew up.

2.3.1.1 Availability of Media Services

Our premise maintains that children's and adolescents' everyday lives are particularly affected by the meta-process of mediatization. An increasing number of media devices, in a child's own bedroom and elsewhere in the family's household, the expanding range of functions offered by new services, the continuous and omnipresent availability of services which overcome temporal and spatial limits—these aspects mark a significant trend in children's and adolescents' media use. Today's children and young people have far more options for communicating than any generation before them (Rideout, 2016, p. 138). The media content and media services available to them are indeed potentially omnipresent.

2.3.1.2 Amount of Media Use
One consequence of the omnipresence of media services seems to be that children continue to spend more and more time with media. For example, in 2009 the 8- to 18-year-olds in the United States spent more than 7.5 hours per day with media (Rideout et al., 2010, p. 11); this was more than one hour longer than five years earlier. Over those years, the proportion of multitasking increased, indicating that young people increasingly use two or even more media simultaneously, so that the total time of media exposure added up to 10.75 hours, some 2.25 hours more than five years earlier.

2.3.1.3 Cross-Media Patterns of Usage
The media industry is increasingly developing cross-media strategies, with the goal of distributing content on as many platforms as possible. Famous media brands for children may originate from games, movies, television, comics, or even books (for example, Harry Potter), but are now available almost everywhere, as the same content is now marketed across different media platforms. Such media brands represent the elements integrating and characterising children's and adolescent's media repertoires (see Paus-Hasebrink & Hasebrink, 2015).

2.3.1.4 Mobility and Connectivity of Media Usage
Connectivity is increasingly moving away from the desktop and towards the mobile and wireless environments (see Horrigan, 2009). The Pew Report from 2010 declares: "cell phones are nearly ubiquitous in the lives of teens" (Lenhart, Purcell, Smith, & Zickuhr, 2010, p. 9). Today, most children and adolescents use smartphones to remain almost permanently connected in some way—be it communicating with friends and peers, be it playing online computer games or just ensuring that they are constantly contactable.

While our study focuses on socially disadvantaged children and adolescents, we will illustrate some of these trends by citing some general findings on the media usage of children and adolescents in Austria and Germany.

Already in 2005, when our study started, almost all adolescents in Austria and Germany used the internet at least occasionally. In this respect, the indicator age is the most relevant factor. Our Fig. 2.1 is based on the KIM survey in Germany and shows that throughout the years of our study the difference between age groups remained stable, with most children starting to use the internet between seven and twelve years.

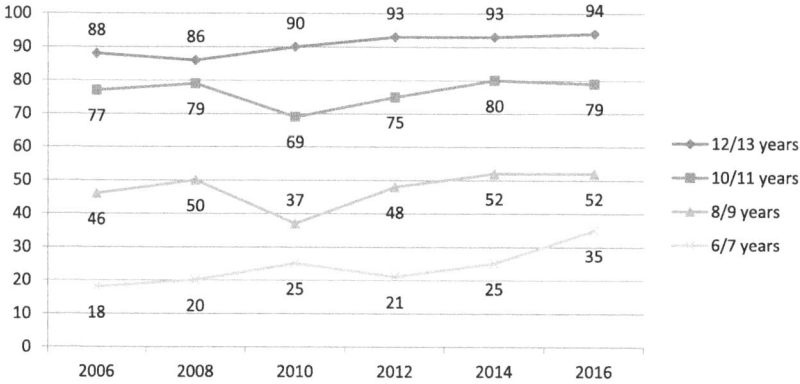

Fig. 2.1 Children (6–13 years) in Germany who use the internet (at least occasionally) (percentages; $n = 1200$) (*Source* KIM 2006–2016; www.mpfs.de)

The main driver of dynamic change in children's and adolescents' media environment has been the rapid spread of smartphones. Figure 2.2 illustrates how many adolescents (12–19 years) in Germany owned a cell phone or smartphone. It took less than five years for nine out of ten adolescents to be identified as owning a smartphone. Today, almost all adolescents have their own mobile smart device. In Upper Austria, the development has been almost the same (see Education Group, 2017): smartphone ownership among adolescents between eight and 11 years in increased from 4% in 2008 to 24% in 2011 and then to 60% in 2013, 77% in 2015 and 85% in 2017.

2.3.2 Mediatization and Its Consequences for Socially Disadvantaged Young People

At first glance, mediatization and social disadvantage do not seem very closely related. But the actual case is that, in general, social and material well-being is strongly connected to a high level of formal education and knowledge about media and communication. This applies particularly to digitalisation, so-called new media, automation, data processing and so on: "**Information and communication technologies** (ICT) have a considerable impact on living and working conditions. Nowadays, an increasing number of businesses rely on ICT for their daily operations

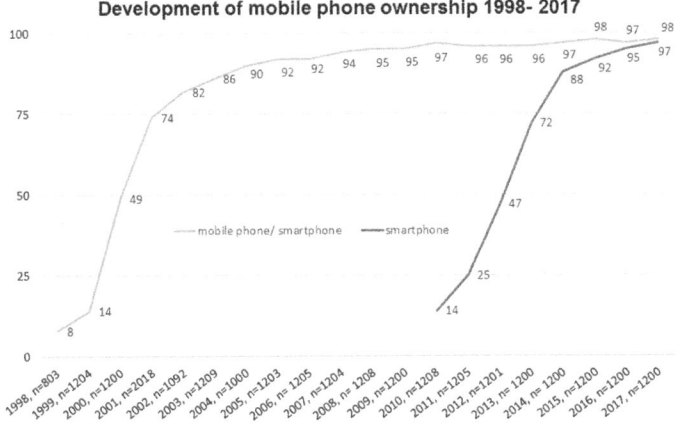

Fig. 2.2 Cell phone and smartphone ownership among adolescents (12–19 years) in Germany (percentages) (*Source* JIM 1998–2017; http://www.mpfs.de)

and this often requires the development and maintenance of ICT systems by specialists" (Eurostat, 2017d, emphasis in original). As a result, unemployment rates in this sector are very low in the European Union; the employment rate for people with ICT training is 91% (EU-28), but it rises to 97% in Germany, Hungary and Estonia and even up to 98% in Malta (Eurostat, 2017d). However, permanent employment is one of the key factors protecting individuals from poverty or social disadvantage (cf. Statistik Austria, 2017a, p. 3; Statistisches Bundesamt, 2017a; UNICEF, 2016, p. 14; van Dijk, 2013, p. 29). This example, then, shows clearly how people and their everyday lives actually are affected by processes of mediatization. The consequences of mediatization, and how to deal with them, have become huge challenges for many people all around the world (see van Dijk, 2013, pp. 29, 34). They reflect processes bringing fundamental change, and they affect virtually every human being, and two groups above all: young people and socially disadvantaged people.

Firstly, children and adolescents growing up are still searching for their identity (see Packer, 2017, pp. 477–487). They are not yet experienced in media usage and are particularly exposed to "content-related risks", "contact-related risks", and "conduct-related risks", but also to "other specified risks", such as for example, "health related risks", "spending too much time online" or a "lack of internet safety in general" (Livingstone, Kirwil, Ponte, & Staksrud, with the EU Kids Online Network, 2013, p. 5) and other contract-related risks. Therefore, they need help and support from adults, in the first instance from their parents, teachers and youth workers, but also from peers, companies, organisations, the state and all other stakeholders involved (see O'Neill, Staksrud, & McLaughlin, 2013, for a broad overview). We here emphasise one context of socialisation applying to these two groups: in mid childhood and especially adolescence, peers are of prime importance for identity formation, but also for wider questions and when practical help is needed (see Packer, 2017, pp. 487–493). But no single context of socialisation fits it all, and, in fact, the interplay of different groups succeeds best. A comparison of international surveys in 2013/14 ("Net Children Go Mobile") and in 2010 ("EU Kids Online") generated evidence that joint information and mediation strategies are helpful and "levels of digital skills are rising slowly" (Livingstone, Mascheroni, Ólafsson, & Haddon, with the networks of EU Kids Online and Net Children Go Mobile, 2014, p. 18).

Secondly, socially disadvantaged people benefit less from the opportunities given by new possibilities for communication, information and participation, even where access is possible. "However, class is an important aspect of the structuring of inequalities, intersecting in complex ways with all inequalities" (Walby, Armstrong, & Strid, 2012, p. 232), in particular in combination with "age" (p. 224). Today, we can benefit from the new possibilities of mass communication and from specific ways of interpersonal communication and we can participate in new fluid public spheres. But there is empirical evidence that this holds good, above all, for those with a better education, whose average income is higher and who live in urban areas with well-developed infrastructure (cf. Vorderer et al., 2015, p. 259; Wessels, 2013, p. 17). This problematic development gains in importance where the freedom of (digital) expression, the freedom of information and the freedom of access to government information and participation are considered to be universal rights for all citizens (cf. Berka & Trappel, 2017, pp. 66–68; see also Dutton, Dopatka, Hills, Law, & Nash, 2011, pp. 22–23; van Dijk, 2013, p. 35). Against this backdrop, the concept of a "second-level digital divide" (Hargittai, 2002) has received much attention. Its premise maintains that differences in people's online skills and access may be affected not only by age and experience but also by education and family income: "In particular, research in both the US and the UK has shown that children from a higher socioeconomic background are more likely to experience educational gains from home computer and internet use than others" (Hargittai & Walejko, 2008, p. 240). We must bear in mind here that, if this applies for online media, it will take on an increased importance with traditional media as well, since people are using a broad set of different media. However, the findings on computer use and the internet cited above "are in line with work on the differentiated uses of more traditional media such as the viewing of educational television programming in earlier decades (Cook et al. 1975)" (Hargittai & Walejko, 2008, p. 240). In addition, "access and use are the main topics of almost all the studies covered" (Paus-Hasebrink et al., 2014, p. 1), as regards online media and socially disadvantaged adolescents. "But for Europe we can state that a lack of access to the internet is not the key problem" (Berka & Trappel, 2017, pp. 116–117; Paus-Hasebrink et al., 2014, p. 1). However, there are differences in the "quality of access" (Livingstone, Haddon, Görzig, & Ólafsson, 2011a, p. 25): for example, mobile access, types of smartphones, data volume and speed of the connection. This equates with concerns by Jenkins, Clinton, Purushotma, Robison and Weigel, as already published in 2006 (p. 3, emphasis in original) and referring to a participation gap: **"The Participation Gap**—the unequal access to the opportunities, experiences, skills, and knowledge that will prepare youth for full participation in the world of tomorrow". Again, socio-economic status is highly relevant for internet usage and vice versa: "The ways in which we use the Internet, our skills and digital background, our digital and social capital, all influence our social status" (Ragnedda, 2017, p. 73). Therefore, it seems reasonable to follow Eszter Hargittai and Gina Walejko (2008, p. 239, emphasis in original) using the term "PARTICIPATION DIVIDE" instead of digital divide, and to "note that access to technology no longer wholly determines potential inequalities derived from differential information and communication technology uses" (p. 241). From research on intersectionality, we know that there might be a strengthening effect when two or more factors come together (Walby et al., 2012, p. 224). There is general agreement that all children and adolescents need our awareness, and that no less where we collect evidence for research. Furthermore, there should be more effective analysis of social disadvantage. However, we should pay special attention if these two factors coincide and we are dealing with socially disadvantaged children and adolescents. "Socially disadvantaged children are at risk in a double way. On the one hand, they suffer from the effects of their parents' socio-structural problems, on the other hand they use media very intensively which means that their socialisation is dominated by media" (Paus-Hasebrink et al., 2014, p. 1). Unfortunately, they are more often left alone when using media or being online and do not have the chance to ask for help or guidance. There is a high correlation between the economic well-being of a family and its educational background. The educational background of the parents has a large influence on the ways media are used in a family (see Livingstone, Haddon, Görzig, & Ólafsson, 2011b, p. 2). Parents' formal education may be named the "key indicator of socioeconomic status" (Paus-Hasebrink, Ponte, Dürager, & Bauwens, 2012, p. 258). However, beside socio-economic aspects as income and educational level, the socio-emotional conditions in a family also play a major role (see Paus-Hasebrink et al., 2012; Paus-Hasebrink, 2017, p. 19). Socio-economic factors include, inter alia, a lack of financial resources or restrictions in the way of living (for example, a lack of healthy food, clothes and spare time activities, low formal education, non-prestigious jobs or bad housing situations). Socio-emotional factors are stable and trustful relationships within the family, strong ties to other important reference persons, competent contact persons in case of problems, or effective approaches to deal with problems and meet challenges. A serious problem occurs in what is termed an "*Unskilled Family*" (Paus-Hasebrink, Bauwens, Dürager, & Ponte, 2013, p. 122, emphasis in original), where parents often cannot support their children and their media usage in an appropriate way. In these families, "parents have a low educational background and SES", and "the parent-child relationships are characterized by low levels of active mediation and a strong tendency to restrictive mediation" (Paus-Hasebrink et al., 2013, p. 122). At this place, active mediation refers to parents talking to their children about what they do on the internet or helping them when something is difficult to do or find on the internet. Restrictive mediation refers to parents limiting or restricting their children's internet use.

2.3.3 *Social Disadvantages and Media Experiences*

In contrast to the importance for the future of our society and of media usage and media socialisation among (socially disadvantaged) adolescents, studies on these topics are currently not the main field of activity in media and communication research. However, there is academic evidence on different aspects of the topics that are relevant to our research interest. In the following, we will provide a brief overview of selected studies that help us to better understand the role of media within children's socialisation, with a particular focus on socially disadvantaged children. It has to be emphasised that these studies are quite heterogeneous in how they define social disadvantaged and which particular aspect of the topic they deal with. Therefore our overview cannot provide a coherent story; instead we demonstrate the range of relevant approaches. In Chapter 3, we will present a comprehensive theoretical framework that allows for integrating the different lines of research.

To cover the field, we primarily used two sources: The European evidence database, made available by The EU Kids Online Network (2018), and the database concerning media socialisation research at https://uni-salzburg.at/mediensozialisation (Paus-Hasebrink, von Reinersdorff, & Sinner, 2017). In addition, a concurrent literature review was conducted. In order to cover a wide range of studies, including those with somewhat marginal topics, we followed a broad approach, using several combinations of search terms (see also Paus-Hasebrink et al., 2014, p. 8).

It is striking that a great many studies originate from Southern European countries or from such countries with greater social inequality as, for example, Brazil or Russia. Simões, Ponte, and Jorge (2013) compared people recruited in a social inclusion centre for vulnerable children and adolescents in Portugal to the results of the EU Kids Online data set. Concerning skills, they found only minor differences: for example, the socially disadvantaged adolescents had less online access at home, but they tended to use more entertainment services. A Spanish study conducted by Cabello (2013, p. 62) paid special attention to the impact of "segregated and stigmatised neighbourhoods". Based on a multi-method approach he tested their abilities to participate and deal with online media—with positive results. However, he highlighted the importance of non-family institutions to teach skills and to empower socially disadvantaged adolescents. Milioni, Doudaki, and Demertzis (2014) compared two parts of a divided country: The Republic of Cyprus/Greek-Cypriot community and Northern Cyprus/Turkish-Cypriot community. They confirm findings on the positive effect of higher education and age as regards experience and skills, but with the unexpected addition that family income is not of importance in this context in Cyprus: "In Cyprus, income does not appear to be related either to access, experience, and use the internet [sic!] or to specific activities online" (Milioni et al., 2014, p. 12). In contrast, in a Dutch study already published in 2006, Peter and Valkenburg confirmed the impact of the socio-economic background, but they underlined the relevance of cognitive resources as well. Concerning aspects of the digital divide, they state: "once access gaps are bridged, other gaps open, most notably in terms of adolescents' use of the internet [...]" (Peter & Valkenburg, 2006, p. 18). Another study on digital parenting in Russia conducted by Ravve (2012) shows both, differences between higher and lower income families in their use of technology and tremendous differences within one country relating to access and costs: "The gap between wealthy and poor parents is significant not only in terms of children's access to devices, but also in their attitudes towards technology. Higher income families tend to see a more positive impact of the digital media on kids' development" (Ravve, 2012, p. 12). Data transfer rates are high in metropolitan areas like Moscow and St. Petersburg but low in rural areas, in particular in the Eastern parts of the country, but the relation is reversed when it comes to the costs (Ravve, 2012, pp. 5, 21). These findings underline the importance of (digital) infrastructure also in more rural areas or such parts of a country that do not belong to the central or capital area in order to provide an equal standard of living. This becomes even more evident when we have a look to South America: One rapidly developing country, and member of the BRICS-states, is Brazil. However, its infrastructure and economic indicators are not yet comparable with the industrialised countries of Western Europe. A comparison of the ICT Kids Online Brazil 2012 data (Barbosa & cgi.br, 2013) with the EU Kids Online data set reveals that the area where people live and their socio-economic status both have a great influence on their access to and use of ICTs in Brazil: "Internet access for the lowest socio-economic households was 6%, while it was 97% for the highest" (Barbosa, O'Neill, Ponte, Simões, & Jereissati, 2013, p. 6). In contrast, three studies from Italy and Turkey underline the important role of usage: Marco Gui (2013) compared high school students ($n=3634$, aged 15–18) and teachers ($n=980$) in Lombardy and Trentino, two rich regions in the Northern part of the country (see also Gui, Micheli, & Tamanini, 2015). The positive impact of the parents' educational and socio-economic background on three aspects stood out: the digital literacy of the children, the use of privacy setting on social networking sites by the children, the choice of personal information to be published on social networking sites. As far as risks and opportunities go, a Turkish study conducted by Akbulut, Sahin, and Eristi (2010) is very interesting. 1470 representatively chosen teenagers (aged 15–18) were interviewed about their online experiences and about victimisation through cyber-bullying: "The victimization scores of the high-income group were significantly higher than those of the middle-income group, whereas the low-income group was in between and did not differ from other groups significantly" (Akbulut et al., 2010, p. 199). This could not be explained by their increased internet usage of the high-income group, but by their making more frequent use of foreign websites. Children with a higher socio-economic background were also at more risk in another study, also conducted in Turkey, on internet addiction (Batigün, Kiliç, Akün, & Özgür, 2010). In the United States, the study, "Ownership and use of new media" (Lauricella, Cingel, Blackwell, Wartella, & Conway, 2014) was conducted among 8- to 17-year-old children and adolescents nation-wide. It covered different internet devices, mobile devices and other forms of newer media technologies in order to analyse the motivation and the ways of usage of the different age groups. The authors are able to demonstrate the diffusion of new mobile devices even among younger children and they point out that they are avid to make use of them. Furthermore, they prove the different functions of internet usage among children and adolescents of different age groups, reflecting their interests and motivations. Another nationally representative study from the United States, "Opportunity for all?" (Rideout & Katz, 2016), is providing a special focus on lower-income families with children attending primary and secondary schools. It reported problems with slow internet connections, which is comparable to Russia or Brazil, and connections turned off due to unpaid bills. Mobile devices like smartphones and tablets are considered substitutes, but they are not suitable when it comes to more complex tasks and acquiring digital skills.

The next study has a similar orientation but with a more lifeworld oriented focus: The qualitative study conducted in Austria pays attention to poor children and adolescents (8–15 years) and sets out their own perspective on poverty and their living conditions compared to other young people, who may be at risk of becoming poor, or to others who do not qualify as poor (Einböck et al., 2015). The subjects report on different access to activities and locations in their leisure time (for example, outdoor activities, sport clubs, youth centres, music schools)

(Einböck et al., 2015, pp. 15–16). The poor children and adolescents report feeling embarrassed, because their parents are not able to support them with money, and furthermore, some of them report becoming victims of bullying due to their poverty (Einböck et al., 2015, p. 5). More detailed, cyberbullying is the specific topic of a German study from 2015 (Stodt, Wegmann, & Brand, 2015), in connection with internet addiction and online skills. It should be emphasised that this study is not dealing with social disadvantage in general, but the authors present highly relevant characteristics and functional mechanisms that are related to the usage of internet and social networking sites as well as to internet addiction and victimisation due to cyberbullying. Particularly introverted and shy persons tend to use internet and social networking sites more intensively. The authors assume that this might be connected to a higher risk for uncontrolled usage. A high level of involvement (active, engaged and creative participation online) is likewise a predictor for being at risk of becoming internet-addicted. When it comes to cyber-bullying, victims tend to more often report timidity, depression and uncertainty in dealing with social contact. These topics are related to a study conducted by Marjon Schols (2015) in the Netherlands that deals with the results of everyday internet usage among 12- to 18-year-old teenagers: intensive usage is able to foster cohesion within peer groups. Being actively online on platforms on the internet is also a starting point for political participation online and offline. However, this study also strongly suggests that an adolescent's higher level of formal education is pointing to a more probable interest in cultural and political activities. In Norway, the digital divide and information literacy among pupils was the topic of a study by Ole Edvard Hatlevik and Greta Björk Gudmundsdottir (2013). They interviewed 3727 pupils at 50 different middle schools characterised by a multi-ethnic student body and relatively high rates of pupils with a migration background. New information and communication technologies were considered as well as "spoken language", "the number of books at home" and the young people's academic aspiration. Their "findings indicate that the number of books at home, the language spoken at home and the students' academic aspirations explain a very large proportion of the variation in information literacy between schools, and a considerable part of the variation between students–within–schools".

In all the studies discussed above, only one country is covered (or rather two communities of a divided country in the case of Cyprus). Such national research is important, but it is equally important to pay special attention to groups of countries for comparison purposes. Since 2006, this has been the aim of the EU Kids Online research dealing with 21, and subsequently 33, countries in Europe (plus affiliated projects in additional countries). In order to better understand how the context of particular countries shapes the situation of children and adolescents, The EU Kids Online Network (2014, p. 8) has proposed five dimensions of country-specific characteristics, based on its work over eight years: "socio-economic stratification", "regulatory framework", "technological infrastructure", "education system" and "cultural values". In the context of poverty and social disadvantage, the economic situation (for example, economic growth, labour market, unemployment rates), the concept of statehood (for example, political system, social system, responsibilities) and the social fabric (for example, harmonious life together, social gap, rate of inequality, integration of refugees and migrants) are of prime importance: "Countries differ heavily in terms of income, education, social welfare and other factors, leading to different perceptions of what counts as being socially disadvantaged between, and even within, countries and regions" (Paus-Hasebrink et al., 2014, p. 8).

2.4 Conclusion

(Child) poverty and social disadvantage are not only problems of so-called poor countries but also of rich Western societies like Austria and Germany. Social disadvantage is in most cases strongly connected to lower formal education and worse future prospects. This goes hand-in-hand with a lack of participation opportunities within society. As regards processes of technological and societal change—framed as the meta-process of mediatization—we have to consider that socially disadvantaged people, in particular children and adolescents, are at risk of falling further and further behind. Therefore, we need to investigate how socially disadvantaged children and adolescents grow up in their specific life situation.

As has been shown in the literature review, the majority of the respective studies deals with differences between socially disadvantaged and non-disadvantaged adolescents in terms of internet access, usage and skills. Only a few of them take a closer look into the particular situation of children and adolescents who grow up in socially disadvantaged contexts. From our own research on the role of media for socially disadvantaged children and young people, we draw the following conclusions.

Firstly, mediatization is closely linked to what we call cross-media. Therefore, we have to ensure we not only pay attention to single media usage but also to "cross-media practices" (Hasebrink & Hepp, 2017, p. 362). In a mediatised cross-media society, doing single-media research, such as, for example, television research, radio research or online research, falls short. We need an integrative approach which allows us to answer the questions as to *which* media services are used by young people, how they are *combined* and *why* young people make use of them (see Vorderer et al., 2015, pp. 272–274). With the concept of "media repertoires", Uwe Hasebrink and Jutta Popp (2006) introduce an idea into the debate on how audience studies might capture people's use of various media. Media repertoires reflect "patterns of behaviour" and "meaningful practices" (Hasebrink & Dohmeyer, 2012, p. 757). Such an approach is able to breathe life into the concept of cross-media because it pays the same attention to more traditional media, like TV, radio, books and newspapers, as it does to online media or new communication tools.

Secondly, we have to focus on children and adolescents within the context of their lifeworld and their social environment. The central question in this respect is how young people make subjective sense of media in general and of the specific kinds of content and services they use in order to deal with their everyday challenges. We need to reflect the interplay between socio-economic and socio-emotional aspects of socialisation and to carefully look at children's and young people's opportunities within their socialisation, which are narrowly connected to the social situation where they grow up. Against this background, the research question of our study is: How do socially disadvantaged life circumstances affect adolescents, their socialisation and their opportunities to participate in society and which role do media play in this context?

In order to answer this question, we developed a theoretical and methodological approach which will be presented in Chapters 3 and 4. As we set out to gain a deeper insight into children's lives—embedded in their families and the families' social situation—we decided to conduct a qualitative long-term study with a panel of socially disadvantaged children and families, extending from 2005, when children were five years old, until 2017, when they were on the edge of adulthood.

References

Akbulut, Y., Sahin, Y. L., & Eristi, B. (2010). Cyberbullying victimization among Turkish online social utility members. *Educational Technology & Society, 13*(4), 192–201.

Atkinson, A. B., Guio, A.-C., & Marlier, E. (2017). Monitoring social inclusion in Europe. In A. B. Atkinson, A.-C. Guio, & E. Marlier (Eds.), *Monitoring social inclusion in Europe—2017 edition* (pp. 33–49). City of Luxembourg, Luxembourg: Publications Office of the European Union. Retrieved from http://ec.europa.eu/eurostat/documents/3217494/8031566/KS-05-14-075-EN-N.pdf/c3a33007-6cf2-4d86-9b9e-d39fd3e5420c.

AWO-ISS. (2012). *"Von alleine wächst sich nichts aus..." Lebenslagen von armen Kindern und Jugendlichen und gesellschaftliches Handeln bis zum Ende der Sekundarstufe I. Abschlussbericht der 4. Phase der Langzeitstudie im Auftrag des Bundesverbandes der Arbeiterwohlfahrt*. Auszug [Living conditions of poor children and adolescents and social action]. Frankfurt am Main, Germany: AWO. Retrieved from http://www.awo-frankfurt.com/fileadmin/user_upload/dokumente/Sozial_und_Politisch/Armut/AWO-ISS-Armutsstudie_zentrale_Ergebnisse.pdf.

AWO-ISS. (2013). *Lebenslagen und Zukunftschancen von (armen) Kindern und Jugendlichen in Deutschland. 15 Jahre AWO-ISS-Studie* [Living conditions and future perspectives of (poor) children and adolescents in Germany]. Frankfurt am Main and Berlin, Germany: Institut für Sozialarbeit und Sozialpädagogik e.V. & AWO Bundesverband. Retrieved from http://www.iss-ffm.de/m_106.

Barbosa, A., & cgi.br. (2013). *ICT Kids Online Brazil 2012: Survey on internet use by children in Brazil*. São Paulo: Comitê Gestor da Internet no Brasil. São Paulo, Brazil: cgi.br. Retrieved from http://cetic.br/media/docs/publicacoes/2/tic-kids-online-2012.pdf.

Barbosa, A., O'Neill, B., Ponte, C., Simões, J. A., & Jereissati, T. (2013). Risks and safety on the internet: Comparing Brazilian and European children. *The EU Kids Online Network*. London, UK: LSE. Retrieved from http://eprints.lse.ac.uk/54801/.

Batigün, A. D., Kiliç, N., Akün, E., & Özgür, P. (2010). Internet addiction: An investigation of personality traits, psychological symptoms, social support and the aspect of related socio-demographic variables. *TÜBITAK Project*. Ankara, Turkey: University of Ankara.

Berka, W., & Trappel, J. (2017). *Internetfreiheit in Österreich. Eine Bestandsaufnahme auf der Grundlage der Empfehlung CM/REC(2016)5 des Ministerkomitees des Europarats an die Mitgliedstaaten zur Internetfreiheit* [Internet freedom in Austria]. Salzburg, Austria: Fachbereich Öffentliches Recht/Verfassungs- und Verwaltungsrecht & Fachbereich Kommunikationswissenschaft der Universität Salzburg.

Bertelsmann Stiftung. (2016). *Kinderarmut. Kinder im SGB-II-Bezug in Deutschland* [Child poverty in Germany]. Gütersloh, Germany: Bertelsmann Stiftung. Retrieved from https://www.bertelsmann-stiftung.de/de/themen/aktuelle-meldungen/2016/september/kinderarmut-in-deutschland-waechst-weiter-mit-folgen-fuers-ganze-leben/.

Cabello, P. (2013). A qualitative approach to the use of ICTs and its risks among socially disadvantaged early adolescents and adolescents in Madrid, Spain. *Communications, 38*(1), 61–83.

Caritas. (2016). *Familienarmut im Land Salzburg. Fakten. Lebenslagen. Wahrnehmungen. 2016* [Poverty of families in Salzburg]. Salzburg, Austria: Erzdiözese Salzburg. Retrieved from https://www.caritas-salzburg.at/fileadmin/storage/salzburg/webseite/aktuell/Kampagnen/ArmutvonFamilieninSalzburgENDFASSUNG.pdf.

Carpentier, N., Schrøder, K. C., & Hallett, L. (2014). Audience/society transformations. In N. Carpentier, K. C. Schrøder, & L. Hallett (Eds.), *Audience transformations: Shifting audience positions in late modernity* (pp. 1–12). New York, NY: Routledge.

Castells, M. (2011). *The rise of the network society: Second edition, with a new preface. The information age: Economy, society and culture* (Vol. 1). Hoboken, NJ and Oxford, UK: Wiley-Blackwell.

Common Sense Media. (2015). *Census media use by tweens and teens*. San Francisco, CA: Common Sense Media. Retrieved from https://www.commonsensemedia.org/research/the-common-sense-census-media-use-by-tweens-and-teens.

Common Sense Media. (2016). *Census plugged-in parents of tweens and teens 2016*. San Francisco, CA: Common Sense Media. Retrieved from https://www.commonsensemedia.org/research/the-common-sense-census-plugged-in-parents-of-tweens-and-teens-2016.

Common Sense Media. (2017). *Census media use by kids age zero to eight 2017*. San Francisco, CA: Common Sense Media. Retrieved from https://www.commonsensemedia.org/research/the-common-sense-census-media-use-by-kids-age-zero-to-eight-2017.

Cook, T. D., Appleton, H., Conner, R. F., Shaffer, A., Tamkin, G., & Weber, S. J. (1975). *'Sesame street' revisited*. New York, NY: Russell Sage Foundation.

Couldry, N. (2008). Mediatization or mediation? Alternative understandings of the emergent space of digital storytelling. *New Media & Society, 10*(3), 373–391.

Couldry, N., & Hepp, A. (2013). Conceptualizing mediatization: Contexts, traditions, arguments. *Journal of Communication Theory, 23*(3), 191–202.

Deacon, D., & Stanyer, J. (2014). Mediatization: Key concept or conceptual bandwagon? *Media, Culture and Society, 36*(7), 1032–1044.

Deacon, D., & Stanyer, J. (2015). 'Mediatization and' or 'mediatization of'? A response to Hepp et al. *Media, Culture and Society, 37*(4), 655–657.
Dutton, W. H., Dopatka, A., Hills, M., Law, G., & Nash, V. (2011). *Freedom of connection, freedom of expression: The changing legal and regulatory ecology shaping the internet*. A report prepared for UNESCO's division for freedom of expression, democracy and peace. Paris, France: United Nations Educational, Scientific and Cultural Organization and Oxford Internet Institute. Retrieved from http://unesdoc.unesco.org/images/0019/001915/191594e.pdf.
Education Group. (2016). *5. Oö. Kinder-Medien-Studie 2016. Das Medienverhalten der 3- bis 10-Jährigen* [Children and media in upper Austria]. Linz, Austria: Education Group.
Education Group. (2017). *5. Oö. Jugend-Medien-Studie 2017. Das Medienverhalten der 11- bis 18-Jährigen* [Youth and media in upper Austria]. Linz, Austria: Education Group.
Einböck, M., Proyer, M., & Fenninger, E. (2015). Lebensbedingungen und Sichtweisen von Kindern und Jugendlichen in und über Armut. Ergebnisse aus einer Erhebung zu den Lebenswelten und Netzwerken armutsbetroffener, armutsgefährdeter und nicht-armutsgefährdeter Kinder und Jugendlicher in zwei österreichischen Regionen [Living conditions and perspectives of children and adolescents in poverty, at risk to poverty and not at risk to poverty in two regions of Austria]. *Projektberichte der Volkshilfe Österreich*. Wien, Austria: Volkshilfe. Retrieved from https://www.volkshilfe.at/cms/download.php?downloadId=348&languageId=1.
Eurostat. (2017a). *Key figures on Europe—2017 edition*. City of Luxembourg, Luxembourg: Publications Office of the European Union. Retrieved from http://ec.europa.eu/eurostat/documents/3217494/8309812/KS-EI-17-001-EN-N.pdf/b7df53f5-4faf-48a6-aca1-c650d40c9239.
Eurostat. (2017b). *17 October: International day for the eradication of poverty. Downward trend in the share of persons at risk of poverty or social exclusion in the EU. But still over 115 million people in this situation*. City of Luxembourg, Luxembourg: Publications Office of the European Union. Retrieved from http://ec.europa.eu/eurostat/documents/2995521/8314163/3-16102017-BP-EN.pdf/d31fadc6-a284-47f3-ae1c-8212a581b0c1.
Eurostat. (2017c). *Eurostatistics. Data for short-term economic analysis—09/2017*. City of Luxembourg, Luxembourg: Publications Office of the European Union. Retrieved from http://ec.europa.eu/eurostat/documents/3217494/8220902/KS-BJ-17-009-EN-N.pdf/8972dccb-9c04-4443-85a4-d0254a8eb31c.
Eurostat. (2017d). *Digital economy & society in the EU. A browse through our online world in figures—2017 edition. Profile of the digital society & businesses. 1.3 Digital skills for a digital world*. City of Luxembourg, Luxembourg:

Publications Office of the European Union. Retrieved from http://ec.europa.eu/eurostat/cache/infographs/ict/bloc-1c.html.

Gui, M. (Ed.). (2013). Indagine sull'uso dei nuovi media tra gli studenti delle scuole superiori lombarde [New media among high school students in Lombardia]. *Dipartimento di Sociologia e Ricerca Sociale - Università di Milano-Bicocca*. Milano, Italy: Regione Lombardia. Retrieved from http://www.orientainsieme.it/wp-content/uploads/2014/10/Indagine-uso-dei-media-studenti-Lombardia.pdf.

Gui, M., Micheli, M., & Tamanini, C. (2015). I media digitali nella vita dei sedicenni delle scuole del Trentino: usi e competenze [Digital media in the lives of the 16 years olds in schools of Trentino: Use and competencies]. *Istituto provinciale per la ricerca e la sperimentazione educativa*. Rovereto, Italy: IPRASE. Retrieved from http://community.formazionescuolatrentina.it/j/file_iprase/attachs/292.pdf.

Guio, A.-C., Gordon, D., & Marlier, E. (2017). Measuring child material deprivation in the EU. In A. B. Atkinson, A.-C. Guio, & E. Marlier (Eds.), *Monitoring social inclusion in Europe—2017 edition* (pp. 209–224). City of Luxembourg, Luxembourg: Publications Office of the European Union. Retrieved from http://ec.europa.eu/eurostat/documents/3217494/8031566/KS-05-14-075-EN-N.pdf/c3a33007-6cf2-4d86-9b9e-d39fd3e5420c.

Hargittai, E. (2002). Second-level digital divide: Differences in people's online skills. *First Monday, 7*(4). Retrieved from http://firstmonday.org/article/view/942/864.

Hargittai, E., & Walejko, G. (2008). The participation divide: Content creation and sharing in the digital age. *Information, Community and Society, 11*(2), 239–256.

Hasebrink, U., & Domeyer, H. (2012). Media repertoires as patterns of behaviour and as meaningful practices: A multimethod approach to media use in converging media environments. *Participations: Journal of Audience & Reception Studies, 9*(2), 757–783.

Hasebrink, U., & Hepp, A. (2017). How to research cross-media practices? Investigating media repertoires and media ensembles. *Convergence: The International Journal of Research into New Media Technologies, 23*(4), 362–377.

Hasebrink, U., & Paus-Hasebrink, I. (2013). Trends in children's consumption of media. In D. Lemish (Ed.), *The Routledge international handbook of children, adolescents and media* (pp. 31–38). Milton Park and London, UK: Routledge and Taylor & Francis.

Hasebrink, U., & Popp, J. (2006). Media repertoires as a result of selective media use: A conceptual approach to the analysis of patterns of exposure. *Communications, 31*(2), 369–387.

Hatlevik, O. E., & Gudmundsdottir, G. B. (2013). An emerging digital divide in urban school children's digital literacy: Challenging equity in the Norwegian school system. *First Monday, 18*. Retrieved from http://firstmonday.org/ojs/index.php/fm/article/view/4232/3641#author.

Hepp, A., & Hasebrink, U. (2018). Researching transforming communications in times of deep mediatization: A figurational approach. In A. Hepp, A. Breiter, & U. Hasebrink (Eds.), *Communicative figurations: Transforming communications in times of deep mediatization* (pp. 15–48). London, UK: Palgrave Macmillan.

Hepp, A., Hjarvard, S., & Lundby, K. (2015). Mediatization: Theorizing the interplay between media, culture and society. *Media, Culture and Society, 37*(2), 314–324.

Horrigan, J. B. (2009). *Wireless internet use*. Washington, DC: Pew Report Center. Retrieved from http://www.pewinternet.org/2009/07/22/wireless-internet-use/.

Jenkins, H., Clinton, K., Purushotma, R., Robison, A. J., & Weigel, M. (2006). *Confronting the challenges of participatory culture: Media education for the 21st century. An occasional paper on digital media and learning*. Chicago, IL: The John D. and Catherine T. MacArthur Foundation. Retrieved from https://www.curriculum.org/secretariat/files/Sept30TLConfronting.pdf.

Jenkins, S. P., & Van Kerm, P. (2017). How does attrition affect estimates of persistent poverty rates? The case of EU-SILC. In A. B. Atkinson, A.-C. Guio, & E. Marlier (Eds.), *Monitoring social inclusion in Europe—2017 edition* (pp. 400–417). City of Luxembourg, Luxembourg: Publications Office of the European Union. Retrieved from http://ec.europa.eu/eurostat/documents/3217494/8031566/KS-05-14-075-EN-N.pdf/c3a33007-6cf2-4d86-9b9e-d39fd3e5420c.

Jokinen, K., & Kuronen, M. (2011). Research on families and family policies in Europe: Major trends. In U. Uhlendorff, M. Rupp, & M. Euteneuer (Eds.), *Wellbeing of families in future Europe: Challenges for research and policy* (pp. 13–118). Dortmund, Germany: Familyplatform. Retrieved from https://eldorado.tu-dortmund.de/bitstream/2003/28914/1/WellbeingOfFamiliesInEurope.pdf.

Krotz, F. (2009). Mediatization: A concept with which to grasp media and societal change. In K. Lundby (Ed.), *Mediatization: Concept, changes, consequences* (pp. 21–40). New York, NY: Peter Lang.

Krotz, F. (2014). Mediatization as a mover in modernity: Social and cultural change in the context of media change. In K. Lundby (Ed.), *Mediatization of communication: Handbook of communication science* (pp. 131–162). Berlin, Germany: de Gruyter.

Lange, A., & Xyländer, M. (2011). Bildungswelt Familie. Disziplinäre Perspektiven, theoretische Rahmungen und Desiderate der empirischen Forschung [Education world family: Disciplinary perspectives, theoretical frames and desideratum for research]. In A. Lange & M. Xyländer (Eds.), *Bildungswelt Familie. Theoretische Rahmung, empirische Befunde und disziplinäre Perspektiven* [Education world family: Theoretical frame, empirical evidence and disciplinary perspectives] (pp. 23–94). Weinheim and München, Germany: Juventa.

Laubstein, C., Holz, G., & Seddig, N. (2016). *Armutsfolgen für arme Kinder und Jugendliche. Erkenntnisse aus empirischen Studien in Deutschland* [Consequences of poverty for children and adolescents: Empirical evidence from research in Germany]. Gütersloh, Germany: Bertelsmann Stiftung. Retrieved from https://www.bertelsmann-stiftung.de/fileadmin/files/BSt/Publikationen/GrauePublikationen/Studie_WB_Armutsfolgen_fuer_Kinder_und_Jugendliche_2016.pdf.

Lauricella, A. R., Cingel, D. P., Blackwell, C., Wartella, E., & Conway, A. (2014). The mobile generation: Youth and adolescent ownership and use of new media. *Communication Research Reports, 31*(4), 357–364.

Lenhart, A., Purcell, K., Smith, A., & Zickuhr, K. (2010). *Social media & mobile internet use among teens and young adults*. Washington, DC: Pew Report Center. Retrieved from http://pewinternet.org/Reports/2010/Social-Media-and-Young-Adults.aspx.

Livingstone, S. (2009). On the mediation of everything: ICA presidential address 2008. *Journal of Communication, 59*(1), 1–18.

Livingstone, S., Haddon, L., Görzig, A., & Ólafsson, K. (2011a). Risks and safety on the internet: The perspective of European children—Full findings and policy implications from the EU Kids Online survey of 9–16 year olds and their parents in 25 countries. *The EU Kids Online Network*. London, UK: LSE. Retrieved from http://eprints.lse.ac.uk/33731/.

Livingstone, S., Haddon, L., Görzig, A., & Ólafsson, K. (2011b). Disadvantaged children and online risk. *The EU Kids Online Network*. London: LSE. Retrieved from http://eprints.lse.ac.uk/39385/.

Livingstone, S., Kirwil, L., Ponte, C., & Staksrud, E., with the EU Kids Online Network. (2013). In their own words: What bothers children online? *The EU Kids Online Network*. London, UK: LSE. Retrieved from http://eprints.lse.ac.uk/48357/.

Livingstone, S., Mascheroni, G., Ólafsson, K., & Haddon, L., with the networks of EU Kids Online and Net Children Go Mobile. (2014). Children's online risks and opportunities: Comparative findings from EU Kids Online and Net Children Go Mobile. *The EU Kids Online Network*. London, UK: LSE. Retrieved from http://eprints.lse.ac.uk/id/eprint/60513.

Lunt, P., & Livingstone, S. (2016). Is 'mediatization' the new paradigm for our field? A commentary on Deacon and Stanyer (2014, 2015) and Hepp, Harvard, and Lundby (2015). *Media, Culture and Society, 38*(3), 462–470.

Milioni, D. L., Doudaki, V., & Demertzis, N. (2014). Youth, ethnicity, and a 'reverse digital divide': A study of internet use in a divided country. *Convergence: The International Journal of Research into New Media Technologies, 20*(3), 316–336.

MPFS (Medienpädagogischer Forschungsverbund Südwest). (2016). *KIM 2016. Kindheit, Internet, Medien. Basisstudie zum Medienumgang 6- bis 13-Jähriger in Deutschland* [KIM 2016. Childhood, internet, media]. Stuttgart, Germany: MPFS. Retrieved from https://www.mpfs.de/fileadmin/files/Studien/KIM/2016/KIM_2016_Web-PDF.pdf.

MPFS (Medienpädagogischer Forschungsverbund Südwest). (2017). *JIM 2017. Jugend, Information, (Multi-)Media. Basisstudie zum Medienumgang 12- bis 19-Jähriger in Deutschland* [JIM 2017. Adolescents, information, (multi-) media]. Stuttgart, Germany: MPFS. Retrieved from. https://www.mpfs.de/fileadmin/files/Studien/JIM/2017/JIM_2017.pdf.

O'Neill, B., Staksrud, E., & Mclaughlin, S. (Eds.). (2013). *Towards a better internet for children: Policy pillars, players and paradoxes*. Research antologies. Gothenburg, Sweden: Nordicom.

Ofcom. (2017). *Children and parents: Media use and attitudes report*. London, UK: Ofcom. Retrieved from https://www.ofcom.org.uk/research-and-data/media-literacy-research/childrens/children-parents-2017.

ORF/APA. (2017). *Österreich weiter viertreichstes EU-Land* [Austria remains on rank four of the richest countries of the European Union]. Wien, Austria: ORF and Austria Presse Agentur. Retrieved from http://orf.at/stories/2395280/.

Packer, M. J. (2017). *Child development: Understanding a cultural perspective*. London, UK, Los Angeles, CA, New Delhi, India, and Singapore: Sage.

Palentien, C. (2003). Armut – Subjekt – Sozialisation. Ein Plädoyer für eine Stärkung sozialisationstheoretischer Perspektiven in der aktuellen Diskussion eines sozialen Phänomens [Poverty—subject—socialisation: A plea to foster a socialisation theoretical perspective]. In J. Mansel, H. M. Griese, & A. Scherr (Eds.), *Theoriedefizite der Jugendforschung. Standortbestimmung und Perspektiven* [Theory gaps in youth research: Determination and perspectives] (pp. 91–101). Weinheim and München, Germany: Juventa.

Paus-Hasebrink, I. (2017). Mediengebrauch in der Sozialisation: Langzeit-Panelstudie zu sozial benachteiligten Heranwachsenden [Media usage and socialisation]. In I. Paus-Hasebrink (Ed.), *Langzeitstudie zur Rolle von Medien in der Sozialisation sozial benachteiligter Heranwachsender. Lebensphase Jugend* [Longitudinal study on the role of media within socialisation of socially disadvantaged adolescents: Phase of adolescence] (pp. 15–20). Baden-Baden, Germany: Nomos.

Paus-Hasebrink, I., & Bichler, M. (2008). *Mediensozialisationsforschung. Theoretische Fundierung und Fallbeispiel sozial benachteiligte Kinder* [Media socialisation research—Theoretical foundation and a case study on socially disadvantaged children]. Assisted by C. Wijnen. Innsbruck, Austria: Studienverlag.

Paus-Hasebrink, I., & Hasebrink, U. (2015). Media brands in everyday lives. In G. Siegert, K. Förster, S. Chan-Olmsted, & M. Ots (Eds.), *Handbook of media branding* (pp. 295–306). Heidelberg, Germany and New York, NY: Springer International Publishing.

Paus-Hasebrink, I., & Kulterer, J. (2014a). *Praxeologische Mediensozialisationsforschung. Langzeitstudie zu sozial benachteiligten Heranwachsenden* [Praxeological media socialisation research. A longitudinal study regarding socially disadvantaged adolescents]. Assisted by P. Sinner. Baden-Baden, Germany: Nomos.

Paus-Hasebrink, I., & Kulterer, J. (2014b). Socially disadvantaged children, media and health. In C. von Feilitzen & J. Stenersen (Eds.), *Risks and rights: Young people, media and health*. The International Clearinghouse on Children, Youth and Media Yearbook (pp. 33–44). Gothenburg, Sweden: Nordicom.

Paus-Hasebrink, I., Bauwens, J., Dürager, A. E., & Ponte, C. (2013). Exploring types of parent–child relationship and internet use across Europe. *Journal of Children and Media—JOCAM, 7*(1), 114–132.

Paus-Hasebrink, I., Ponte, C., Dürager, A. E., & Bauwens, J. (2012). Understanding digital inequality: The interplay between parental socialization and children's development. In S. Livingstone, L. Haddon, & A. Görzig (Eds.), *Children, risk and safety on the internet: Research and policy challenges in comparative perspective* (pp. 257–271). Bristol, UK: Policy Press.

Paus-Hasebrink, I., Sinner, P., & Prochazka, F. (2014). Children's online experiences in socially disadvantaged families: European evidence and policy recommendations. *The EU Kids Online Network*. London, UK: LSE. Retrieved from http://eprints.lse.ac.uk/57878/1/EU_Kids_Online_Disadvantaged_children.pdf.

Paus-Hasebrink, I., von Reinersdorff, D., & Sinner, P. (2017). *Forschungsüberblick Mediensozialisationsforschung 2017* [Literature review on research concerning media socialisation 2017]. Salzburg, Austria: Universität Salzburg. Retrieved from https://uni-salzburg.at/fileadmin/multimedia/Kommunikationswissenschaft/documents/Abteilungen/Mediensozialisation/Literaturstudie_2017/Literaturu%CC%88berblick_Mediensozialisation_2017.pdf.

Peter, J., & Valkenburg, P. M. (2006). Adolescents' internet use: Testing the "disappearing digital divide" versus the "emerging digital differentiation" approach. *Poetics, 34*(4–5), 293–305.

Ragnedda, M. (2017). *The third digital divide: A Weberian approach to digital inequalities*. London, UK and New York, NY: Routledge.

Ravve, R. (2012). *Digital parenting Russia I: How Russian parents view and capitalize on digital media*. Moscow: Anketki Research. Retrieved from https://de.slideshare.net/digitalparentingrussia/dpr1-en.

Rideout, V. (2016). Measuring time spent with media: The common sense census of media use by US 8- to 18-year-olds. *Journal of Children and Media—JOCAM, 10*(1), 138–144.

Rideout, V., Foehr, U. G., & Roberts, D. F. (2010). *Generation M²: Media in the lives of 8- to 18-year-olds*. A Kaiser Family Foundation study. Menlo Park, CA: The Henry J. Kaiser Family Foundation. Retrieved from https://kaiserfamilyfoundation.files.wordpress.com/2013/04/8010.pdf.
Rideout, V., & Katz, V. S. (2016). *Opportunity for all? Technology and learning in lower-income families*. A report of the families and media project. New York, NY: The Joan Ganz Cooney Center at Sesame Workshop. Retrieved from http://digitalequityforlearning.org/wp-content/uploads/2015/12/jgcc_opportunityforall.pdf.
Schols, M. (2015). *Young, online and connected: The impact of everyday internet use of Dutch adolescents on social cohesion*. Rotterdam, The Netherlands: Erasmus Research Centre for Media, Communication and Culture.
Simões, J. A., Ponte, C., & Jorge, A. (2013). Online experiences of socially disadvantaged children and young people in Portugal. *Communications, 38*(1), 85–106.
SOS Kinderdorf. (2017). *Verstärkte Maßnahmen gegen Kinderarmut. Unsere Forderung an die zukünftige Regierung, zentrale Maßnahmen gegen Kinderarmut zu setzen* [Enhanced measures against child poverty: Demands on policies of the new government]. Innsbruck, Autria: SOS Kinderdorf. Retrieved from https://www.sos-kinderdorf.at/so-hilft-sos/kinderrechte/downloads/verstarkte-ma%C3%9Fnahmen-gegen-kinderarmut#.
Statistik Austria. (2017a). *Statistics Brief Armut* [Poverty]. Wien, Austria: Statistik Austria. Retrieved from http://www.statistik-austria.at/wcm/idc/idcplg?IdcService=GET_PDF_FILE&RevisionSelectionMethod=LatestReleased&dDocName=114988.
Statistik Austria. (2017b). *Tabellenband EU-SILC 2016. Einkommen, Armut und Lebensbedingungen* [EU-SILC 2016. Income, poverty and living conditions]. Wien, Austria: Statistik Austria. Retrieved from https://www.sozialministerium.at/cms/site/attachments/7/0/0/CH3434/CMS1493709119968/tabellenband_eu-silc_2016.pdf.
Statistisches Bundesamt. (2016). *Datenreport 2016. Ein Sozialreport für die Bundesrepublik Deutschland* [Data report 2016. A social report for the Federal Republic of Germany]. Bonn, Germany: Statistisches Bundesamt & Bundeszentrale für politische Bildung. Retrieved from https://www.destatis.de/DE/Publikationen/Datenreport/Downloads/Datenreport2016.pdf?__blob=publicationFile.
Statistisches Bundesamt. (2017a). *19.7% der Bevölkerung Deutschlands von Armut oder sozialer Ausgrenzung bedroht* [19.7% of the population in Germany are at risk of poverty or marginalisation]. Wiesbaden, Germany: Statistisches Bundesamt. Retrieved from https://www.destatis.de/DE/PresseService/Presse/Pressemitteilungen/2017/11/PD17_392_634.html.

Statisches Bundesamt. (2017b). *Armutsgefährdung in den Bundesländern weiter unterschiedlich* [Risk of poverty remains different in the German Länder]. Wiesbaden, Germany: Statistisches Bundesamt. Retrieved from https://www.destatis.de/DE/PresseService/Presse/Pressemitteilungen/2017/08/PD17_298_122.html.

Stodt, B., Wegmann, E., & Brand, M. (2015). *Geschickt geklickt?! Zum Zusammenhang von Internetnutzungskompetenzen, Internetsucht und Cybermobbing bei Jugendlichen und jungen Erwachsenen* [Competencies of usage, internet addiction and cyberbullying among adolescents and young adults]. Leipzig, Germany: Vistas.

The EU Kids Online Network. (2014). EU Kids Online: Findings, methods, recommendations. *The EU Kids Online Network*. London, UK: LSE. Retrieved from http://eprints.lse.ac.uk/id/eprint/60512.

The EU Kid Online Network. (2018). European evidence database. *The EU Kids Online Network*. London, UK: LSE. Retrieved from http://www.lse.ac.uk/media@lse/research/EUKidsOnline/DB/home.aspx.

UNICEF. (2016). Fairness for children. A league table of inequality in child well-being in rich countries. *Innocenti Report Card 13. Children in the Developed World*. Florence, Italy: UNICEF Office of Research—Innocenti. Retrieved from https://www.unicef-irc.org/publications/pdf/RC13_eng.pdf.

van Dijk, J. A. G. M. (2012). *The network society* (3rd ed.). London, UK, Thousand Oaks, CA, New Delhi, India, and Singapore: Sage.

van Dijk, J. A. G. M. (2013). A theory of the digital divide. In M. Ragnedda & G. W. Muschert (Eds.), *The digital divide: The internet and social inequality in international perspective* (pp. 29–52). London, UK and New York, NY: Routledge.

Vorderer, P., Klimmt, C., Rieger, D., Baumann, E., Hefner, D., & Knop, K., …, Wessler, H. (2015). Der mediatisierte Lebenswandel: Permanently online, permanently connected [A mediatised living]. *Publizistik, 60*(3) 259–276.

Walby, S., Armstrong, J., & Strid, S. (2012). Intersectionality: Multiple inequalities in social theory. *Sociology, 46*(2), 224–240.

Wessels, B. (2013). The reproduction and reconfiguration of inequality: Differentiation and class, status and power in the dynamics of digital divides. In M. Ragnedda & G. W. Muschert (Eds.), *The digital divide: The internet and social inequality in international perspective* (pp. 17–28). London, UK and New York, NY: Routledge.

Open Access This chapter is licensed under the terms of the Creative Commons Attribution 4.0 International License (http://creativecommons.org/licenses/by/4.0/), which permits use, sharing, adaptation, distribution and reproduction in any medium or format, as long as you give appropriate credit to the original author(s) and the source, provide a link to the Creative Commons licence and indicate if changes were made.

The images or other third party material in this chapter are included in the chapter's Creative Commons licence, unless indicated otherwise in a credit line to the material. If material is not included in the chapter's Creative Commons licence and your intended use is not permitted by statutory regulation or exceeds the permitted use, you will need to obtain permission directly from the copyright holder.

CHAPTER 3

The Role of Media Within Young People's Socialisation: A Theoretical Approach

3.1 Introduction

Contemporary societies are characterised by rapid social change, which is furthered by developments in media and technology. Mediatization, as a societal meta-process (Krotz & Hepp, 2013; Livingstone & Lunt, 2014), is regarded as a highly "transformative process" (Silverstone, 2002, p. 761); it refers to "how changes occur when communication patterns are transformed due to the communication tools and technologies" (Lundby, 2014, p. 3). Mediatization has not only changed the everyday lives of adults but accompanies far-reaching changes in the lives of children and adolescents. In Western societies at least, media are omnipresent companions in the everyday lives of young people, at home and at school, during training and in leisure time. From the earliest years of childhood, today's young people are confronted with media devices and media content in a vast diversity that would have been nearly inconceivable in previous generations. Rideout refers to the growth in media activities among children as "phenomenal" (2016, p. 138). As with adult life, contemporary childhood and youth are, in their essence, deeply mediatised (Hasebrink & Paus-Hasebrink, 2013; Livingstone, 2014). Such increasing mediatization means that we need to understand how it is transforming the interplay of structural and individual aspects in everyday life for young people (see Hoffmann, Krotz, & Reißmann, 2017, p. 7). What does this mean for research that sets out to understand young people's *socialisation*?

© The Author(s) 2019
I. Paus-Hasebrink et al., *Social Inequality, Childhood and the Media*,
Transforming Communications – Studies in Cross-Media Research,
https://doi.org/10.1007/978-3-030-02653-0_3

Due to the increasing relevance of mediatization in society as a whole, and for young people in particular, scholars have to pay attention to the ways in which adolescents relate to media in the course of their everyday socialisation: "It seems rather obvious to state that children's use of media and exposure to media content does not happen in a vacuum, it occurs in the wider contexts in which they live their lives" (Vandewater, 2013, p. 51). Therefore, researching the role of media in socialisation requires an integrative approach that conceptualises socialisation as a contextual, interwoven process, in which children and adolescents construct their approach to life against the background of the specific social place, in which they grow up, and of their psycho-social development as individuals. On this basis, we will argue that we need to conceptualise and operationalise socialisation in terms of the interaction between the individual child, or, respectively, adolescent, and the relevant contexts of its growing up. This seems necessary because of the two parent disciplines underpinning previous research on socialisation: psychology, which discusses the individual side of socialisation processes, and sociology, which sheds light on the socio-structural side. Both have long been characterised by their isolated and specific disciplinary perspectives (for a deeper insight, see Prout, 2008). They do, however, have two things in common: firstly, viewing several socialisation agents as "next to" others (for examples of this, see Prout et al., 2015), particularly parents and peers, educational institutions and extracurricular socialisation agents, and such as youth centres, secondly, by and large they do not attend to media at all. This is unsatisfactory because children grow up in interwoven contexts, all of which are saturated by media.

Before we look at socialisation processes as they relate to media and communications, we will discuss the relevant perspectives of psychology and sociology, in order to bolster our argument on the need for an interactive perspective on the process of socialisation in general.

3.2 Socialisation from Different Disciplinary Perspectives

Psychology and/or sociology have developed theories on socialisation from an individual and/or societal perspective, and further research on socialisation processes derives from them.

Many contemporary theories and models dealing with the psychology of personality have substantial biological components (Krueger &

Johnson, 2010). And a field recently become popular, neuroscience and genetics, also offers insights, which play an important role in understanding human behaviour (Grusec & Hastings, 2015, p. xii). Here, the focus is on the interdependence between biological conditions and experiences, an issue also relevant in socialisation research. While we acknowledge the relevance of biological conditions, we will not discuss them in more detail, because our main objective in this chapter is to conceptualise the way children are situated in their relevant contexts.

3.2.1 Socialisation from a Psychological Perspective

From the psychological perspective, socialisation has been described using such examples as the maturationist theory (for example, Gesell, 1933), constructivist theories (for example, Bruner, Goodnow, & Austin, 1962; Piaget, 1980; Wygotski, 1977), psychodynamic theories (for example, Freud, see Mayer, 2017; Erikson, 1959, 1968; Adler, see Hoffman, 1994) and ecological theory (for example, Bronfenbrenner, 1977, 1979).

The history of psychology suggests that psychoanalysis has tended to neglect how people perform as active agents. The perspective of agency has not been considered relevant in the psychology of perception and in cognitive psychology until the *cognitive turn* of the last forty years. These theories then proceeded to reject biological models of personality development and instead examined social and societal influences, returning to the active subject as premise. Agency has also been considered relevant in the developmental psychology pioneered by Piaget, which focuses on the "physical, cognitive, and social-emotional changes that occur during the life span" (Piotrowski & Valkenburg, 2016, p. 1). Bronfenbrenner developed Piaget's thoughts into an "ecological model" to place the ecology of human development in the context "of the progressive, mutual accommodation, throughout the life span, between a growing human organism and the changing immediate environments in which it lives, as this process is affected by relations obtaining within and between these immediate settings, as well as the larger social contexts, both formal and informal, in which the settings are embedded" (1977, p. 514). This viewpoint sees human development taking place within "a set of social contexts, including local ones such as family, household and neighbourhood, and more distant ones such as social structure and policy" (Prout, 2008, p. 28). The revised Ecological Systems Theory

(EST) (Neal & Neal, 2013) describes children's development in the context of several environmental systems, which can be seen as an overlapping arrangement of structures. This model constructs social contexts as "environments", in which individuals develop their identities on the basis of social patterns. According to these theories, socialisation is a "bidirectional process" (Smetana, Robinson, & Rote, 2015, p. 60): "The shift is part of the more general change from the top-down perspective of early behaviourists and psychoanalytic theories to interactive viewpoints which place increasing emphasis on the agency of the child as well as the parent in socialization" (Maccoby, 2015, p. 25). However, EST does not cover the process of transforming social contexts into personal characteristics.

3.2.2 Socialisation from a Sociological Perspective

Sociology's initial theories on socialisation considered how an individual may internalise successfully social values and norms (Abels, 2015). Abels emphasised that the verb "to socialise" had first arisen in 1846 and meant "to make fit for living in society" (Abels, 2015, p. 51). Sociology looked for aspects of social order (for example, Cooley, 1902); Simmel (1908) and researched different forms of sociality and social control. For many years, sociology focused on individuals as objects (or even victims) of external, societally determined influences on their socialisation. According to a functionalist point of view (Durkheim, 1972), individuals were believed to simply adopt the roles given to them. Parsons focused on the relevance of the roles and norms dominating society; in this sense socialisation means integration into a social order as default setting (Parsons, 1951).

However, the concept of socialisation has changed since the end of the 1960s, initiated by the idea of an "active subject" (see for overview Hurrelmann, Bauer, Grundmann, & Walper, 2015). Theories of action were developed by Berger and Luckmann (1966), who based their work on Weber (see Schöllgen, 1998), and Mead (1934). Berger and Luckmann outlined the reality of everyday life as "an intersubjective world, a world that I share with others" (1966, p. 37). They showed how social reality is constituted through social actions and can be understood as the practice of everyday life, which, in turn, influences the development of individual actors.

During the 1980s, the socialisation researcher Klaus Hurrelmann (2009) developed these insights into a model of "productive processing of reality" that connects sociological and psychological elements. Hurrelmann states that "personality does not form independently from society any of its functions or dimensions but is continuously being shaped, in a concrete, historically conveyed life world, throughout the entire space of the life span" (Hurrelmann, 2009, p. 42). This model puts the human subject into a social and ecological context, which is subjectively perceived and processed. While the social and ecological contexts influence individuals, the latter also always influence, change and co-create the former (Hurrelmann & Bauer, 2015). Thus, this approach is characterised by a multi-dimensional perspective, taking into account both subjective and objective factors of personality development. The objective factors are the circumstances of the social and physical environment (exterior reality), whereas the subjective factors encompass a subject's bodily and mental qualities and traits (interior reality). From this perspective, children are neither "becomings" nor "full beings" (James, Jenks, & Prout, 1998) but "active constructers of social knowledge" (Laible, Thomson, & Froimson, 2015, p. 47).

Whether emphasis is placed on individual or social perspectives, socialisation is always an "interactive process" (Hurrelmann & Bauer, 2015, p. 146) and is contextualised in a dynamic process of interwoven macro and microstructural factors within the framework of social interaction between individuals and the specific social context of their everyday lives. Specific practices of socialisation are mainly developed in social contexts (for example, family, peers or friendships), in institutional contexts (for example, kindergarten, schools, job training), or in non-institutional, recreational contexts. Communicative practices, including media-based practices, are developed as integral parts of these social practices.

3.2.3 *Perspectives on the Process of Socialisation in Media and Communications Research*

Media and communications research provides rich empirical evidence on young people's use of media devices and products (for example, Lauricella, Cingel, Blackwell, Wartella, & Conway, 2014; Rideout, Foehr, & Roberts, 2010). Particularly in recent years, many researchers have fundamentally questioned how children use media within their process of identity construction (Buckingham, 2008; see Hoffmann et al., 2017, p. 6).

Studies show that children and adolescents use media to acquire a view of the world, to build contacts with peers and friends, and to deal with the self (Paus-Hasebrink, 2010; Subrahmanyam & Šmahel, 2011). As agencies of symbols and meanings, media offer children orientation and the potential for identification (Lemish, 2007; Livingstone & Bovill, 2001; Paus-Hasebrink & Kulterer, 2014), and the internet offers a particularly wide range of opportunities for self-presentation. When using "the Internet the self is presented without bodily presence [(…)], the presentation of the self requires resources to mediate not only the setting and appearance but also the manners, the dramatic realization" (Skaar, 2009, p. 252).

Media can have a supporting function in young people's socialisation and further the development of social understanding (Livingstone, d'Haenens, & Hasebrink, 2001, p. 5; Paus-Hasebrink & Kulterer, 2014). This "means they can offer children stimuli and suggestions for an active engagement with themselves and their surroundings" (Charlton & Neumann, 1986, p. 32). In formal education, inserting "popular culture, media and/or new technologies into the communications, language and literacy curriculum have a positive effect on the motivation and engagement of children in learning" (Marsh et al., 2005, p. 6).

In addition, many researchers have, particularly in recent years, questioned how, given the background of different social contexts they are involved in, children and adolescents make sense of media within their everyday life. So, such research fundamentally investigates how children use media within their process of identity construction (Buckingham, 2008; see Hofmann et al., 2017, p. 6). Here, Drotner, and Livingstone (2008) and Lemish (2013), for example, have made a positive advance by demonstrating how research is needed to "strengthen the depth of contextualisation within studies of media and of childhood both in theoretical and empirical terms" (Drotner & Livingstone, 2008, p. 4). With reference to increasing mediatization, we have to take transformation processes within the interplay of structural and individual aspects of young people's everyday life into account and show how they interact (see Hofmann et al., 2017, p. 7). Therefore, it is not sufficient to do cross-sectional research only, because this cannot trace how socialisation processes occur over a number of years and indicate which roles different media play within this process. In order to understand young people holistically as they engage in a range of specific social contexts (see Furlong & Davies, 2012), we need, on the one hand, a theoretical approach, taking into account immediate and broader social contexts and providing deeper insights into the interplay between relevant contexts within the process of socialisation (James, 2013). These questions correspond to Ien Ang's understanding of contextualism (2006). As she emphasises, the key challenge for such an approach is to identify the relevant contexts, which shape the structure of the child's everyday life (Ang, 2006, p. 69). On the other hand, we need a methodology which is able to empirically show how the process of transfer between social contexts and personal characteristics—and vice versa—takes place within young people's socialisation processes as they grow up, in order to illustrate these interactions in relation to the role of media within socialisation. Against this background, we intend to deal more broadly with socialisation within children's and adolescents' relevant socio-cultural contexts (see Wartella et al., 2016) and to shed light on the role of media in today's mediatised socialisation. This approach takes account of the fact that media infiltrate *all* contexts of socialisation, considered here as a contextual, interlinked process. In it, children and adolescents construct their approach to life against the background of the specific social situation in which they are growing up and of their individual biological and psycho-social development.

In order to examine these processes, we will firstly discuss the concept of developmental tasks. Secondly, we will focus on the family as the most relevant social context for most children and adolescents, which at the same time also reflects the other social contexts, such as peers and friendships, institutional contexts like kindergarten, school, job training and non-institutional, recreational contexts. Thirdly, we propose, therefore, a praxeological approach built on three analytical concepts developed by Paus-Hasebrink (see, for example, Paus-Hasebrink, 2017, 2018), which help to analyse the interaction between the individual child and its social contexts and are based on Bourdieu's "Theory of Practice" (1977; see also Weiß, 2000).

3.3 On the Role of Developmental Tasks in the Framework of Socialisation Processes

At the centre of an adolescent's socialisation is the process of identity formation, in which it develops its personal as well as its social identity (Erikson, 1968; Krappmann, 2016). According to Erikson, identity construction is a basis for growing up: "In the social jungle of human existence there is no feeling of being alive without a sense of identity" (1970). Against the theoretical framework of developmental tasks, as presented by Havighurst (1972), children grow up and learn to deal with the age-specific challenges they encounter in their everyday lives. Development is conceived of as a learning or working process. In order to cope with the relevant developmental tasks related to the different stages of growing up and with various daily life experiences, young people seek to acquire expertise. Hence the process of growing up is built on dealing un/successfully with developmental tasks, for example building stable social relationships with peers and dealing with the self. "Erving Goffman describes 'the presentation of self in everyday life' (1959) as a perpetual process of social performance" (Skaar, 2009, p. 251). Developmental tasks—closely linked to children's and adolescents' age, gender and social background—shape their perception and action when dealing with their environment. This process takes place within the framework of developmental tasks shaped by a person's biography and guiding an individual's perception, cognition and action (Havighurst, 1972), while not wholly determining it. "A developmental task is a task which arises at or about a certain period in the life of the individual, successful achievement of which leads to his happiness and to success with later tasks, while failure leads to unhappiness in the individual, disapproval by the society, and difficulty with later tasks" (Havighurst, 1972, p. 2). This concept was developed within developmental psychology and has since been frequently applied to societal changes and adapted to explain them (see Hurrelmann, 2009). For our purposes, it serves as a relevant insight into how children build their identity in the context of their everyday lives. Heckhausen and Schulz (1999) have stressed that Havighurst's concept does not only apply to children but to adults as well. In order to distinguish between children's and adults' tasks, we use the term developmental tasks with reference to children and the term life tasks with reference to adults.

3.3.1 Childhood and Adolescence—More Than Age-Based Phases

The concept of developmental tasks recognises children's active role in co-constructing the symbolic and material world in which they live and grow up (James et al., 1998). At the same time, it reflects James' (2013, p. 15) recent argument that children's individual agency has, in fact, been somewhat overemphasised, as children's agency cannot fully override socio-structural conditions. Following this perspective, identity formation can be regarded as a dynamic process of construction, in which children form their beliefs and their attitudes towards themselves, including cognitive, emotional and motivational components. In this process, a child is confronted with basic challenges that arise from his or her particular situation and biographical context: the "developmental tasks" (Havighurst, 1972). These tasks include finding one's place in life, learning about oneself by relating to others, and interacting with and positioning oneself within the family, the peer group, and other social contexts (Hurrelmann, 2009, p. 42).

When children grow older, they have to cope with the special challenges of adolescence; socialisation research calls this phase a "distinct developmental period" (Smetana et al., 2015, p. 60).

Historically, the phase of adolescence is a fairly recent concept. A transitional phase between childhood and adulthood has been identified since antiquity, but in its current form this phase is the result of massive changes in productive and social structures caused by the industrial revolution in Western societies. In this sense, adolescence has developed into a phase not marked by gainful work, but by education and preparation for adulthood (see Kimmel & Weiner, 1995, p. 7; Oerter & Dreher, 2008, p. 271). During the post-war years especially, adolescence continued to be differentiated and has expanded at the expense of adulthood, until it has today become a central phase in an individual's life cycle (see Hurrelmann, 2010, pp. 17, 36).

In terms of its duration, the phase of adolescence is very ambiguous and hard to define. Simple age in years is often used to set its boundaries, especially in legal contexts, but a look at the extensive literature on it shows that definitions vary greatly with regard to any framing by age (see Göppel, 2005, pp. 3–5). On the social level, many societies maintain certain rites of passage (often linked to religious rituals like, for example, the bar mitzvah or the Christian confirmation) that mark the beginning of adolescence. Other definitions concentrate on biological factors to mark at least the beginning of adolescence with the beginning of the biological and physical changes associated with puberty, which do not always correspond with definitions based on age, since such development varies among individuals (see Kimmel & Weiner, 1995, pp. 2–3).

Each and every age-based definition is, thus, first and foremost an artificial and pragmatic limitation and does not necessarily correspond with an individual's reality. It is, therefore, much more feasible to focus on a definition that concentrates on shared patterns of experiences or crises, in the sense of developmental tasks as characteristic for adolescence in today's society. In this sense, dealing with the same developmental challenges can be used as a marker to subsume individuals in the same developmental phase. At the same time, it must be pointed out that youth or adolescents do not exist as a homogenous mass; even with shared developmental tasks, these collective terms cover a heterogeneous group of individuals.

3.3.2 Adolescence—A Phase of Transition

What most definitions of adolescence do, however, have in common, is the notion of transition, the transition between childhood and adulthood (Kimmel & Weiner, 1995, p. 15). Where young people have to cope with "with unstable forms of community integration, identity is seen as much more dynamic, multiplistic, relativistic, fluid, context-specific, and fragmented" (Mayseless & Keren, 2014, p. 64). Arnett (2007, p. 69) describes the end of this phase of transition as a time "between": "no longer adolescent but only partly adult, emerging into adulthood but not there yet" (Arnett, 2007, p. 70). This phase is characterised by "unsettledness, exploration, and instability" (Arnett, 2006, p. 7). Issues such as the context in which this transition takes place, what is expected from adolescents and what is deemed "successful" or "unsuccessful" coping with developmental tasks are subject to cultural and historic differences (see Kimmel & Weiner, 1995, p. 4).

In 1972, Havighurst first formulated developmental tasks that are specific to various periods in life. His work serves as the basis for later adaptations that account for social changes in the years since the tasks were first formulated. Despite social changes in the past decades, literature shows that the core topics remain fairly stable, but recently we have observed that dealing with certain tasks is being pushed backwards by dint of, for example, longer periods in education and a later entry into work, women becoming mothers at a later age and so on, all coupled with changing priorities (see Fend, 2005, p. 152; Noller & Atkin, 2014, pp. 5–10; Oerter & Dreher, 2008, p. 283). Mayseless and Keren (2014) point out coping with love and work as the central developmental task: "(...) love and work, are described as the focus of identity exploration in emerging adulthood. (...) Current postmodern processes in Western industrialized countries set the stage for the saliency of a new developmental task in emerging adulthood: finding the meaningful life" (Mayseless & Keren, 2014, p. 63). With regard to Havighurst's conception, and to further differentiations from other authors, we can subsume the relevant developmental tasks for adolescents in today's Western societies as follows: coming to terms with one's body, establishing and negotiating relationships with peers, forming an idea of one's role in society, developing first romantic relationships, dealing with one's sexual identity, detachment/independence from parents, gathering resources to build a personal economic basis, developing an idea of one's self, obtaining values, thinking about forming a family and making plans for the future (see Havighurst, 1972, p. 45; Kimmel & Weiner, 1995, pp. 15f.; Noller & Atkin, 2014, pp. 2–10; Oerter & Dreher, 2008, p. 279).

3.3.3 "Meta-Developmental Tasks"

Above all this stands one large "meta-developmental task" (Friedemann & Hoffmann, 2013, p. 375; translated by the authors) that basically influences all other areas and tasks: the construction of a unique identity to set oneself apart from others (see Friedemann & Hoffmann, 2013, p. 375). It can be argued that this task is one that continues throughout life, and one's identity is, in this context, never ultimately fixed. Nevertheless, the phase of adolescence is where this task becomes especially prominent.

Young people often live under particular pressure (see Quenzel, 2015, p. 23); they have to cope with many changes, both on an individual and a social level. When we look at the employment market and the insecure employment situations today, it is evident that young people have to face numerous demanding situations, such as the need for flexibility and more and more higher qualifications. Hence, the task of acquiring qualifications for a career has gained importance in recent years. This is highly relevant for less educated adolescents especially and frequently leads to pressure on them to perform (see Albert, Hurrelmann, & Quenzel, 2015, p. 40). So, socially disadvantaged young people often have to deal with frustration and disappointment (see Quenzel, 2015, p. 23). Confronting situations like these leads to strain and emotional pressure and quite often to capacity overload. In this context, Quenzel talks about another relevant developmental task for young people: they have to know how to recuperate and to relax and, in this context, to manage leisure time competently and deal with consumer culture (see Quenzel, 2015, p. 34).

3.3.4 Developmental Tasks and Media Contexts

By coping with developmental tasks, young people develop and stabilise their capacity for action. Where they are confronted with specific developmental tasks during the socialisation process, they attribute specific meanings to media and communicative practices. The context for coping with developmental tasks is an individual's everyday life. In this sense, young people are always moving in fields of tension and are challenged by crises, which can also be understood as possible turning points. They must cope with these challenges to make daily life liveable. To do so, they require information and orientation, as well as support, and counsel. The process often includes an increased desire for experience, while such desires and needs also typify an individual adolescent's situation in the world. Against this backdrop, and the range of available media options, young people select media products and services based on their individual preferences and aversions and with regard to their usefulness in coping with everyday life challenges.

So far, we have discussed socialisation as the process of interaction between individual adolescents and their relevant social contexts. We have referred to the concept of developmental tasks to specify how children form identity by coping with these tasks, in part by using media. We will now proceed to examine the most relevant social context, the family, and its role in children's and young peoples' socialisation. As mentioned above, there are several relevant contexts, such as the family, peer-groups or friends (and later, romantic partners), institutional contexts, such as kindergarten, school or job training, alongside the overall societal context (Hurrelmann, 2009) and the media system (Lange, 2015). These contexts will be discussed later on by considering children's and parents' perspective on them against the background of our empirical data. As our study progressed, we focused on the family, because our empirical research indicated how the families of the children in our panel crystallised as the main socialisation context, and, with this, the fundamental basis for children in developing their view on the world. Against this background, the interaction between the individual children and their family contexts will be discussed more explicitly, before we present our empirical conceptualisation of our study.

3.4 The Family Context in Socialisation

The family is the most relevant context of (most) young people's everyday lives because their lives are deeply embedded in it (see Noller & Atkin, 2014). Keeping in mind that the concept of "family" cannot be understood as referring only to a stable, nuclear group of mother and father and children, we use this term in the wide sense of the core group, in which a child grows up. Particularly in early childhood, the family, and especially the parents, remain the most important actor in most children's socialisation (Grusec & Hastings, 2015, p. xiii; Huston & Wright, 1997). This also continues as they grow older and enter the often turbulent and challenging phase of adolescence (see Noller & Atkin, 2014). Accordingly, we will now proceed to discuss children's and young people's socialisation in greater depth.

3.4.1 On the Relevance of the Parent–Child Relationship

We recognise the relevance of the interaction between family members (Goldberg, Grusec, & Jenkins, 1999), given how the degree of proximity, trust and reciprocity that parents and children show towards each other shapes the styles of parenting and family communication. Parenting styles and practices are observable in the specific way parents interact with and manage their children and indicate how highly relevant they are to children's socialisation (Schofield Clark, 2013; Smetana et al., 2015, p. 66). Given the correlation between parents' socio-structural background and their specific ways of interacting with their children and managing them, it can be assumed that the cognitive, social and cultural resources that parents acquire from their education, professional lives, and social networks influence their ability to support their children in their socialisation: the socio-cultural capital of parents shapes the acquisition of that capital by their children (Paus-Hasebrink, Bauwens, Dürager, & Ponte, 2013). In this regard, we emphasise how families differ in their abilities to cope with and to support children in growing up and tackling their own developmental tasks, especially when they begin to seek independence and strive for individuality during adolescence (Noller & Atkin, 2014, p. 2).

3.4.2 On the Relevance of Doing Family

The ways family members interact with each other—Jordan calls this the "family system" (2003)—are connected to "family 'climate', family paradigms, family coordinated practices, and family myths and rituals" (Maccoby, 2015, p. 24). Analogously to what Livingstone and Sefton-Green (2016, p. 169) show for the area of education, this process may also have longer roots reaching back to earlier generations. This dynamic and affective process takes place every day, is continually renegotiated and reconstituted by the family members, and includes specific communication practices and media-based practices of sense-making. Taken together, these practices characterize the specific way of "doing family" (Morgan, 2011).

However, the process of *doing family* is influenced not only by children coping with biographically determined developmental tasks but also by the way their parents and other family members cope. In this process, the parents and/or other reference persons participate against the background of their own life tasks: for instance, they have to deal with the role distribution between mothers and fathers, to cope with the particular challenges of being a single parent or of unemployment, to manage potential new relationships, to find a balance between work life and family life, to fulfil their personal ambitions, or to maintain, or even improve, their position within the broader societal context. In this respect, the family also reflects other social contexts of children's socialisation, such as the neighbourhood, the parents' professional environment, and the family's position within the wider societal structure. In this way, the family sets the framework for a child's growing up and learning to deal with everyday challenges and to realise his or her own interests.

Furthermore, research also shows that there is a correlation between the relationships among family members, the ways in which they interact with each other, and the children's own ability to form their own relationships with peers, as well as in a romantic sense later in life. As Noller and Atkin (2014, p. 2) point out: "It appears that adolescents may model their dating relationships on what they have seen in relationship between their parents (Steinberg, 2005). Thus, adolescents whose families have poor relationships and relationships that are highly conflicted are less likely than those from harmonious families to learn the skills necessary for successful relationships outside the family. In addition, the quality of their adolescents' relationships with both parents and peers influences the quality of their romantic relationships (Brown, 2004)".

As regards media usage, a rich body of research on family communication and media has shown that a child's actions in general, and media related actions in particular, cannot be understood adequately without reflecting on families' specific modes of "doing family" (see, for example, Jennings & Wartella, 2013; Lull, 1980; Wilson & Drogos, 2013), which is, in turn, influenced by their socio-economic backgrounds. As Nathanson (2013, p. 304) emphasises, "family dynamics can shape children's vulnerability to the media and, likewise, media use can influence family dynamics".

Having said that, social contexts—the family as well as others–shape children's and adolescents' socialisation (Kimmel & Weiner, 1995; Lamb, Ketterlinus, & Fracasso, 1992, p. 465; Noller & Atkin, 2014; see also Packer, 2017). Our study will demonstrate conclusively that we need to specify how these contexts, and the underlying social structures, are transformed into an individual child's personal orientation and identity. In the following section, we will propose a praxeological approach that allows us to understand how the socio-structural conditions influencing the everyday life of all members of a family are transformed into the specific ways children see and experience the world, how they orient themselves in this world, how they develop individual goals and plans, and, in doing so, how they make sense of media within their everyday life.

3.5 A Praxeological Approach to Researching Children's Socialisation

The following questions are central to the praxeological approach of researching the role of media within socialisation: *How* do children make sense of their media usage? How is this sense-making process connected to the children's interaction with their immediate reference persons in the context of the family? A fruitful starting point for our research lies in the perspective of Cultural Studies on society, individuals and the media: "The central emphasis here is not on the effects of the media on behaviour and attitudes, but on the ways in which meanings are established, negotiated and circulated (…) this research regards children's uses and interpretations of the media as inherently social processes to be characterized by forms of power and difference" (Buckingham, 2008, pp. 221–222).

However, as Ralph Weiß (2000) argues, research conducted in the sphere of Cultural Studies has not successfully demonstrated the link between the "maps of meanings", which show how subjects appropriate and interpret mediated points of view, and the practical rules that individuals use to organise their everyday lives in their specific social places (Weiß, 2000, p. 44). As early as 1992, David Morley, one of the proponents of Cultural Studies, stressed this point: "What is needed here is an approach that links differential interpretation back to the socio-economic structure of society, showing how members of different groups and classes, sharing different 'cultural codes', will interpret a given message differently not just at the personal, idiosyncratic level, but in a way systematically related to their socio-economic position" (Morley, 1992, p. 54). Nevertheless, the question of how social structures transform an individual's "subjective sense" remains a challenge for Cultural Studies because researchers lack a theory that systematically explains how to translate the objective structure of the relationship between power and social inequality into the subjective structure of points of view, habits of feeling and need to experience (Weiß, 2001, p. 12). The praxeological approach serves to answer this question.

Our focus is on young people and their reference persons in their everyday lives and thus in the particular social places that are materially and symbolically at their disposal. It is in these social places that individuals invest their "capital" and gain their competences for the action, through which they then make sense of everyday life, including, as one aspect of it, their use of media. In the following, we will set out the theoretical components of our approach systematically.

3.5.1 The Lifeworld and Related Contexts

As stated above, socialisation processes are shaped by social contexts, ranging from the inner circle of family and the most significant reference persons to the societal level characterised by the medially permeated political, economic and cultural contexts of a region or a country, such as the labour market, family-related laws and support programmes, educational institutions, and the availability of recreational facilities. Everyday life derives its specific character from the social situation of the family and the factors that characterise it: income, job, formal education and the living situation of the parents (Hradil, 1987). The social space in which the child learns to act is marked by the family's social situation, while that space's specific structure arises from the different fields of everyday life.

Socio-phenomenological or social-constructivist conceptions of everyday life provide an opportunity to avoid both a one-dimensional objectivist perspective on social phenomena and a purely subjectivist one. In his concept of the *Lebenswelt*, the "lifeworld", Alfred Schütz laid the foundation for a phenomenological sociology which strives to uncover the universal structures in the everyday. Following Schütz and Luckmann, the *Lebenswelt* may be conceived of as what individuals consider to be the given sphere in which they act (2003, p. 30). The lifeworld is realised in the "conduct of everyday life" (Jurczyk et al., 2015). This term goes back to Max Weber, and it is defined "primarily as practice (it means the structure of activities that are part of life on an everyday basis)" (Jurczyk et al., 2015, p. 45). The "conduct of everyday life" is understood as both the individually constructed and the institutionalised ordering of everyday life over time. Both endow daily actions with direction, efficiency and meaning and lend stability, coherence and continuity to life as a whole (Kudera, 2001, p. 51). As discussed earlier, the way children conduct their everyday lives is influenced by how they cope with impending developmental tasks; the same holds good for the children's adult reference persons and their respective life tasks.

The individual's activities, with their connections and consequential effects, are at the centre; however, based on patterns of interpretation and biographical schemata, how individuals classify these activities meaningfully cannot be ignored (Hörning, 2001, p. 158). So, beyond subjective representation, the conduct of everyday life is shaped by "classifying practices", which are a symbolic order presenting significant distinctions (Bourdieu, 1996, p. 175). These practices are connected to the social space where children and their parents gain their experiences (both medial and non-medial), build their identities, gain *competences for action*, and judge, value and classify themselves and their social space. Bourdieu's work on social fields provides a theoretical framework for understanding the interaction between structure and action. Each field values particular sorts of resources (Bourdieu & Wacquant, 1992), which Bourdieu metaphorically calls "capital". He distinguishes three different types of resources: economic, cultural and social capital. Furthermore, he introduces symbolic capital, which is related to honour and recognition and is earned on an individual basis (Bourdieu, 1989). "Thus, on a social field, economic, social and cultural capital is converted to symbolic capital" (Walther, 2014, p. 10).

The composition of the different forms of capital is always unevenly distributed, leading to the formation of specific social milieus. These are shaped by fundamental points of view, which are shared by members of a milieu and through which they distinguish themselves from other social milieus (Weiß, 1997, p. 259). In this way, social milieus demonstrate the social arrangement and structure of a society (Weiß, 1997, p. 246).

The different types of capital are gained through education and socialisation (Bourdieu, 1986). With respect to the social milieu in which social action takes place, Bourdieu explains how certain aims are followed, how certain patterns of orientation and perspectives can be formed, and how particular patterns of action are socially accepted (Weiß, 2000, p. 47). In the framework of socialisation, the patterns of action and orientation that are developed during childhood are culturally rooted, refer to individuals' particular societal status and their social milieu, and shape their specific habitus, which is developed through common social contexts and formed by similar existential backgrounds. As Benson (2016, p. 3) maintains, it is via their habitus that individual agents internalise their experiences of social structure; "habitus-endowed agents constitute and reconstitute the fields of which they are a part" (Benson, 2016, p, 3). In Bourdieu's own words: "The habitus (...) enables an intelligible and necessary relation to be established between practices and a situation, the meaning of which is produced by the habitus through categories of perception and appreciation that are themselves produced by an observable social condition" (Bourdieu, 1996, p. 110). As the habitus operates "at the unconscious level of taken-for-granted assumptions, tastes, and bodily hexis (embodied practice or way of using one's body)" (Benson, 2016, p. 4), it can be understood as an incorporated social structure (Weiß, 1997, p. 246), or as "socialized subjectivity", which can be seen as "a system of dispositions" (Bourdieu, 1996, p. 6). These dispositions are shaped by conditions for the conduct of everyday life that are socially unequal and structurally distributed (Weiß, 1997, p. 246).

Patterns of action are culturally rooted and refer to people's social status. Transformed into everyday opportunities and competences, they influence individual actions and the processes of social and personal identity development and interact with people's subjective ways of making sense of societal conditions (Weiß, 2000; Willis, 1977). To conclude, the habitus as a concept following Bourdieu's ideas and provisions has a dual nature: It covers the individual predisposition of a single person on the one hand, but also it incorporates the conditions of the social environment of living and the social surroundings during the process of growing up and socialisation within a social milieu (see also Paus-Hasebrink, 2013, p. 80).

Within this general praxeological perspective on socialisation, we are focusing especially on young people's relation to the media, because these provide a way to deal subjectively with topics arising from developmental and family-related challenges.

When considering the ensemble of practices that are used to conduct everyday life and to cope with everyday challenges, our focus shifts to the individual context. At the same time, we go beyond subjective representations and take into account the social milieus which are—actually or symbolically—at an individual's disposal. In their practical actions, meaning their specific conduct of everyday life, individuals use their capital to seize opportunities in their social spheres (Habermas, 1988, p. 473), such as their working life (employment, income, capital), in politics and law (social order, law, morality), and the private sphere (love, personal relationships, happiness), as efficiently as possible (Weiß, 2000, p. 47). Individuals, including children, attempt to employ their own capital to realise the opportunities of their specific social places (Weiß, 2000, p. 48). The objective structure of socially unequal conditions for action is transformed into the subjective structure of diverging *outlines for action*. This transformation takes place as a psycho-social process within the identity formation outlined above. It is co-determined by factors such as formal education, gender and the bodily experience of growing up in the framework of an individual biography. In this respect, the media fulfil several functions in the process of a child's socialisation, and these are connected to its specific developmental tasks against the backdrop of its own and its parents' conduct of everyday life within the process of *doing family*.

3.5.2 Three Analytic Concepts: **Options, Outlines and Competences for Action**

The conduct of everyday life is manifested in social milieus where individuals attempt to realise their specific goals in life, including their own particular plans and wishes. An individual's subjective perception of the *options for action* available, based on his/her social milieu, is crucial here, as is the way an individual forms his/her *outlines for action* within the framework of the identified *options for action* and thereby acquires *competences for action*, which make it possible for him/her to apply his/her resources to the task of realising the *outlines for action*.

Thus, the following three concepts must be integrated (for an overview see Table 3.1):

- *Options for action* are, on the one hand, related to the individual's specific socio-structural conditions and, on the other, to the socio-structural aspects of society as a whole and its political, economic, cultural and media contexts. *Options for action* describe the objective characteristics of an individual's social conditions, which are shaped by the rules of the social field(s) in which he/she operates. *Options for action* represent an ordered arrangement of possible (and impossible) actions.
- *Outlines for action* are related to subjective perceptions of social conditions and represent the ways in which the subject transforms the objective characteristics of his/her situation into a subjective guide for action. These *outlines* reflect what makes sense to the subject and indicate the viewpoints from which he/she structures his/her perceptions and interpretations of the world. Thus, all of the family's or the individual's goals and plans are closely tied to a subjective perception of the social milieu.
- *Competences for action* are related to the resources at the individual's disposal to accomplish the above *outlines for action*. As Bourdieu maintains, these competences characterise the material, cultural and social resources available to an individual and serve as cognitive or motivational prerequisites for his/her actions, including the use of media. These competences are reflected in the realisation of the individual's *outlines for action*.

Based on the *options for action*, *outlines for action* and *competences for action*, it is theoretically and empirically possible to understand the connection between a social milieu, and the subjective structure of making sense of one's life. Our approach to young people's socialisation, as presented here, provides answers through a combined analysis of both the subjective and structural components of practice. It is focused on the lifeworld of a child in the family, where he/she conducts his/her

Table 3.1 Options for action, outlines for action and competences for action

Options for action	• Related to the individual's specific socio-structural conditions and to the socio-structural aspects of society as a whole (political, economic, cultural and media contexts) • Describe the objective characteristics of an individual's social conditions, which are shaped by the rules of the social field(s) in which he/she operates • Represent an ordered arrangement of possible (and impossible) actions
Outlines for action	• Related to subjective perceptions of social conditions • Represent the ways in which the subject transforms the objective characteristics of his/her life situation into a subjective action guide • Reflect what makes sense to the subject and indicate the viewpoints from which he/she structures perceptions and interpretations of the world
Competences for action	• Related to the resources at the individual's disposal • Reflect the competences characterised by an individual's material, cultural and social resources • Represent cognitive or motivational prerequisites for an individual's actions, including the use of media • Reflect competences in the realisation of the individual's *outlines for action*

everyday life and where, starting in early childhood, media activity is given its meaning. This approach helps in examining the everyday structures of a child's life, which are shaped by the family's social situation, in order to describe the "arrangements" for conducting everyday life and the process of *doing family*. It is through these arrangements that practices, including media practices, are formed and media actions gain structure and meaning. So it is possible to reconstruct the transmission process, namely, how socio-structural conditions transform into an individual's subjective perception and (media-related) actions and how this perception leads to an independent orientation towards the world.

3.6 Conclusion

This chapter contends that, in order to understand the role of media within young people's socialisation, we need to conceptualise and operationalise socialisation as the interaction between an individual child and the relevant contexts of growing up. Referring to the concept of developmental tasks, we have specified the way children, by coping with these tasks, partly by making use of media, form identity. In order to conceptualise the interaction between the individual child and social contexts, we have focused on the family as the most relevant context for young people's growing up. In order to specify how the underlying social structures in families and other contexts are transformed into a child's personal orientation and identity, we have proposed a praxeological approach that distinguishes three analytical concepts: *options for action*, *outlines for action*, and *competences for action*. Based on these concepts, it is theoretically and empirically possible to understand the connection between a social milieu and the subjective structure of making sense of one's life. In specifying the "arrangements" of the conduct of everyday life and the process of *doing family*, this approach enables us to examine the everyday structures of an adolescent's life. It is through these arrangements that practices, including media practices, are formed and media actions gain structure and meaning. So it is possible to reconstruct the transmission process, namely how socio-structural conditions transform into an individual's subjective perception and (media-related) actions and how this perception leads to an independent orientation towards the world.

As presented in this chapter, our theoretical approach provides a fruitful basis for research on the role of media within young people's socialisation. The role of other contexts we empirically investigated in our longitudinal study, such as peers, romantic partners, kindergarten or schools, professional training, will be discussed in more detail in Chapter 6.

The next chapter (Chapter 4) illustrates both the methods we applied in our longitudinal study on children's, or respectively adolescents', socialisation in socially disadvantaged families and how this approach can be operationalised.

References

Abels, H. (2015). Der Beitrag der Soziologie zur Sozialisationsforschung [Contribution of sociology on socialisation]. In K. Hurrelmann, U. Bauer, M. Grundmann, & S. Walper (Eds.), *Handbuch Sozialisationsforschung* [Handbook of socialisation research] (8th Rev. ed., pp. 50–79). Weinheim, Germany: Beltz.

Albert, M., Hurrelmann, K., & Quenzel, G. (2015). *Jugend 2015: Eine pragmatische Generation im Aufbruch. 17. Shell Jugendstudie* [Adolescence 2015: A pragmatic generation moving on 17th Shell adolescence study]. Frankfurt am Main, Germany: S. Fischer Verlag.
Ang, I. (2006). Radikaler Konstruktivismus und Ethnografie in der Rezeptionsforschung [Radical constructivism and ethnography in reception research]. In A. Hepp & R. Winter (Eds.), *Kultur – Medien – Macht. Cultural Studies und Medienanalyse* [Culture—media—power: Cultural studies and the analysis of media] (3rd ed., pp. 61–79). Wiesbaden, Germany: VS Verlag für Sozialwissenschaften.
Arnett, J. J. (2006). Emerging adulthood: Understanding the new way of coming of age. In J. J. Arnett & J. L. Tanner (Eds.), *Emerging adults in America: Coming of age in the 21st century* (pp. 3–19). Washington, DC: American Psychological Association.
Arnett, J. J. (2007). Emerging adulthood: What is it and what is it good for. *Child Development Perspectives, 1*(2), 68–73.
Benson, R. (2016). Bourdieu, Pierre. In K. B. Jensen & R. T. Craig (Eds.), *International encyclopaedia of communication theory and philosophy*. Hoboken, NJ: Wiley.
Berger, P. L., & Luckmann, T. (1966). *The social construction of reality: A treatise in the sociology of knowledge*. London, UK: Penguin Books.
Bourdieu, P. F. (1977). *Outline of a theory of practice*. New York, NY: University Press.
Bourdieu, P. F. (1986). The forms of capital. In J. Richardson (Ed.), *Handbook of theory and research for the sociology of education* (pp. 241–258). New York, NY: Greenwood Publishing Group.
Bourdieu, P. F. (1989). Social space and symbolic power. *Sociological Theory, 7*(1), 14–25.
Bourdieu, P. F. (1996). *Distinction: A social critique of the judgement of taste* (8th ed., R. Nice, Trans.). London, UK: Routledge.
Bourdieu, P. F., & Waquant, L. (1992). *An invitation to reflexive sociology*. Chicago, IL: The University of Chicago Press.
Bronfenbrenner, U. (1977). Toward an experimental ecology of human development. *American Psychologist, 32*(7), 513–531.
Bronfenbrenner, U. (1979). *The ecology of human development: Experiments by nature and design*. Cambridge, MA: Harvard University Press.
Brown, B. B. (2004). Adolescents' relationships with peers. In R. J. Lerner & L. D. Steinberg (Eds.), *Handbook of adolescent psychology* (2nd ed., pp. 363–394). New York; NY: Wiley.
Bruner, J. S., Goodnow, J., & Austin, G. A. (1962). *A study of thinking*. New York, NY: Wiley (Science Editions, A Wiley Publication in Psychology).

Buckingham, D. (2008). Children and media: A cultural studies approach. In K. Drotner & S. Livingstone (Eds.), *The international handbook of children, media and culture* (pp. 219–236). Los Angeles, CA, London, UK, and New Dehli, India: Sage.

Charlton, M., & Neumann, K. (1986). *Medienkonsum und Lebensbewältigung in der Familie: Methode und Ergebnisse der strukturanalytischen Rezeptionsforschung. Mit fünf Darstellungen* [Media consumption and coping with life: Methods and outcomes of structure-analytical reception research]. München, Germany: Psychologie-Verlags-Union.

Cooley, C. H. (1902). *Human nature and the social order*. New Brunswick, Canada: Transaction Books.

Drotner, K., & Livingstone, S. (Eds.). (2008). *The international handbook of children, media and culture*. London, UK, Thousand Oaks, CA, and New Dehli, India: Sage.

Durkheim, É. (1972). *Selected writings*. Edited, translated, and with an introduction by A. Giddens. Cambridge, UK: Cambridge University Press.

Erikson, E. H. (1959). *Identity and the life cycle*. New York, NY: International Universities Press.

Erikson, E. H. (1968). *Identity: Youth and crisis*. New York, NY: Norton.

Fend, H. (2005). *Entwicklungspsychologie des Jugendalters. Ein Lehrbuch für pädagogische und psychologische Berufe* [Developmental psychology of adolescence: A textbook for pedagogic and psychologic professionals] (3rd ed.). Wiesbaden, Germany: VS Verlag.

Friedemann, S., & Hoffmann, D. (2013). Musik im Kontext der Bearbeitung von Entwicklungsaufgaben des Jugendalters [Music in the context of coping with developmental tasks of adolescence]. In R. Heyer, S. Wachs, & C. Palentien (Eds.), *Handbuch Jugend – Musik – Sozialisation* [Handbook of adolescence—music—socialisation] (pp. 371–393). Wiesbaden, Germany: Springer.

Furlong, J., & Davies, C. (2012). Young people, new technologies and learning at home: Taking context seriously. *Oxford Review of Education, 38*(1), 45–62.

Gesell, A. (1933). Maturation and the patterning of behaviour. In C. Murchison (Ed.), *The international university series in psychology: A handbook of child psychology* (2nd ed., pp. 209–235). Worcester, MA: US Clark University Press.

Goffman, I. (1959). *The presentation of self in everyday life*. New York, NY: Doubleday.

Goldberg, S., Grusec, J. E., & Jenkins, J. M. (1999). Confidence in protection: Arguments for a narrow definition of attachment. *Journal of Family Psychology, 13*(4), 475–483.

Göppel, R. (2005). *Das Jugendalter. Entwicklungsaufgaben – Entwicklungskrisen – Bewältigungsformen* [Adolescence: Developmental tasks—Developmental crises—Forms of coping]. Stuttgart, Germany: Verlag W. Kohlhammer.

Grusec, J. E., & Hastings, P. D. (2015). Preface. In J. E. Grusec & P. D. Hastings (Eds.), *Handbook of socialization: Theory and research* (2nd ed., pp. XI–XIII). New York, NY: Guilford Press.

Habermas, J. (1988). *Theorie des kommunikativen Handelns. Band 1 und 2* [Theory of communicative action: Volume 1 and 2] (4th Rev. ed.). Frankfurt am Main, Germany: Suhrkamp.

Hasebrink, U., & Paus-Hasebrink, I. (2013). Trends in children's consumption of media. In D. Lemish (Ed.), *The Routledge international handbook of children, adolescents and media* (pp. 31–38). Milton Park and London, UK: Routledge and Taylor & Francis.

Havighurst, R. J. (1972). *Developmental tasks and education* (3rd ed.). New York, NY: McKay.

Heckhausen, J., & Schulz, R. (1999). Biological and societal canalizations and individuals' developmental goals. In J. Brandtstadter & R. Lerner (Eds.), *Action and self-development: Theory and research through the life-pan* (pp. 67–103). Thousand Oaks, CA, London, UK, and New Dehli, India: Sage.

Hoffman, E. (1994). *The drive for self: Alfred Adler and the founding of individual psychology.* New York, NY: Addison-Wesley.

Hoffmann, D., Krotz, F., & Reißmann, W. (2017). Mediensozialisation und Mediatisierung. Problemstellung und Einführung [Media socialisation and mediatization]. In D. Hoffmann, F. Krotz, & W. Reißmann (Eds.), *Mediatisierung und Mediensozialisation. Prozesse – Räume – Praktiken* [Mediatization and media socialisation: Processes—spaces—practices] (pp. 3–18). Wiesbaden, Germany: Springer.

Hörning, K. H. (2001). *Experten des Alltags* [Experts in everyday life]. Weilerswist, Germany: Velbrück.

Hradil, S. (1987). *Sozialstrukturanalyse in einer fortgeschrittenen Gesellschaft* [Analysis of social structure in an advanced society]. Opladen, Germany: Leske und Budrich.

Hurrelmann, K. (2009). *Social structure and personality development.* Cambridge, UK: Cambridge University Press.

Hurrelmann, K. (2010). *Lebensphase Jugend. Eine Einführung in die sozialwissenschaftliche Jugendforschung* [Life period adolescence: An introduction into social scientific youth research] (10th ed.). Weinheim and München, Germany: Juventa Verlag.

Hurrelmann, K., & Bauer, U. (2015). Das Modell des produktiv realitätsverarbeitenden Subjekts [The model of the subject productively processing reality]. In K. Hurrelmann, U. Bauer, M. Grundmann, & S. Walper (Eds.), *Handbuch Sozialisationsforschung* [Handbook of socialisation research] (8th Entirely Rev. ed., pp. 144–161). Weinheim, Germany: Beltz.

Hurrelmann, K., Bauer, U., Grundmann, M., & Walper, S. (Eds.). (2015). *Handbuch Sozialisationsforschung* [Handbook of socialisation research] (8th Entirely Rev. ed.). Weinheim, Germany: Beltz.

Huston, A. C., & Wright, J. C. (1997). Mass media and children's development. In I. Sigel & K. A. Renninger (Eds.), *Handbook of child psychology: Child psychology in practice* (5th ed., Vol. 4., pp. 999–1058). New York, NY: Wiley.

James, A. (2013). *Socialising children*. Basingstoke, UK: Palgrave Macmillan.

James, A., Jenks, C., & Prout, A. (1998). *Theorizing childhood*. Cambridge, MA: Polity Press.

Jennings, N., & Wartella, E. (2013). Technology and the family. In A. Vangelisti (Ed.), *The handbook of family communication* (2nd ed., pp. 448–462). Mahwah, NJ: Lawrence Erlbaum Associates.

Jordan, A. B. (2003). A family systems approach to examining the role of the internet in the home. In J. Turow & A. L. Kavanaugh (Eds.), *The wired homestead: MIT press sourcebook on the internet and the family* (pp. 141–160). Cambridge, MA: MIT Press.

Jurczyk, K., Voß, G. G., & Weihrich, M. (2015). Conduct of everyday live in subjective-oriented sociology. In E. Schraube & C. Højholt (Eds.), *Psychology and conduct of everyday life* (pp. 34–64). London, UK: Routledge.

Kimmel, D. C., & Weiner, I. B. (1995). *Adolescence: A developmental transition* (2nd ed.). New York, NY: Wiley.

Krappmann, L. (2016). *Soziologische Dimensionen der Identität. Strukturelle Bedingungen für die Teilnahme an Interaktionsprozessen* [Sociological dimensions of identity processes]. Stuttgart, Germany: Klett-Cotta.

Krotz, F., & Hepp, A. (2013). A concretization of mediatization: How mediatization works and why, mediatized worlds' are a helpful concept for empirical mediatization research. *European Journal for the Philosophy of Communication, 3*(2), 37–152.

Krueger, R., & Johnson, W. (2010). Behavioral genetics and personality: A new look at the integration of nature and nurture. In O. P. John, R. W. Robins, & L. A. Pervin (Eds.), *Handbook of personality: Theory and research* (3rd ed., pp. 287–310). New York, NY: Guilford.

Kudera, W. (2001). Anpassung, Rückzug oder Restrukturierung – Zur Dynamik alltäglicher Lebensführung in Ostdeutschland [Adaption, retreat or restructuring—On dynamic conduct of everyday life in Eastern Germany]. In B. Lutz (Ed.), *Entwicklungsperspektiven von Arbeit* [Perspectives on development of work] (pp. 46–82). Berlin, Germany: Akademie Verlag.

Laible, D., Thomson, R. A., & Froimson, J. (2015). Early socialization: The influence of close relationships. In J. E. Grusec & P. D. Hastings (Eds.), *Handbook of socialization: Theory and research* (pp. 35–59). New York, NY: Guilford Press.

Lamb, M. E., Ketterlinus, R. D., & Fracasso, M. P. (1992). Parent–child relationships. In M. H. Bornstein & M. E. Lamb (Eds.), *Developmental psychology: An advanced textbook* (pp. 465–518). Mahwah, NJ: Lawrence Erlbaum Associates.

Lange, A. (2015). Sozialisation in der mediatisierten Gesellschaft [Socialisation in a mediatized society]. In K. Hurrelmann, U. Bauer, M. Grundmann, & S. Walper (Eds.), *Handbuch Sozialisationsforschung* [Handbook of socialisation research] (8th Entirely Rev. ed., pp. 537–556). Weinheim, Germany: Beltz.

Lauricella, A. R., Cingel, D. P., Blackwell, C., Wartella, E., & Conway, A. (2014). Mobile generation: Youth and adolescent ownership and use of new media. *Communication Research Reports, 31*(4), 357–364.

Lemish, D. (2007). *Children and television: A global perspective.* Malden, MA: Blackwell.

Lemish, D. (Ed.). (2013). *The Routledge international handbook of children, adolescents and media.* Milton Park and London, UK: Routledge and Taylor & Francis.

Livingstone, S. (2014). The mediatization of childhood and education: Reflections on the class. In L. Kramp, N. Carpentier, A. Hepp, I. T. Trivundža, H. Nieminen, R. Kunelius, ..., R. Kilborn (Eds.), *Media practice and everyday agency in Europe* (pp. 55–68). Bremen, Germany: Edition lumière.

Livingstone, S., & Bovill, M. (Eds.). (2001). *Children and their changing media environment: A European comparative study.* Mahwah, NJ: Lawrence Erlbaum Associates.

Livingstone, S., d'Haenens, L., & Hasebrink, U. (2001). Childhood in Europe: Contexts for comparison. In S. Livingstone & M. Bovill (Eds.), *Children and their changing media environment: A European comparative study* (pp. 3–30). Mahwah, NJ: Lawrence Erlbaum Associates.

Livingstone, S., & Lunt, P. (2014). Mediatization: An emerging paradigm for media and communication studies. In K. Lundby (Ed.), *Mediatization of communication: Handbook of communication science* (pp. 703–723). Berlin, Germany: Walter de Gruyter.

Livingstone, S., & Sefton-Green, J. (2016). *The class: Living and learning in the digital age.* New York, NY: New York University Press.

Lull, J. (1980). Family communication patterns and the social uses of television. *Human Communication Research, 6*(3), 197–209.

Lundby, K. (2014). Mediatization of communication. In K. Lundby (Ed.), *Mediatization of communication: Handbook of communication science* (pp. 3–35). Berlin, Germany: Walter de Gruyter.

Maccoby, E. E. (2015). Historical overview of socialization research and theory. In J. E. Grusec & P. D. Hastings (Eds.), *Handbook of socialization: Theory and research* (2nd ed., pp. 3–32). New York, NY: Guilford Press.

Marsh, J., Brooks, G., Hughes, J., Ritchie, L., Roberts, S., & Wright, K. (2005). *Digital beginnings: Young children's use of popular culture, media and new technologies.* Report of the 'Young Children's Use of Popular Culture, Media and New Technologies' study, funded by BBC Worldwide and the

Esmée Fairbairn Foundation. Sheffield, UK: Literacy Research Centre of the University of Sheffield, BBC Worldwide and Esmée Fairbairn. Retrieved from http://www.digitalbeginnings.shef.ac.uk/DigitalBeginningsReport.pdf.

Mayer, A. (2017). *Sigmund Freud. Zur Einführung* [Sigmund Freud: An introduction]. Hamburg, Germany: Junius Verlag.

Mayseless, O., & Keren, E. (2014). Finding a meaningful life as a developmental task in emerging adulthood: The domains of love and work across cultures. *Emerging Adulthood, 2*(1), 63–73.

Mead, G. H. (1934). *Mind, self, and society*. Chicago, IL: The University Chicago Press.

Morgan, D. H. J. (2011). *Rethinking family practices*. Basingstoke, UK: Palgrave Macmillan.

Morley, D. (1992). *Television, audiences and cultural studies*. London, UK: Routledge.

Nathanson, A. I. (2013). Media and the family context. In D. Lemish (Ed.), *The Routledge international handbook of children, adolescents and media* (pp. 299–306). London, UK: Routledge.

Neal, J. W., & Neal, Z. P. (2013). Nested or networked? Future directions for ecological systems theory. *Social Development, 22*(4), 722–737.

Noller, P. & Atkin, S. (2014). *Family life in adolescence*. Berlin, Germany and Boston, MA: Sciendo Migration.

Oerter, R., & Dreher, E. (2008). Jugendalter [Adolescence]. In R. Oerter & L. Montada (Eds.), *Entwicklungspsychologie* [Developmental psychology] (6th Entirely Rev. ed., pp. 271–332). Weinheim, Germany and Basel, Switzerland: Beltz.

Packer, M. J. (2017). *Child development: Understanding a cultural perspective*. London, UK, Los Angeles, CA, New Dehli, India, and Singapore: Sage.

Parsons, T. (1951). *The social system*. New York, NY: Free Press.

Paus-Hasebrink, I. (2010). Das Social Web im Kontext der Entwicklungsaufgaben junger Menschen [Social media in the context of developmental tasks of young people]. *Medien Journal: Zeitschrift für Kommunikationskultur, 34*(4), 20–34.

Paus-Hasebrink, I. (2013). Audiovisuelle und Online-Kommunikation – Theoretische Wege zur Analyse der komplexen Zusammenhänge von Produktions-, Angebots- und Aneignungsweisen [Audiovisual and online-communication]. In I. Paus-Hasebrink, S. Trültzsch, A. Pluschkowitz, & C. Wijnen (Eds.), *Integrative AV- und Online-Kommunikationsforschung. Perspektiven – Positionen – Projekte* [Integrative AV- and online-communication research: Perspectives—Positions—Projects] (pp. 60–99). Baden-Baden, Germany: Nomos.

Paus-Hasebrink, I. (2017). Praxeologische (Medien-)Sozialisationsforschung [Praxeological approach on media socialisation research]. In D. Hoffmann, F. Krotz, & W. Reißmann (Eds.), *Mediatisierung und Mediensozialisation.*

Prozesse – Räume – Praktiken [Mediatization and media socialisation: Processes—Spaces—Practices] (pp. 103–118). Wiesbaden, Germany: Springer Fachmedien.

Paus-Hasebrink, I. (2018). The role of media within children's socialization: A praxeological approach. *Communications: The European Journal of Communication Research.* Ahead of print, 17.10.2018 (pp. 1–20). DOI: https://doi.org/10.1515/commun-2018-2016.

Paus-Hasebrink, I., Bauwens, J., Dürager, A. E., & Ponte, C. (2013). Exploring types of parent–child relationship and internet use across Europe. *Journal of Children and Media—JOCAM, 7*(1), 114–132.

Paus-Hasebrink, I., & Kulterer, J. (2014). *Praxeologische Mediensozialisationsforschung. Langzeitstudie zu sozial benachteiligten Heranwachsenden* [Praxeological media socialisation research: A longitudinal study regarding socially disadvantaged adolescents] Assisted by P. Sinner. Baden-Baden, Germany: Nomos.

Piaget, J. (1980). *Psychologie der Intelligenz* [Psychology of cognitive development]. Stuttgart, Germany: Klett-Cotta.

Piotrowski, J. T., & Valenburg, P. M. (2016). Psychology, development. In K. B. Jensen & R. T. Craig (Eds), *International encyclopedia of communication theory and philosophy.* Hoboken, NJ: Wiley.

Prout, A. (2008). Culture-nature and the construction of childhood. In K. Drotner & S. Livingstone (Eds.), *The international handbook of children, media and culture* (pp. 21–35). Los Angeles, CA, London, UK, and New Dehli, India: Sage.

Prout, S., Anderson, A. A., Gentile, D. A., Warburton, W., Saleem, M., Groves, C. L., & Brown, S. C. (2015). Media as agents of socialization. In J. E. Grusec & P. D. Hastings (Eds.), *Handbook of socialization: Theory and research* (2nd ed., pp. 276–300). New York, NY: Guilford Press.

Quenzel, G. (2015). *Entwicklungsaufgaben und Gesundheit im Jugendalter* [Developmental tasks and health during adolescence]. Weinheim, Germany: Beltz Juventa.

Rideout, V. J. (2016). Measuring time spent with media: The common sense census of media use by US 8- to 18-year-olds. *Journal of Children and Media—JOCAM, 10*(1), 138–144.

Rideout, V., Foehr, U. G., & Roberts, D. F. (2010). *Generation M^2: Media in the lives of 8- to 18-year-olds: A Kaiser family foundation study.* Menlo Park, CA: The Henry J. Kaiser Family Foundation. Retrieved from https://kaiserfamilyfoundation.files.wordpress.com/2013/04/8010.pdf.

Schofield Clark, L. (2013). *The parent app: Understanding families in the digital age.* Oxford, UK: University Press.

Schöllgen, G. (1998). *Max Weber.* München, Germany: Beck.

Schütz, A., & Luckmann, T. (2003). *Strukturen der Lebenswelt* [Structures of the lifeworld]. Konstanz, Germany: UVK Verlagsgesellschaft.

Silverstone, R. (2002). Complicity and collision in the mediation of everyday life. *New Literary History, 33*(4), 745–764.
Simmel, G. (1908). *Soziologie. Untersuchungen über die Formen der Vergesellschaftung* [Sociology: Studies on the forms of socialisation]. Berlin, Germany: Duncker & Humblot.
Skaar, H. (2009). Branded selves. *Journal of Children and Media—JOCAM, 3*(3), 249–267.
Smetana, J. G., Robinson, J., & Rote, W. (2015). Socialization in adolescence. In J. E. Grusec & P. D. Hastings (Eds.), *Handbook of socialization: Theory and research* (2nd ed., pp. 60–84). New York, NY: Guilford Press.
Steinberg, L. (2005). *Adolescence* (7th ed.). New York, NY: McGraw-Hill.
Subrahmanyam, K., & Šmahel, D. (2011). *Digital youth: The role of media in development.* New York, NY: Springer.
Vandewater, E. A. (2013). Ecological approaches to the study of media and children. In D. Lemish (Ed.), *The Routledge international handbook of children, adolescents and media* (pp. 46–53). Milton Park and London, UK: Routledge and Taylor & Francis.
Walther, M. (2014). *Repatriation to France and Germany: A comparative study based on Bourdieu's theory of practice.* Wiesbaden, Germany: Springer Gabler.
Wartella, E., Beaudoin-Ryan, L., Blackwell, C. K., Cingel, D., Hurwitz, L. B., & Lauricella, A. R. (2016). What kind of adults will our children become? The impact of growing up in a media-saturated world. *Journal of Children and Media—JOCAM, 10*(1), 13–20.
Weiß, R. (1997). Auf der Suche nach kommunikativen Milieus [Searching for communicative milieus]. In H. Scherer & H.-B. Brosius (Eds.), *Zielgruppen, Publikumssegmente, Nutzergruppen* [Target groups, audience segments, user groups] (pp. 239–261). München, Germany: Reinhard Fischer.
Weiß, R. (2000). Praktischer Sinn, soziale Identität und Fern-Sehen [Practical sense, social identity and tele-vision]. *Medien und Kommunikationswissenschaft, 48*(1), 42–62.
Weiß, R. (2001). *Fern-Sehen im Alltag. Zur Sozialpsychologie der Medienrezeption* [Tele-vision in everyday life: On social psychology of media reception]. Opladen, Germany: Westdeutscher Verlag.
Willis, P. (1977). *Learning to labor: How working class kids get working class jobs.* Tiptree, UK: Anchor Press.
Wilson, B. J., & Drogos, K. L. (2013). The mass media and family communication. In A. Vangelisti (Ed.), *The handbook of family communication* (2nd ed., pp. 424–447). Mahwah, NJ: Lawrence Erlbaum Associates.
Wygotski, L. S. (1977). *Denken und Sprechen* [Thinking and speaking]. Edited by J. Helm with an introduction by T. Luckmann. Frankfurt am Main, Germany: Fischer.

Open Access This chapter is licensed under the terms of the Creative Commons Attribution 4.0 International License (http://creativecommons.org/licenses/by/4.0/), which permits use, sharing, adaptation, distribution and reproduction in any medium or format, as long as you give appropriate credit to the original author(s) and the source, provide a link to the Creative Commons licence and indicate if changes were made.

The images or other third party material in this chapter are included in the chapter's Creative Commons licence, unless indicated otherwise in a credit line to the material. If material is not included in the chapter's Creative Commons licence and your intended use is not permitted by statutory regulation or exceeds the permitted use, you will need to obtain permission directly from the copyright holder.

CHAPTER 4

The Methodological Approach of the Long-Term Study

4.1 Introduction

Lasting from 2005 to 2017, this study's methodological approach to the role of media in the socialisation of socially disadvantaged children and adolescents in Austria illustrates how the complex praxeological approach to researching children's and adolescent's media usage within the process of socialisation can be operationalised. The approach we selected for dealing with this challenge involved a qualitative longitudinal panel and was conducted successfully in six waves of data collection over a period of twelve years. The starting point was the question: How to operationalise the theoretical approach presented in the preceding chapter, in order to provide a fruitful basis for analysing the role of media within socialisation on a methodological level? As growing up in a mediatised world is a complex process, it is abundantly clear that looking merely superficially at how children deal with media will not suffice. Instead, it is essential to investigate how they subjectively make sense of media as a source for coping with factors of which they are not yet aware. The question: "How do children, and also their parents, make sense of media?" is closely connected with the structures of their everyday lives on the micro-level of the child or adolescent, on the meso-level of the family, but also of peers and friends, as well as on the macro-level of the country/society (see Fig. 4.1). Their media-related practices may be understood as subjectively given answers to the challenges of their everyday

© The Author(s) 2019
I. Paus-Hasebrink et al., *Social Inequality, Childhood and the Media*,
Transforming Communications – Studies in Cross-Media Research,
https://doi.org/10.1007/978-3-030-02653-0_4

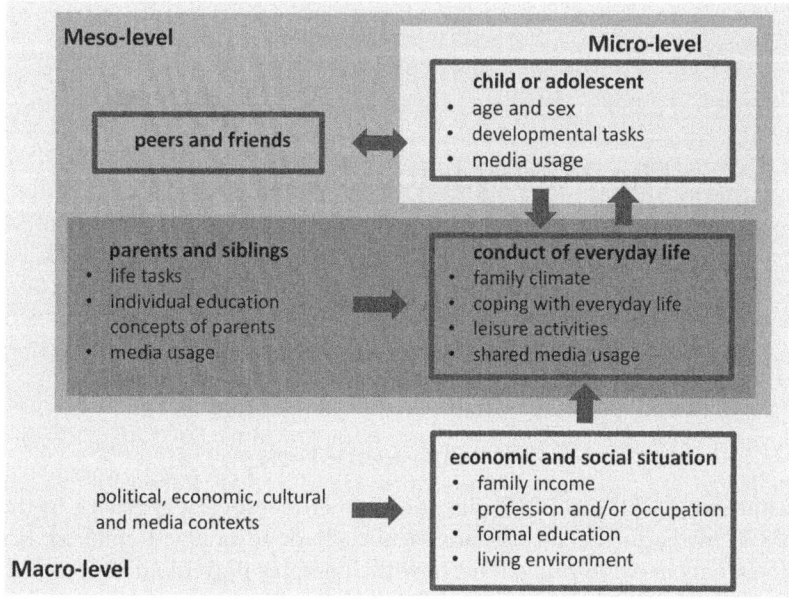

Fig. 4.1 Relevant contextual factors for children's socialisation

lives. Against this background, we consider media usage a practice within a socially constructed everyday life and thus a form of observable practical ability.

To sum up, the approach implies the following four methodological requirements: first and foremost, since the main analytical concepts refer to entangled and interlinked processes of interaction between children and their parents within their everyday lives, the methodological approach has to be located within a qualitative research paradigm (Clarke, 2005, 2011; Flick, 2014; Wilson, 1970). Researching within this paradigm allows us to retrace and reconstruct how individuals subjectively make sense of their social contexts and act in them. Furthermore, it allows us to detect the underlying structures of individuals' utterances and actions. Secondly, in order to be able to reconstruct and to review the processes of *doing family*, data have to be collected from children as well as from parents. Thirdly, in order to include the broader social contexts that have an impact on a family, particular attention has to be paid to its socio-structural conditions. And fourthly, in order to grasp the dynamic character of the socialisation processes, a longitudinal design is needed.

4.2 Recruitment of the Families

We conducted a panel study of twenty (reduced to 18 after the second wave due to drop-outs) socially disadvantaged families with children (boys and girls), who were, respectively, almost five or six years old in 2005 (see Paus-Hasebrink & Bichler, 2008, pp. 132–141; Paus-Hasebrink & Kulterer, 2014; Paus-Hasebrink, Sinner, Kulterer, & Oberlinner, 2017, pp. 48–49). They were not yet in school and still attending kindergarten. So, from the preparatory theoretical work, we deduced the following selection criteria as being central to researching social inequality and then recruited the 20 families accordingly.

- Apparent markers of social disadvantage following Hradil (1987, 1999): for example, unemployment, low income (defined as relatively poor, less than 50% of the national median income, and as at risk of poverty, less than 60% of the national median income), lower formal education, residential neighbourhood, bad housing conditions—singly or in combination.
- Family structure: families were so chosen that the sample would contain different family configurations, like single-parent families, large families (more than five children) and nuclear families.
- Migrant background: households with at least one foreign member (understood as a non EU- or EFTA-citizen) belong to the groups at risk of poverty or being marginalised (see Statistik Austria, 2017, pp. 21, 25).
- Area of living: urban and rural areas/areas with a poor infrastructure (for example, mountain areas, areas with bad public transport connections, no accessible railway stations) (see Table 4.1).

It was not our aim to depict statistical distribution throughout the population but to select typical and *"information-rich cases"* (Patton, 2002, p. 230, emphasis in original) in our field of research, a procedure that is called "purposeful sampling" (Rapley, 2014, p. 56): "Information-rich cases are those from which one can learn a great deal about issues of central importance to the purpose of inquiry, thus the term *purposeful* sampling" (Patton, 2002, p. 230, emphasis in original). Based on a

Table 4.1 The families—An overview

Family	Sex of the child (m/f)	Urban/rural area	Single-parent-family	Extended family	Migration background
1	M	Urban			
2	M	Rural		×	
3	M	Urban			
4	F	Urban	×	×	
5	F	Rural			
6	F	Rural			
7	F	Rural	×		
8	M	Rural		×	
9	F	Rural			
10	F	Rural			
11	F	Urban	×		
12	M	Urban	×	×	
13	F	Urban	×		
14	M	Urban		×	
15	M	Rural	×		
16	F	Urban	×		×
17	M	Urban			
18	M	Urban	×		
19	F	Rural	×	×	
20	M	Urban		×	

literature review (Paus-Hasebrink & Bichler, 2008, pp. 135–136) conducted to acquire "knowledge of the phenomenon" (Rapley, 2014, p. 50), we selected markers that define the characteristic living conditions of socially disadvantaged families, in order to make a "thoughtful and rigorous" (Rapley, 2014, p. 49) choice.

Lack of money is the most important marker of social disadvantage. On the one hand, family income depends on the specific living conditions of a family's wage earners, on the other hand, the availability of material resources defines the living conditions of a family as a whole. In order to include families in our sample, we had to be able to easily survey suitable markers, but with the provision that they would be capable of representing a wide range of socially disadvantaged families. Accordingly, for our sampling we decided to consider those factors that increase the risk of poverty (see Chapter 2): low income, unemployment, lower formal education of the parents, single-parent families, large families and families with migrant background. In addition, we decided to select children between five and six years old, who were not yet attending school, in order to capture the important transition period from kindergarten to primary school in our second wave of surveying our panel. We decided in advance on a total of 20 cases and based our decision on the qualitative orientation of the study, the complex methodological approach and the available resources (temporal, personal and financial). Both the distribution of families across rural and urban areas and the distribution between the sexes were to be equal. For practical reasons, we recruited families in the Federal States of Salzburg and Upper Austria.

The process of recruitment was supported by a number of social organisations and social facilities like the *Organisation of Single Mothers and Single Fathers*, *Caritas*, the *Youth Welfare Office* and numerous *kindergartens*, as well as by public authorities like the *Department of Families* and the relevant ministers from the two states. We informed potential participants about the project, invited them to contact the principal investigator and offered an expense allowance (50€ per data collection) to the families, an amount which remained unchanged until 2016. The children, and later the adolescents, received small non-monetary gifts (for example, sweets, pens or handicraft kits). However, socially disadvantaged people do have a record of rejecting government institutions and participation in research projects, so that the process of recruitment was quite hard and time-consuming (see also Patton, 2002, pp. 310–311). In order to achieve our goals, we were forced to take further action: we started to cooperate with additional social organisations and social facilities, used personal contacts and political support, and we placed advertisements in local and regional newspapers and journals.

Table 4.1 provides an overview of the sample's main characteristics at the beginning of the study (see Chapter 5 for a description of the families). Due to the fact that low income in the beginning was a major selection criterion to become a part of the panel this criterion is not listed in the table—at that time all families had a low income.

The focus of the research was on one child at the right age from each family. However, the siblings figured in the interviews, too. Since two families did not participate throughout, by the end of the project the sample consisted of ten boys and eight girls. Over the study period, the families' changing circumstances altered other characteristics as well, so the sample looked different at the end of the project, a point extensively discussed below (see Chapter 8). The aim of choosing children between the ages of five and six was to be able to investigate the relevant phases of a child's development from kindergarten, through mid-childhood to youth over six waves of data collection (2005, 2007, 2010, 2012, 2014, and 2016). To complete it, we conducted a telephone survey in winter 2016/2017, in order to get the latest information about the development of the adolescents and their families.

4.3 THE CHALLENGES OF MANAGING A LONG-TERM STUDY

The whole project consists of three separate phases (waves 1 and 2, waves 3 and 4, waves 5 and 6 and call-back interviews). All three project phases had to be applied for singly. Not only did they have to pass the blind peer-review process, but they also had to fulfil the requirements and restrictions of the OeNB Anniversary Fund (2015) (Fund of the Austrian National Bank). In addition, the proposals needed the approval of Department of Communications of the University of Salzburg, the approval of the Research Service of the University of Salzburg (2018) and the approval of the Rectorate of the University of Salzburg. Due to the limited time frames, we had to plan the three project waves separately, not as a single twelve-year project. However, we did manage to acquire three consecutive grants, but there was always the risk of terminating the study after its first or second phase. Financing over a period of years is one of the most challenging tasks in conducting long-term research, due to reduced overall funding for research, but also given the existing structures (in Austria) for research funding. As a consequence, we had to work hard on maintaining our panel. On the one hand, we had to keep contact-data up to date, as our clients moved house and changed telephone numbers, email addresses and other contact details quite often. Furthermore, they often neglected official letters, sometimes not even opening them. Consequently, we had to visit some of the families over the time, just in order to stay in touch and to re-recruit them for our next wave of data collection. On the other hand, we had to deal with the uncertainties over the project funding. Every time we had to invite the families to participate again in future, even though we could not guarantee if, and when, the next wave of data collection would take place. This required great commitment from both sides, families and researchers, but in the end, we were able to achieve a very low drop-out quota.

4.4 Data Collection

In order to reconstruct, describe and explain how children make sense of media against the background of their everyday lives, we have applied a broad repertoire of qualitative methods (Morse & Maddox, 2014, pp. 524–525; see also Paus-Hasebrink et al., 2017, pp. 51–58; see Figs. 4.2 and 4.3). However, we have gone one step further, using a rich design which is characterised "as one that is not restricted to one theory and method, or one set of categories or instruments, but which embraces diverse and multiple perspectives brought together with coherence and harmony. It is more than a multi-method design per se" (Paus-Hasebrink, Prochazka, & Sinner, 2013, p. 23): we conducted guided in-depth interviews (semi-structured) with the children. Commencing with the fifth wave (beginning of adolescence, 2014), we added three more methods of data collection:

(1) Thinking aloud about a social networking tool (for example Facebook or WhatsApp) selected by each child, (2) In addition, we asked them to produce their own network maps of media and relationship structures, and (3) to take a set of photos (favourite spot, place of work, preferred spot for media usage). We also conducted guided in-depth interviews (semi-structured) with the parents or one single parent. In addition, we asked them to independently complete a standardised

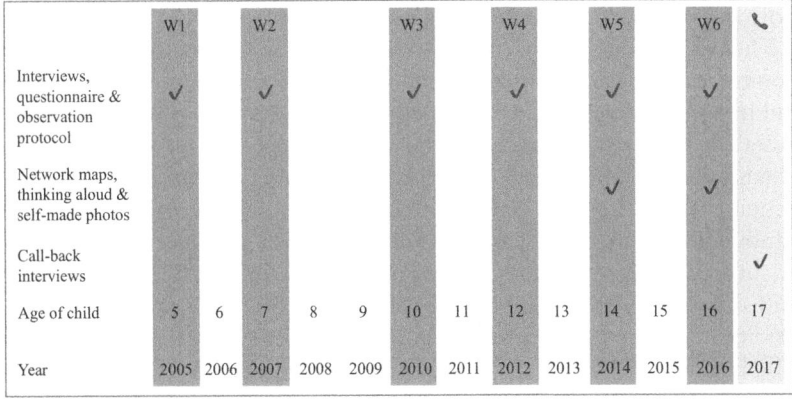

Fig. 4.2 Methods of data collection in the different waves of research at a glance

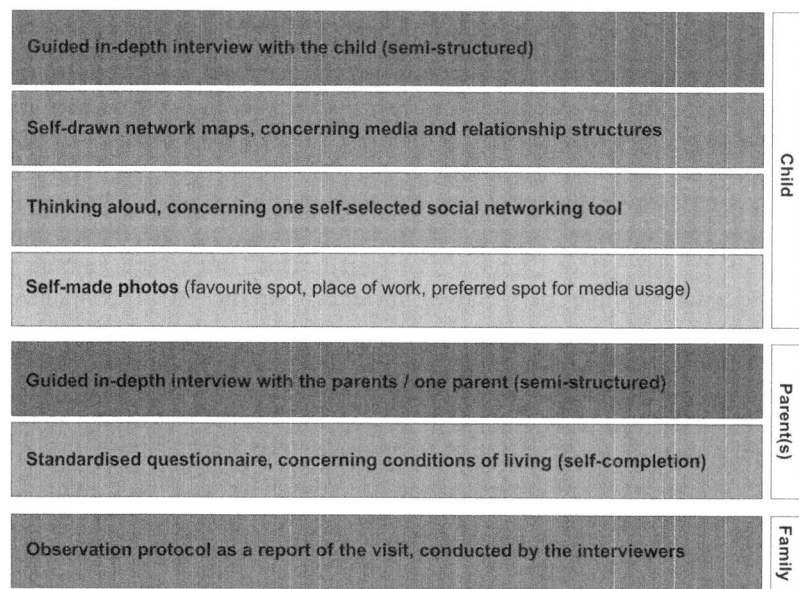

Fig. 4.3 Methods of data collection

questionnaire on their living conditions. In order to get an overall impression of the respective families, we used observation protocols to provide a report on the visit by the interviewers.

These components of our rich design draw on, complement, and monitor each other during data collection and analysis, a process which simultaneously makes the research transparent and intersubjectively traceable: "The goal of such rich design approaches may be to eliminate weaknesses and blind spots perceived in one method by using complementary approaches that have specific strengths in such areas. A sensitive combination of methods can therefore shed light on aspects that cannot be covered adequately by only one method. Such rich designs feature a high density of data and a high level of reflection on the research process itself" (Paus-Hasebrink et al., 2013, p. 23). This is in accordance with Denzin's (1989, p. 307) concept of triangulation: "By combining multiple observers, theories, methods, and data sources, [researchers] can hope to overcome the intrinsic bias that comes from single-methods, single-observer, and single-theory studies" (see also Denzin & Lincoln,

2011, p. 2). The capacity for "comparing and cross-checking the consistency of information" (Patton, 2002, p. 559) allows researchers to generate greater added value.

The strategies of research were guided by the analytical concepts presented in Chapter 3: *options for action, outlines for action* and *competences for action*. In order to operationalise these concepts, we used several reactive and non-reactive methods. The standardised questionnaire for the parents was used in order to examine the *options for actions*. Observational methods served as an additional tool to investigate how the child and the parents conduct their everyday life and how they deal with the conditions of their specific social situation in *doing family* (for example, conflicts, proximity and so on). In order to define the *outlines for action*, we combined these questionnaires and the named observations with guided in-depth interviews conducted separately with the child and the parents—mostly the mother, in some cases both parents—on different aspects of their everyday lives and their usage of media. In order to gather evidence regarding *competences for action*, we used indications from interviews and observations of a wide range of aspects, for instance, a child's cognitive and motivational resources, their attitudes towards kindergarten, as well as school and education in general, parents' strategies for bringing up their children, together with their ability to implement them, and for mediating their media usage, and both children's and parents' media-related skills. All these aspects were investigated from both the children's and the parents' perspective. This made it possible to discover discrepancies or commonalities in how children and parents mutually perceive their competences. Differences between the answers of parents and children suggested conclusions regarding family climate and *doing family* (relationships between parents and children and within the family as a whole). Furthermore, this approach allowed conclusions concerning the applied mediation strategies and their acceptance, as well as their relevance for the process of socialisation. In addition, it became possible to track the process of growing up and the process of distancing from parents as the children became older and subsequently adolescent (at the beginning of puberty and youth) (see Paus-Hasebrink et al., 2017, p. 51). All the data collected from these different methods were used to create and to update a *global characteristic* (Charlton & Neumann, 1986; Schütze, 1977; see also Paus-Hasebrink & Bichler, 2008, pp. 142–145; Paus-Hasebrink & Kulterer, 2014, pp. 57–59; Paus-Hasebrink et al., 2017, p. 51) for each family investigated.

4.4.1 Standardised Questionnaire

At each visit, the parents were asked to complete a standardised questionnaire on their living conditions. These questionnaires covered central aspects about living together, the constellation within individual families, housing and socio-economic circumstances. It consisted of the following main categories:

- family constellation and family characteristics: marital status, number of family members living together, number of children, overall and in residence, ages of children and parents, nationality, religious affiliation;
- professional career and activity of the parents: school education and apprenticeship, (un)employment and self-employment, training courses;
- economic situation of the family: household income (single earner or not), social benefits, further sources of income (for example, rental income, interest, inheritances), assets and/or estates, amount of pocket money (children), later on also, income of the adolescents;
- housing situation: residential area and neighbourhood, size and state of flat or house, ownership or renting a flat or house, duration of residence, plans for relocation.

4.4.2 Guided In-Depth Interview with the Parents

Since its inception, we tried to keep changes or modifications to the guideline at a minimum, in order to sustain a maximum of comparability throughout the investigation period. The guidelines for both parents and children were closely coordinated. However, we questioned the parents more intensively about their children than the other way round. Our interviews included questions about how, in the first instance, the parents—but then, to a lesser extent, their children and other family members—dealt with and experienced possible challenges, such as unemployment or poorly-paid jobs, shortage of money, bad housing conditions, living in a single parent family and/or in the context of a large family, and so on. We also asked them how they interacted with their family and if they felt integrated in it, in their neighbourhood, peer-groups, friendships, kindergarten or class, and social life in general,

4 THE METHODOLOGICAL APPROACH OF THE LONG-TERM STUDY   87

and what kinds of media offerings they used, to what extent, for what purposes, and with whom. Additionally, we asked children and parents in each wave of data collection for their ideas, preferences, goals, plans and motives for action and what they were planning for their future. However, in the interviews with parents some topics were examined more intensively than they were with the children. There were, for example, questions about their mediation strategies, questions not only about the child of particular interest but also about the siblings, and questions concerning developments in different aspects of individual families' lives. In order to provide an overview, the guidelines for parents followed four main themes:

- how the family felt situated socially—the everyday life of the family—the participation of parents and children within society, that is, the social conditions of growing up, the changes that have happened in living conditions, the climate and relationships within the family, daily routines and aspects of everyday life, the preferred leisure activities of parents, and of children, their shared interests, social activities and involvement in associations, cultural life and active citizenship;
- their attitudes towards the media—the media usage of parents, child and siblings—the behaviour within the family as regards the media, meaning the importance of different media for the parents, the individual patterns of media usage of the family members, the relevance of joint media practices, the sources of information, the expertise within the family when dealing with the media;
- media repertoires: the media ownership of the family and of single members of the family, the financing of access to the media, the media usage of parents and children, the individual media repertoires of the family members, the importance of media for the children in general/in their everyday lives, the roles and functions of the media for the children, but also for the parents, the modes of media usage (for example, where, when, how long, with whom, on which device), the existence of mediation strategies, the importance of media education for parents, the regulation of media usage by the parents;
- the communication and transferring of values—the extent, importance and credibility of the family—the extent, importance and credibility of other contexts of socialisation (for example, media,

kindergarten, school, friends, peers) and the changes over time, the sources of knowledge transfer, the sources of value transfer, role models and idols, the importance of the family along with other players, the changes due to the development of the child.

4.4.3 Guided In-Depth Interview with the Children and Adolescents

In order to sustain maximum comparability, changes were reduced to a minimum, with the main themes remaining the same over time. Although the main aim of the interviews with the children was to investigate their media usage within a mediatised world, we also asked them about the circumstances of their lives (for example, family life, kindergarten and school, friends and peers, financial worries, housing, their own room, wishes and dreams and so on). Special attention was paid to the growing importance of online media and internet-based (communication) services. We did not enquire about the usage of single devices, but rather more about individual media repertoires, based on functions and interests (see Hasebrink, 2014; Hasebrink & Domeyer, 2012; Hasebrink & Popp, 2006). Thus, some aspects of our guidelines were restructured over time. This meant specifically adding new questions, removing others, or rewording some, in order to cater for new technological developments. In the interests of a pleasant and more relaxed atmosphere, boys were always interviewed by male members of the team and girls by female members. Whenever possible, we tried to send the same interview teams to the same families over several years and waves of investigation. On the one hand, the interviewer gained special knowledge about the respective family and its members, on the other hand, this approach created a particular relationship of trust. For the same reasons, we tried to send more experienced interviewers to more challenging families (see Chapter 8).

- The situation of the child's life in society—the everyday life of the family—the participation of the child within society—leisure activities—the social conditions of growing up and living conditions, the climate and relationships within families, the daily routines and aspects of everyday life, the preferred leisure activities of the children, their social activities, involvement in associations, cultural life and active citizenship;

- Media ownership—their media repertoires—their media usage and media behaviour—the importance of media—the roles and functions of media for the child—the structure of media repertoires, the accessibility of media for the children, the personal ownership of media, the media used by the children and the role of media in the children's everyday lives;
- The behaviour of parents and siblings as regards the media—their attitudes towards media—the media usage within the family—media education and the regulation of media usage—the role of different media for individual members of the family, the behaviour of individual family members as regards the media, the media practices shared within the family, the mediation strategies, media education and the media expertise within the family;
- The ways of adopting values—the role of the family concerning communication and transfer of knowledge and values—the role of other contexts of socialisation (for example, media, kindergarten, school, friends, peers)—the contexts in which children adopt values and codes of practice—the role models and idols for children.

In contrast to the guidelines for parents, the guidelines for children contained so-called role-playing questions, in order to better understand the importance of media and media personalities for the children. Different layers of media processing—cognitive, emotional and social—formed our analytic distinctions. However, in real life they are closely linked and intertwined. Therefore, it is quite difficult for the adolescents to articulate themselves concerning these fields (Cakici & Bayir, 2012, pp. 1076–1077; Cohen, Manion, & Morrison, 2011, pp. 513–522; Jörg, 1994; Paus-Haase, 1998, p. 104; Stahlke, 2005, pp. 496–507; Tilemann, 2017, p. 393). To answer role-playing questions may be helpful in expressing complex contexts of experience and subjective understanding (Paus-Haase, 1998, p. 165; Sader, 1995, p. 194). We used three different types of role-playing questions. In an "island-question", the adolescents were asked to explain which persons and which objects they would take with themselves to a desert island and why. In the "100 Euro-question" (later "500 Euro-question") they were asked to tell us what they would do with 100 (or 500) Euro. In the "wishing question", they were asked at the end of the interview what they would do if they had one wish. We found the answers to these questions were particularly important sources of information.

4.4.4 Observation Protocol

Finally, we will now outline our observation protocol (Mason, 2002, pp. 96–98). This completed our survey of the families from the interviewers' point of view by basically fulfilling two purposes: on the one hand, it systematically recorded the respective families' living and housing conditions and their media hardware. On the other hand, it served as a guideline for the participatory observation, in order to grasp how all family members were *doing family*. We kept the criteria of the protocol the same over time (see also Paus-Hasebrink & Bichler, 2008, pp. 131–132; Paus-Hasebrink & Kulterer, 2014, p. 381):

- the state of the house or flat and rooms: cleanliness, neatness, furniture, differences between the children's rooms and the rest of the rest of the houses or flats;
- the media hardware: devices, number of them, their positioning, media-related items, media hardware in the children's bedrooms;
- the pets: species, number, location, behaviour, cleanliness;
- the family members: garments, smoking, alcohol, behaviour and manner of children, parents and siblings;
- any further particular features.

As criteria like cleanliness, neatness or the conditions of furniture and clothing may be viewed subjectively, it was essential to reach a common understanding. Therefore, we applied a two-step procedure: firstly, both interviewers had to fill out the protocol together, immediately after finishing the visit in the family. They were instructed to compare their personal impressions with their experiences in other families they visited. Secondly, in order to consolidate a common understanding of a given sample, the research team discussed all recent observation protocols and compared them to the data from the previous waves.

4.4.5 Complementary Methods for Adolescents: Thinking Aloud, Network Maps, Photos

With the fifth wave of data collection in 2014, the children we were observing entered on a new stage of life, adolescence. So, we decided to add three more qualitative methods of data collection to our already existing range. On the one hand, we wanted to do justice to our adolescents by acknowledging the changes in their everyday lives, their new interests, behavioural patterns and options. On the other hand, we had to adjust to the technological and medial changes in a mediatised world between our waves of interviews. These newly added methods, then, allowed a better understanding of the media behaviour of the adolescents and their social inclusion in family and non-family relationships. This approach was successful in revealing hidden information, not only when it was difficult for the adolescents to express their thoughts and ideas, but also when they were not fully aware of certain facts and structures (see Paus-Hasebrink, 2005, p. 224; 2017, pp. 277–278; Paus-Hasebrink et al., 2017, pp. 55–56).

4.4.5.1 Thinking Aloud About Favourite Social Media Tools
With the first supplementary method, we could stay abreast of changes caused by the increasing importance of social networking tools. Based on the method of thinking aloud (Bilandzic, 2005, pp. 362–364; 2017, pp. 407–408), we asked the adolescent to talk about their favourite social networking tools (for example, Facebook, WhatsApp, YouTube). They were asked to show us their profiles and settings (for example, privacy settings, friends list, photos, groups, single chats, followed pages and channels and so on) and to talk about how they make use of the applications and features (see Rose, 2016, pp. 301–302). Our aim was to better understand what is really important to the adolescents (see Marotzki, Holze, & Verständig, 2014, p. 457), so the guideline for this method contained only a few questions and topics (Toerien, 2014, pp. 330–331), but did include questions about the structures of the respective social networking tools, for example core or advanced features but also restrictions (see also Trappel, 2007, pp. 156–158). However, we likewise used the method of thinking aloud in order to reveal how competent and knowledgeable the adolescents were about the social networking tools, although they had not been willing or able to talk about them during the formal interview.

4.4.5.2 Network Maps Drawn by Our Subjects
In order to cater for the increased relevance of social relationships within the everyday lives of the adolescents (Cotterell, 2007, p. 91), we decided to integrate network maps into our repertoire of methods (Coffey, 2014, p. 367; Samuelsson, Thernlund, & Ringström, 1996, pp. 327–330) as these can visualise connections and communication paths and routines

(Hepp & Düvel, 2010, p. 271). Hence, they are suitable for researching not only media repertoires but also information repertoires and relationship structures. We decided to apply a two-step approach by firstly asking the adolescents to write down the names of all relevant persons on a sheet of paper with the word "me" already printed in its centre to symbolise the position of the respective adolescents, around which they then grouped other relevant persons. The number of persons, their position in relation to the adolescents and the links between them were up to the adolescents (Crosnoe, 2000, p. 379). When they had finished, we asked them to elaborate on the spatial distances, on the choice of people (maybe on people who had been left out or forgotten and so on) and on the connections between themselves and the people nominated. In a second step, we asked the adolescents to add the media services they used and their media devices to the map. If possible, they might indicate connections between certain media (devices and services) and (groups of) persons (for example, PlayStation with friend XY, WhatsApp group for best friends, TV-series with brother and sister). All this resulted in network maps about everyday communication, the media used (devices and services) and connections among the elements cited. This method shed light on the importance of (groups of) persons and media thus selected, in order to visualise their status (see Hepp & Düvel, 2010, pp. 271–273; Hepp, Berg, & Roitsch, 2011, pp. 10–12). However, it was also very informative to note the persons and media not present, or no more than distant from the respective adolescents.

4.4.5.3 Photos by Our Subjects
Inspired by the concept of "bedroom culture" (Bovill & Livingstone, 2001, p. 2; Lincoln, 2013, p. 315), we asked the adolescents to take a set of photos in their own room, in order to better understand their personalities and their media behaviour. In practical terms, they were asked to take three pictures (see Harper, 2005, pp. 231, 233; Marshall & Rossman, 2016, pp. 184–187; Rose, 2016, pp. 310–312): a photo of their favourite spot, a photo of their place of work and a photo of their preferred spot for media usage. However, they could also indicate where one photo could cover two or even three spots (Mason, 2002, pp. 112–113). Such photos do provide deep insights into the private spheres of the adolescents (Rose, 2016, pp. 360–362). They reveal rooms where they spend a lot of time, and ones which are today strongly affected by media (see Bovill & Livingstone, 2001, p. 3). In their own

realm within the house or flat they can realise their own ideas and express themselves (see Lincoln, 2013, pp. 318–320). Examples of their self-expression are individual schemes for painting walls and the positioning of media devices, but also the use of posters or merchandising products and selected furniture and how these are set out in the room.

4.4.6   *Final Call-Back Interview*

The sixth and last planned wave of surveys had already taken place in January and February 2016. Since it was our aim to bring the data up to date before completing the study, we shortened our guidelines and conducted an additional call-back interview in January 2017. To integrate the results with preceding waves, we talked to the adolescents and also to at least one of the guardians, in most cases the mothers. We kept to our protocol of girls being interviewed by a female team member and boys by a male team member. The focus in these call-back interviews was on the current living situations, life-changing experiences and our subjects' perception of the changes. However, against the backdrop of the sixth wave, questions about future prospects and developments, working life and unemployment were particularly important. At this time, some of the adolescents had to face a period of uncertainty. They had to decide about their plans for the future, whether to continue schooling or start an apprenticeship or even working life itself. Finding a (appropriate) training place was not easy for all of them, so they had to deal with unemployment and with training activities at job centres. The following topics were part of our guidelines:

- current living situation;
- school education or apprenticeship;
- future prospects and unemployment;
- family life and satisfaction;
- friends, peers and (new) relationships;
- favourite media;
- role of the media in everyday life.

In the data processing, we processed the call-back interviews just like the guided interviews from the previous six waves of data collection. This included, in particular, transcription, anonymisation of data and subsequent analysis. However, we did not intend the call-back interviews as a substitute for a seventh wave of data collection, due to temporal, financial and personal restrictions. They were only used to record the latest developments in the topics mentioned above to wrap up before finishing the study. Compared to the sixth wave of data collection, we had to accept two adolescents dropping out: one boy was not reachable in any way, one girl missed all appointments for a telephone call.

4.5 Data Processing and Data Analysis

The wide range of data collection methods required a common strategy to analyse the huge amount of heterogeneous data from different sources. The guided interviews and their analysis were at the heart of the process, but all other sources were taken into account at every stage of the analysis as well (Banks, 2014, pp. 394, 402; Bilandzic, 2005, pp. 362–364; 2017, pp. 407–408; Coffey, 2014, pp. 367, 377–373; Crosnoe, 2000, pp. 379, 387; Marotzki, Holze, & Verständig, 2014, p. 457; Marvasti, 2014, pp. 359–361; Samuelsson et al., 1996, pp. 327–330). We divided the analysis of the collected data into a number of steps (see Fig. 4.4), which are closely linked to each other, so

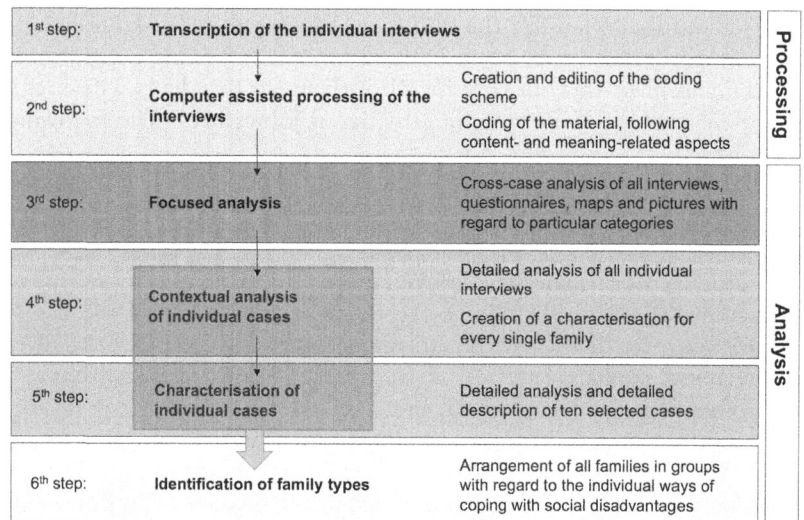

Fig. 4.4 Overview of data processing and data analysis

that the team is able to go back and forth between original data and, for example, the coded material, in order to clarify issues of interpretation (see Paus-Hasebrink, Sinner, Prochazka, & Kulterer, 2018 for a more detailed description of the process of analysing qualitative data in a long-term study).

(1) *The transcription of interviews, including consistent and thorough anonymisation of names and places throughout all successive waves of interviews with panel members*: The literary transcription of the audio files of the interviews (including the call-back interviews) was the starting point in each wave. Due to the sensitive character of the data and the possibility of unmasking our interview partners within small-scale communities, we rigorously practiced a strict and consistent anonymisation, including the separate storage of the original audio files, the anonymised transcripts and the anonymisation protocol with proper names and aliases (see Marshall & Rossman, 2016, pp. 212–213; Mertens, 2014, p. 510). However, we made use of anonymisation not only for proper names (family, friends, peers, teachers and so on) but also for pets' names, locations (stores, schools, facilities) and locations of leisure activities. Strict rules were essential for us to coordinate our subjective impressions from all stages of the project. However, over time we had to pass material from one staff member to another. To maintain transparent processes, we, therefore, conducted employee training and meetings of the coders at regular intervals. In order to support the process of transcription, we used the advanced transcription software *f4transkript* (Windows) and *f5transkript* (MacOS) (for example, automated switching of speakers, time-markers, slowed playback speed (Dresing, Pehl, & Schmieder, 2015; Marshall & Rossman, 2016, pp. 209–210).

(2) *The development of a comprehensive coding scheme for the analyses of all the forms of data, and computer-assisted coding of data using qualitative data analysis software (MAXQDA)*: We applied thematic coding (Flick, 2013; Kuckartz, 2010, p. 10) combining deductive and inductive steps. Based on theoretical considerations of grounded theory research (Strauss & Corbin, 1996, 1998), we made use of open coding, axial coding and selective coding. Categories were defined partly deductively, based on the above-mentioned considerations, and inductively, based on the

actual material. The coding schemes (one for parents, one for children) were continuously enhanced throughout the successive waves of interviews with panel members, in order to grasp new phenomena (for example, new media services). However, we tried to keep it consistent over time, and coders were not authorised to make changes on their own. Instead, we used memos and meetings of the coders to discuss any changes within our schemes and any later additions.

(3) *The data analysis followed an approach developed by Paus-Haase and Keuneke* (Paus-Haase, Hasebrink, Mattusch, Keuneke, & Krotz, 1999, pp. 143, 147) *As a first step, we conducted a "focused analysis" of all data across all families:* This was conducted in alignment with the main categories of the coding schemes: the role of family, of friends and peers, school, media usage, leisure activities, financial aspects and personal ambitions. Comparability across the waves of data collection was ensured by thematically structured matrices for each family, which included data from all waves and all methods of data collection. These matrices are organised by year (2005, 2007, 2010, 2012, 2014, and 2016) and category. Due to the long-term character of the study, the knowledge we generated was not always linear and chronological. In some cases, we were able to clarify situations in later years, or we were able to find out more about past events. In such cases, we updated not only the matrix of the family but also family profiles and cases. In order to support the processing, we also made use of the summary-function and the summary-grid-function included in MAXQDA. This meant we were able to portray developments over the years systematically.

(4) *For the next step, we conducted a "contextual in-depth analysis"* (Paus-Haase et al., 1999, pp. 143, 191) *using the three analytical concepts, options for action, outlines for action, and competences for action*: Based on a qualitative analysis of the entire data set, we created a characterisation for each of our children within its respective family. By accounting for the contexts, we were able to understand how the child developed its cognitive and motivational resources and gained *competences for action*, which, against the backdrop of the *options for action*, are reflected in the realisation of the child's and the parents' *outlines for actions* (see

Paus-Hasebrink et al., 2017, pp. 64–66; 2018, pp. 218–221; Paus-Hasebrink & Kulterer, 2014, p. 70).

(5) *Case studies*: On completion of the second wave, we went on to select families of particular significance. We examined these case studies even more intensively as regards *options for action, outlines for action*, and *competences for action*. In order to assure that this qualitative analysis was comprehensible to all our researchers, we applied two safety mechanisms: on the one hand, we used strict guidelines for composing these particular cases and describing them. On the other hand, two team members always dealt with these case examples together, in order to check each other's approach, but also in order to support each other's understanding. Later on, we compiled fact sheets for all the other families too and developed them into full family profiles. Consequently, there is no difference in our treatment of the individual families in this study as we applied identical methodology to all of them (see Chapter 5).

(6) *The family characterisations, as determined in the two previous steps, served as the basis for identifying family types* (Kluge, 2000): Using our three analytical concepts, we defined three criteria, which, in turn, indicated meaningful differences between the families: socio-economic circumstances as indicator of *options and for action*; socio-emotional climate as indicator of *outlines for action*; coping resources as indicator of *competences for action*. Each family was characterised by these criteria indicating a specific pattern for each, and based on them, we were able to define similar cases as types (see Chapter 8 and Paus-Hasebrink et al., 2018, pp. 221–222).

4.6 Ethical Challenges

As we have shown above, conducting a qualitative long-term study over twelve years means intensive and close contact to the families studied, because our data collection was conducted at their homes and not in a laboratory or at a neutral location (see Marshall & Rossman, 2016, pp. 146–147). Conducting (qualitative) research with children and subsequently with adolescents does, then, require particular care (see also Marshall & Rossman, 2016, p. 162). Qualitative researchers "situate themselves in consciously value-laden territory in which human relationships and critical self-reflection loom prominently. This positioning leads to the emergence of ethical dilemmas throughout the conduct of research that go beyond legal requirements or many professional standards for ethically responsible research" (Mertens, 2014, p. 510). How do researchers interact with their subjects without being either patronising or didactic? How do they retain their role and not become a form of consultant, who might influence the subjects of research? How do they deal with severe problems and conflicts within the families, for example, psychiatric disorders, physical violence, experiences of abuse or suspicion about (sexual) abuse? At what point are previously defined limits exceeded, so that researchers cannot remain in their role and are obligated to interfere or to provide support (see also Mertens, 2014, pp. 516–518; Patton, 2002, pp. 326–327, 405–415)? Furthermore, we had to deal with the small-scale structures of Austrian communities, where individuals might be recognised easily. Given the sensitive topic of our study, we had to find ways to guarantee absolute anonymity to our participants while going deeper and deeper into their personal spheres (see data processing; see Marshall & Rossman, 2016, p. 126).

All the difficulties outlined in the paragraph above occurred during the twelve years of research. Each time, we had to deal with a particular case based on individual circumstances. We discussed each situation before carefully deciding whether or not to interfere. Any intervention then resulted from further discussion of the correct procedure. In some cases, we involved a psychologist at the university, not only to request support in deciding our own action, but also to possibly offer professional help to affected families (see also Lobe, Livingstone, Ólafsson, & Simões, 2008, pp. 29–31, 47–49, 52–53, 57–59; Ólafsson, Livingstone, & Haddon, 2013, pp. 39–42, 75–76; Paus-Hasebrink, 2008, p. 57).

4.7 Conclusion

In this chapter, we have explicated the methodological design behind operationalising our theoretical approach to researching the role of media within children's and adolescents' socialisation in socially disadvantaged families. We conducted a longitudinal study to understand the complex interplay of subjective and structural factors which shape the lives of children as they grow up. We applied a complex design, convinced that "triangulation (…) increases credibility and quality by countering the concern (or accusation) that a study's findings are simply an artefact of a single method, a single source or a single investigator's blinders" (Patton, 2002, p. 563). However, we stress that "it is important to avoid the use of triangulation simply as an end in itself. Rich design or triangulation is only valid if it is applicable to the research question" (Paus-Hasebrink et al., 2013, p. 23). Over the years of our study, this challenging approach proved suitable for researching complex processes. Our experience shows, however, how important it is, when conducting a qualitative long-term study, to follow strict rules and to work intersubjectively traceable, ensuring that all aspects remain comprehensible to the researchers involved. At the same time, we found it essential to react to the new challenges presented not only by medial and technological changes but also by social changes and by the development of the children themselves.

Conducting a complex research project is always a sophisticated process. Methodical procedures and ethical guidelines need to be followed and fulfilled. Moreover, the research team has to deal with restriction in relation to financial, temporal and personnel resources. But every kind of project has specific peculiarities. To conclude, we want to highlight two aspects that turned out to be of particular relevance conducting our longitudinal study over twelve years. At the same time, to meet these aspects was extremely challenging: The first point concerns the maintenance of the panel. Not only we had to convince our families to remain part of our project over and over again, but also, we had to engage in keeping the contacts alive. Therefore, we had to learn to gather as much contact details as possible (for example, different e-mail addresses and telephone numbers of mothers and fathers, not only a single one), because the contact details were changing quite quickly. Furthermore, when the children were older, it turned out to be purposeful to ask them for contact details and the permission to contact them, too. The second point concerns the handling but also the storage of the data. As said before, the strict compliance of rules and intersubjective working methods are indispensable in order to generate valid data in a qualitative longitudinal study. In this context, a major challenge was to handle our sensitive data with care, this included not only the processing of data, but also the safe storage of data and the administration of access rights. Our solution included a mirrored database with backups on different hard drives in spatially separate rooms and strict access rules to the entire data. As mentioned above, this included as well the separate storage of anonymised data and the anonymisation protocol. Furthermore, we had to deal with rapidly increasing volumes of data. This development was caused by additional methods of data collection on the one hand, but also by more extensive answers of our subjects (due to more complex media repertoires and living situations) on the other hand. Having these experiences in mind, it seems to be essential to plan data handling, data storage and panel maintenance very carefully from the beginning, when it comes to developing a longitudinal research project comparable to our study.

References

Banks, M. (2014). Analysing images. In U. Flick (Ed.), *The SAGE handbook of qualitative data analysis* (pp. 394–408). London, UK, Thousand Oaks, CA, New Dehli, India, and Singapore: Sage.

Bilandzic, H. (2005). Lautes Denken [Thinking aloud]. In L. Mikos & C. Wegener (Eds.), *Qualitative Medienforschung. Ein Handbuch* [Qualitative media research: A handbook] (pp. 362–370). Konstanz, Germany: UVK UTB.

Bilandzic, H. (2017). Lautes Denken [Thinking aloud]. In L. Mikos & C. Wegener (Eds.), *Qualitative Medienforschung. Ein Handbuch* [Qualitative media research: A handbook] (2nd ed., pp. 406–412). Konstanz, Germany: UVK UTB.

Bovill, M., & Livingstone, S. (2001). Bedroom culture and the privatization of media use. *LSE Research Online*. London, UK: LSE Research Online. Retrieved from http://eprints.lse.ac.uk/archive/00000672. First published in *Children and their changing media environment: A European comparative study* (pp. 179–200). Mahwah, NJ: Lawrence Erlbaum Associates.

Cakici, Y., & Bayir, E. (2012). Developing children's views of the nature of science through role play. *International Journal of Science Education, 34*(7), 1075–1091.

Charlton, M., & Neumann, K. (1986). *Medienkonsum und Lebensbewältigung in der Familie. Methode und Ergebnisse der strukturanalytischen Rezeptionsforschung - mit fünf Fallbeispielen* [Media consumption and coping with life in the family: Method and results of structural-analytical reception research—With five case studie]. München and Weinheim, Germany: Psychologie Verlags Union.

Clarke, A. D. (2005). *Situational analysis: Grounded theory after the postmodern turn*. Thousand Oaks, CA, London, UK, and New Dehli, India: Sage.

Clarke, A. D. (2011). Von der Grounded-Theory-Methodologie zur Situationsanalyse [From Grounded theory-based methodology to situational analysis]. In G. Mey & K. Mruck (Eds.), *Grounded theory reader* (pp. 207–229). Wiesbaden, Germany: VS Verlag für Sozialwissenschaften.

Coffey, A. (2014). Analysing documents. In U. Flick (Ed.), *The SAGE handbook of qualitative data analysis* (pp. 367–379). London, UK, Thousand Oaks, CA, New Dehli, India, and Singapore: Sage.

Cohen, L., Manion, L., & Morrison, K. (2011). *Research methods in education* (7th ed.). Assisted by R. Bell, S. Martin, G. McCulloch, & C. O'Sullivan. New York, NY: Routledge.

Cotterell, J. (2007). *Social networks in youth & adolescence* (2nd ed.). New York, NY: Routledge.

Crosnoe, R. (2000). Friendships in childhood and adolescence: The life course and new directions. *Social Psychology Quarterly, 63*(4), 377–391.

Denzin, N. K. (1989). *The research act: A theoretical introduction to sociological methods* (3rd ed.). Englewood Cliffs, NJ: Prentice Hall.

Denzin, N. K., & Lincoln, Y. S. (2011). Introduction. In N. K. Denzin & Y. S. Lincoln (Eds.), *The SAGE handbook of qualitative research* (pp. 1–20). Los Angeles, CA, London, UK and New Dehli, India: Sage.

Dresing, T., Pehl, T., & Schmieder, C. (2015). *Manual (on) transcription: Transcription conventions, software guides and practical hints for qualitative researchers* (3rd English ed.). Marburg, Germany: Audiotranskription. Retrieved from http://www.audiotranskription.de/english/transcription-practicalguide.

Flick, U. (2013). *Qualitative Sozialforschung. Ein Handbuch* [Qualitative social research: A handbook]. Reinbek bei Hamburg, Germany: Rowohlt.

Flick, U. (2014). Mapping the field. In U. Flick (Ed.), *The SAGE handbook of qualitative data analysis* (pp. 3–18). London, UK, Thousand Oaks, CA, New Dehli, India, and Singapore: Sage.

Harper, D. (2005). Photography as social science data. In U. Flick, E. von Kardorff, & I. Steinke (Eds.), *A companion to qualitative research* (pp. 231–236) (B. Jenner, Trans. Originally published 2000). London, UK, Thousand Oaks, CA and New Dehli, India: Sage.

Hasebrink, U. (2014). Medienrepertoires: Ein analytischer Rahmen zur Untersuchung des "Nebeneinander" verschiedener Medien [Media repertoires: An analytical framework for studying the "juxtaposition" of different media]. In K. Kleinen-von-Königslöw & K. Förster (Eds.), *Medienkonvergenz und Medienkomplementarität aus Rezeptions- und Wirkungsperspektive* [Media convergence and media complementarity from the perspective of research into reception and effects] (pp. 15–36). Baden-Baden, Germany: Nomos.

Hasebrink, U., & Domeyer, H. (2012). Media repertoires as patterns of behaviour and as meaningful practices: A multimethod approach to media use in converging media environments. *Participations: Journal of Audience & Reception Studies, 9*(2), 757–783.

Hasebrink, U., & Popp, J. (2006). Media repertoires as a result of selective media use: A conceptual approach to the analysis of patterns of exposure. *Communications, 31*(2), 369–387.

Hepp, A., & Düvel, C. (2010). Die kommunikative Vernetzung in der Diaspora: Integrations- und Segregationspotenziale der Aneignung digitaler Medien in ethnischen Migrationsgemeinschaften [Communicative networking in the diaspora: Integration and segregation potentials of the adoption of digital media in ethnic migration communities]. In J. Röser, T. Thomas, Tanja, & C. Peil (Eds.), *Alltag in den Medien – Medien im Alltag* [Everyday life and the media—Media and everyday life] (pp. 261–281). Wiesbaden, Germany: VS Verlag für Sozialwissenschaften.

Hepp, A., Berg, M., & Roitsch, C. (2011). Mono-thematic and multi-thematic horizons of mediatized communitization: Patterns of communicative networking and mediated belonging. *SCM—Studies in Communication and Media, 1*(2), 1–34. Retrieved from http://www.scm.nomos.de/fileadmin/scm/doc/SCM_11_02_Hepp_engl.pdf.

Hradil, S. (1987). *Sozialstrukturanalyse in einer fortgeschrittenen Gesellschaft* [Analysis of social structure in an advanced society]. Opladen, Germany: Leske und Budrich.

Hradil, S. (1999). *Soziale Ungleichheit in Deutschland* [Social inequality in Germany]. Opladen, Germany: Leske und Budrich.

Jörg, S. (1994). Entwicklungspsychologische Voraussetzungen der Medienrezeption bei Kindern [Developmental-psychological prerequisites of media reception of children]. In Deutsches Jugendinstitut (Ed.), *Handbuch Medienerziehung im Kindergarten, Teil 1: Pädagogische Grundlagen.* [Handbook media education in Kindergarten, Part 1: Pedagogical basics] (pp. 188–202). Opladen, Germany: Leske und Budrich.

Kluge, S. (2000). Empirisch begründete Typenbildung in der qualitativen Sozialforschung [Empirically based typification in qualitative social research]. *Forum: Qualitative Social Research/Qualitative Sozialforschung, 1*(1). Retrieved from http://www.qualitative-research.net/index.php/fqs/article/view/1124.

Kuckartz, U. (2010). *Einführung in die computergestützte Analyse qualitativer Daten* [Introduction to the computer-aided analysis of qualitative data] (3rd ed.). Wiesbaden, Germany: VS Verlag für Sozialwissenschaften.

Lincoln, S. (2013). Media and bedroom culture. In D. Lemish (Ed.), *The Routledge international handbook of children, adolescents and media* (pp. 315–321). New York, NY: Routledge.

Lobe, B., Livingstone, S., Olafsson, K., & Simões, A. J. (2008). Best practice research guide: How to research children and online technologies in comparative perspective. *The EU Kids Online Network.* London, UK: LSE. Retrieved from http://eprints.lse.ac.uk/21658/.

Marotzki, W., Holze, J., & Verständig, D. (2014). Analysing virtual date. In U. Flick (Ed.), *The SAGE handbook of qualitative data analysis* (pp. 450–463). London, UK, Thousand Oaks, CA, New Dehli, India, and Singapore: Sage.

Marshall, C., & Rossman, G. B. (2016). *Designing qualitative research* (6th ed.). Los Angeles, CA, London, UK, New Dehli, India, Singapore, Washington, DC and Boston, MA: Sage.

Marvasti, A. B. (2014). Analysing observations. In U. Flick (Ed.), *The SAGE handbook of qualitative data analysis* (pp. 354–366). London, UK, Thousand Oaks, CA, New Dehli, India, and Singapore: Sage.

Mason, J. (2002). *Qualitative researching* (2nd ed.). London, UK, Thousand Oaks, CA, and New Dehli, India: Sage.

Mertens, D. M. (2014). Ethical use of qualitative data and findings. In U. Flick (Ed.), *The SAGE handbook of qualitative data analysis* (pp. 510–523). London, UK, Thousand Oaks, CA, New Dehli, India, and Singapore: Sage.

Morse, J. M., & Maddox, L. J. (2014). Analytical integration in qualitative driven (QUAL) mixed and multiple methods designs. In U. Flick (Ed.), *The SAGE handbook of qualitative data analysis* (pp. 524–539). London, UK, Thousand Oaks, CA, New Dehli, India, and Singapore: Sage.

OeNB Anniversary Fund. (2015). *Funding applications*. Vienna, Austria: Oesterreichische Nationalbank. Retrieved from https://www.oenb.at/en/About-Us/Research-Promotion/The-OeNB-Anniversary-Fund/funding-applications.html.

Ólafsson, K., Livingstone, S., & Haddon, L. (2013). How to research children and online technologies: Frequently asked questions and best practice. *The EU Kids Online Network*. London, UK: LSE. Retrieved from http://eprints.lse.ac.uk/50437/.

Patton, M. Q. (2002). *Qualitative research & evaluation methods* (3rd ed.). Thousand Oaks, CA, London, UK and New Dehli, India: Sage.

Paus-Haase, I. (1998). *Heldenbilder im Fernsehen und ihre Symbolik. Zur Bedeutung von Serienfavoriten in Kindergarten, Peer-Group und Kinderfreundschaften* [Heroes on TV and their symbolism: On the importance of series favorites in kindergarten, peer group and children's friendships]. Opladen, Germany: Westdeutscher Verlag.

Paus-Haase, I., Hasebrink, U., Mattusch, U., Keuneke, S., & Krotz. F. (1999). *Talkshows im Alltag von Jugendlichen. Der tägliche Balanceakt zwischen Orientierung, Amüsement und Ablehnung* [Talkshows and everyday life of adolescents: A balancing act between orientation, amusement and rejection] Schriftenreihe Medienforschung der Landesanstalt für Rundfunk Nordrhein-Westfalen, Band 32. Opladen, Germany: Leske und Budrich.

Paus-Hasebrink, I. (2005). Kinder- und Jugendforschung [Research on children and adolescents]. In L. Mikos & C. Wegener (Eds.), *Qualitative Medienforschung. Ein Handbuch* [Qualitative media research: A handbook] (pp. 222–231). Konstanz, Germany: UVK UTB.

Paus-Hasebrink, I. (2008). Researcher's experience. In B. Lobe, S. Livingstone, K. Olafsson, & A. J. Simões (Eds.), Best practice research guide: How to research children and online technologies in comparative perspective. *The EU Kids Online Network*. London, UK: LSE. Retrieved from http://eprints.lse.ac.uk/21658/.

Paus-Hasebrink, I. (2017). Forschung mit Kindern und Jugendlichen [Research with Children and adolescents]. In L. Mikos & C. Wegener (Eds.), *Qualitative Medienforschung. Ein Handbuch* [Qualitative media research: A handbook] (2nd ed., pp. 276–282). Konstanz, Germany: UVK UTB.

Paus-Hasebrink, I., & Bichler, M. (2008). *Mediensozialisationsforschung. Theoretische Fundierung und Fallbeispiel sozial benachteiligte Kinder* [Media socialisation research—Theoretical foundation and a case study on socially disadvantaged children]. Assisted by C. Wijnen. Innsbruck, Austria: Studienverlag.

Paus-Hasebrink, I., & Kulterer, J. (2014). *Praxeologische Mediensozialisationsforschung. Langzeitstudie zu sozial benachteiligten Heranwachsenden* [Praxeological media socialisation research: A longitudinal study regarding socially disadvantaged adolescents]. Assisted by P. Sinner. Baden-Baden, Germany: Nomos.

Paus-Hasebrink, I., Prochazka, F., & Sinner, P. (2013). What constitutes a, 'rich design' in qualitative methodology? In M. Barbovschi, L. Green, Lelia, & S. Vandoninck (Eds.), *Innovative approaches for investigating how children understand risk in new media: Dealing with methodological and ethical challenges. The EU Kids Online Network* (pp. 23–26). London, UK: LSE. Retrieved from http://eprints.lse.ac.uk/53060/.

Paus-Hasebrink, I., Sinner, P., Kulterer, J., & Oberlinner, A. (2017). Methodologische und methodische Herausforderungen: Zum Design der Langzeit-Panelstudie [Methodical and methodological challenges: The design of the long-term study]. In I. Paus-Hasebrink (Ed.), *Langzeitstudie zur Rolle von Medien in der Sozialisation sozial benachteiligter Heranwachsender. Lebensphase Jugend* [Longitudinal study on the role of media within socialisation of socially disadvantaged adolescents: Phase of adolescence] (pp. 45–68). Baden-Baden, Germany: Nomos.

Paus-Hasebrink, I., Sinner, P., Prochazka, F., & Kulterer, J. (2018). Auswertungsstrategien für qualitative Langzeitdaten: Das Beispiel einer Langzeitstudie zur Rolle von Medien in der Sozialisation Heranwachsender [Processing of qualitative long-term data: The example of a long-term study on media socialisation of socially disadvantaged adolescents]. In A. M. Scheu (Ed.), *Auswertung qualitativer Daten. Strategien, Verfahren und Methoden der Interpretation nicht-standardisierter Daten in der Kommunikationswissenschaft* [Processing of qualitative data: Strategies, techniques and methods in order to process non-standard data in communication science] (pp. 209–225). Wiesbaden, Germany: Springer VS.

Rapley, T. (2014). Sampling strategies in qualitative research. In U. Flick (Ed.), *The SAGE handbook of qualitative data analysis* (pp. 49–63). London, UK, Thousand Oaks, CA, New Dehli, India, and Singapore: Sage.

Rose, G. (2016). *Visual methodologies: An introduction to researching with visual materials* (4th ed.). London, UK, Thousand Oaks, CA, New Dehli, India, and Singapore: Sage.

Sader, M. (1995). Rollenspiel [Role-playing games]. In U. Flick, E. von Kardorff, H. Keupp, L. von Rosenstiel, & S. Wolff (Eds.), *Handbuch qualitative Sozialforschung. Grundlagen, Konzepte, Methoden und Anwendungen* [Handbook qualitative social research: Basics, concepts, methods and practical approaches] (pp. 193–198). Weinheim, Germany: Beltz Psychologie Verlags Union.

Samuelsson, M., Thernlund, G., & Ringström, J. (1996). Using the five field map to describe the social network of children: A methodological study. *International Journal of Behavioral Development, 19*(2), 327–345.

Schütze, Y. (1977). *Innerfamiliale Kommunikation und kindliche Psyche. Eine exemplarische Analyse der Kommunikations- und Rollenstrukturen zweier Familien* [Communication in the family and the psyche of children: A case study on structures of communication and roles in two families]. Berlin, Germany: Schriften des Max-Planck-Instituts für Bildungsforschung.

Stahlke, I. (2005). Rollenspiel [Role-playing games]. In L. Mikos & C. Wegener (Eds.), *Qualitative Medienforschung. Ein Handbuch* [Qualitative media research: A handbook] (pp. 496–507). Konstanz, Germany: UVK UTB.

Statistik Austria. (2017). *Tabellenband EU-SILC 2016. Einkommen, Armut und Lebensbedingungen* [EU-SILC 2016: Income, poverty and living conditions]. Wien, Austria: Statistik Austria. Retrieved from https://www.sozialministerium.at/cms/site/attachments/7/0/0/CH3434/CMS1493709119968/tabellenband_eu-silc_2016.pdf.

Strauss, A. L., & Corbin, J. (1996). *Grounded theory: Grundlagen Qualitativer Sozialforschung* [Basics of qualitative social research]. Weinheim, Germany: Beltz Psychologie Verlags Union.

Strauss, A. L., & Corbin, J. (1998). *Basics of qualitative research: Techniques and procedures for developing grounded theory* (2nd ed.). Thousand Oaks, CA, London, UK and New Dehli, India: Sage.

Tilemann, F. (2017). Szenisches Spiel [Role-playing]. In L. Mikos & C. Wegener (Eds.), *Qualitative Medienforschung. Ein Handbuch* [Qualitative media research: A handbook]. (2nd ed., pp. 389–396). Konstanz, Germany: UVK UTB.

Toerien, M. (2014). Conversations and conversation analysis. In U. Flick (Ed.), *The SAGE handbook of qualitative data analysis* (pp. 327–340). London, UK, Thousand Oaks, CA, New Dehli, India, and Singapore: Sage.

Trappel, J. (2007). *Online-Medien - Leistungsprofil eines neuen Massenmediums* [Online-Media—Performance profile of a new mass medium]. Konstanz, Germany: UVK.

University of Salzburg. (2018). *Research service*. Salzburg, Austria: University of Salzburg. Retrieved from https://uni-salzburg.at/index.php?id=200125&MP=200029-200945&L=1.

Wilson, T. P. (1970). Normative and interpretive paradigms in Sociology. In J. D. Douglas (Ed.), *Understanding everyday life: Toward the reconstruction of sociological knowledge* (pp. 57–79). Chicago, IL: Aldine Publications Company.

Open Access This chapter is licensed under the terms of the Creative Commons Attribution 4.0 International License (http://creativecommons.org/licenses/by/4.0/), which permits use, sharing, adaptation, distribution and reproduction in any medium or format, as long as you give appropriate credit to the original author(s) and the source, provide a link to the Creative Commons licence and indicate if changes were made.

The images or other third party material in this chapter are included in the chapter's Creative Commons licence, unless indicated otherwise in a credit line to the material. If material is not included in the chapter's Creative Commons licence and your intended use is not permitted by statutory regulation or exceeds the permitted use, you will need to obtain permission directly from the copyright holder.

CHAPTER 5

Family Descriptions

5.1 Introduction

Our overview of our 18 families begins with a short summary of the developments in each family's situation during the study. They appear in alphabetical order, with an initial focus on the original criteria for selecting the families (see Chapter 4): the socio-economic situation of each family, with particular attention being paid to income, the job situation, the housing situation, the formal education (of parents), the family constellation (nuclear family, patchwork family, single-parent households, extended families, migration background etc.); a description of the core characteristics of the families, with any subsequent developments, then follows.

5.2 The Families of the Panel

5.2.1 *The Aufbauer Family with Their Daughter, Amelie*

When first recruited, Ms. Aufbauer, a qualified goldsmith, was living together with her then partner and her two daughters, each of whom had a different biological father. Amelie was the younger of the two siblings, and subsequent interviews with her took place at 5, 7, 10, 12, 14, 16 and 17. The family constellation changed several times, as Ms. Aufbauer gave birth to another child in 2007, but was already separated from the father by that time. In 2014, Ms. Aufbauer had another child, while no longer being involved with the father. Ms. Aufbauer always made clear that she was a single mother by choice and claimed that she was only interested in the children, not in the men. In 2016, Ms. Aufbauer was living together with daughter Amelie—the oldest daughter had moved out in the meantime—and with her two younger sons. Ms. Aufbauer was either unemployed (2005, 2012), only briefly working in a sales position (2010), or on maternal leave (2007, 2014, 2016). She, therefore, had to rely largely on social welfare support. As a consequence, the Aufbauer family moved frequently, since financial allowances for housing—one of the main pillars of the Austrian social welfare system—often ran out, and a new apartment had to be found. When the study began, Ms. Aufbauer and her children were living in the city, later they moved to the country, and by the end, they were about to move back to their old neighbourhood in the city. The décor of their apartments made a pleasant impression, within the limitations of a small budget, being notably neat and tidy. By the time the study ended, Amelie was pursuing a general qualification for university entrance with a special focus on business and economy.

5.2.2 The Boll Family with Their Son, Gregor

The Boll family is an extended family, and at the study's onset consisted of the parents and ten children—four girls and six boys (the oldest son had already moved out since he was already grown up). Our subject, Gregor, is the third youngest; interviews with him took place at 5, 7, 11, 13, 15, 16 and 17. Initially, the family was renting a run-down farm house in rural northern Austria, where the poor local infrastructure meant that the children experienced a certain degree of isolation before going to kindergarten or school. The family's previous house had been forcibly sold in a court-ordered auction.

When our study began, Mrs. Boll was at home with the children, and Mr. Boll was on parental leave. Later on, he started working as a massage therapist. In addition, the parents had a dog and horse breeding business, together with some farming to generate additional income. By our second wave, Mrs. Boll was also working as a cleaner in her oldest son's bar. The family experienced a crisis when Mrs. Boll was diagnosed with cancer, had to undergo chemotherapy and was unable to work afterwards. While she was in treatment, her husband had an affair, which led her to leave him and take some of the children with her. They filed for divorce after 22 years of marriage, and in 2011 Mrs. Boll moved back to her old home in Northern Germany, together with the six youngest children. She has been receiving 1000 €/month disability allowance since then, but her ex-husband did not pay any alimony. The low prices for houses in her home region enabled Mrs. Boll to buy an old house (25,000 €) to rebuild her dog breeding business, in order to create a second source of income. This income was often used to pay the bigger bills, like heating oil. Gregor adjusted well to the new environment, completed school and started training as a retail salesman.

5.2.3 The Dornbacher Family with Their Daughter, Gudrun

Gudrun's parents remained married throughout the study; apart from Gudrun—interviews with her took place at 5, 6, 10, 12, 14, 15 and 16—they have another daughter three years younger than Gudrun. The Dornbacher family was fairly stable as a family throughout, but the job situation, especially for the father, was sometimes uncertain, which meant that the financial situation fluctuated, leading to minor conflicts. The mother remained employed part-time throughout, while the father was on paternity leave during our first wave, unemployed during the second and was participating in professional retraining in the third, although he later abandoned it. Finally, he was able to secure a full-time position in a local industry, which substantially improved their financial situation, so that at the study's close, the family was no longer at risk of poverty. Over all the years, the Dornbacher family lived in the same owner-occupied apartment on the outskirts of their town, which they had paid off by our fifth visit. Although the apartment tended to be crowded towards the end, the family members were always satisfied with their housing situation. The proximity to the town and the good public transport were especially perceived as extremely positive. Daughter Gudrun was attending a secondary school by the time the study ended and had plans to study at the academy of music.

5.2.4 The Ebner Family with Their Daughter, Elisabeth

The Ebner family and their daughter Elisabeth—interviews with her took place at 5, 6, 9, 11, 14, 15, 16 years—had been living together as a nuclear family, including a brother two years her elder, since the study began. The parents married in 2013, and Mr. Ebner, who had trained to be a farmer, worked as such throughout. Mrs. Ebner is a qualified cook, but she worked as a cleaner from wave one to four. As of the fifth wave, she was working full-time on the farm with her husband. The financial situation remained fairly stable throughout the study, but the family was still at risk of poverty when it ended. At the onset, the family was living in an old farmhouse in need of renovating, without any heating and riddled with mould. This caused asthma in Elisabeth's brother, so that the housing situation became unbearable. By our second wave, they had moved into a newer house on the same property. Elisabeth was training to become a florist after the fifth wave. She is very good at her profession, winning an award for apprentices, and wants to gain the master craftswoman's[1] certificate.

5.2.5 The Fein Family with Their Daughter, Olivia[2]

Ms. Fein, a qualified hairdresser, was a single mother with two kids when the study began: daughter Olivia—interviews with her took place at 5, 7, 10, 12 and 15—and a younger son. They were living in a small apartment on the outskirts of their town. Due to the very low household income, she largely had to rely on social welfare. Between the second and fourth wave, Ms. Fein acquired a new partner, a qualified carpenter. She moved to his house in a rural village. They had a daughter together, and her partner undertook professional retraining, so Ms. Fein could only work very few hours a day, so that the household income meant the overall financial situation of the family remained precarious. During most of this time, Olivia was living in a supervised living facility for young people due to an incident in school and an intervention by the child protection agency. When Ms. Fein's relationship ended, she became a single mother again and unemployed. As she was suffering from psychological problems, she was able to receive an early pension, following a long time of sick leave at the age of 33. She and her children moved to the nearest city, and by our sixth wave, Ms. Fein was having an open relationship with a man twice her age. Olivia was in a special school at this time to prepare her for later job training and was earning some pocket money there (80 € a month).

5.2.6 The Grubert Family with Their Son, Erich[3]

Ms. Grubert was a single mother when the study began and was living together with her son, Erich—interviews with him took place at 6, 8, 11, 13, 15 and 17—in what she considered a problem neighbourhood.

Hence, she would not allow her son to play outside or have contact with the neighbours' kids. The apartment was small and untidy. Ms. Grubert was working part-time (15 hours/week) as a switchboard operator, so that their financial situation was precarious. By the second wave, Ms. Grubert had a new partner and had already moved with him to a new and bigger apartment in a nicer neighbourhood. This newly formed, patchwork family continued to live in the same apartment until the end of the study. The socio-economic situation of the family improved slowly but steadily, especially after Ms. Grubert's partner, an IT technician, managed to get a better paid job with a new employer after our fourth wave. From then on, the family was not at risk of poverty anymore. Erich has completed his years of compulsory education and started job training as a cook and was making his own money, but he continued to live at home with his parents. He did not have to contribute to the living expenses and could use his money for himself.

5.2.7 The Hirtner Family with Their Son, Mario[4]

At the beginning of the study, the Hirtner family consisted of Ms. Hirtner, her partner, son, Mario—the interviews with him took place at 5, 11, 13, 16 and 17—and the youngest son. The family had been living in a very small flat (45 sqm) during the recruitment phase and was later able to move to a subsidised flat twice the size near their town's train station. Ms. Hirtner has not completed any form of job training, while her partner actually had, but both were unemployed at the first wave. So the family had to get by on social welfare. Between the first and the third waves—the Hirtners could not be interviewed in 2007 for the second wave—both Ms. Hirtner and her partner found full-time jobs, which improved the financial situation.

Yet Ms. Hirtner was unemployed again by the time of the fourth interview. A big change for the family happened, when, by our fifth wave, Ms. Hirtner and her partner had split up. Mario always thought that his mother's partner was his biological father and learned that this was not the case after the separation, when the partner was no longer responsible for the children. By the end of the study—the family again did not participate in an interview in 2014—Ms. Hirtner had a new partner, was living in the same flat and was working full-time again, which was again followed by an improvement of the financial situation. By this time, her son, Mario, who had previously started training as an electrician only to quit due to health issues, had been able to get into new training in the IT sector.

5.2.8 The Holzner Family with Their Son, Benedikt

At the first and second waves, Ms. Holzner was living alone with her son, Benedikt—interviews with him took place at 5, 7, 10, 14 and 16—and his two older siblings in a sublet apartment in a terraced house. Benedikt had been traumatised by Ms. Holzner's previous partner being violent. Ms. Holzner was unemployed, and the financial situation was precarious, so the family had to rely on social welfare; later Ms. Holzner briefly worked in a toy store in 2007.

By the second wave, Ms. Holzner had met a new partner, who was working full-time, and had moved in with him. Benedikt, like his older siblings, had meanwhile been taken into a supervised living facility for young people and was only visiting on weekends—so that an interview with him was not possible in 2010 and only Ms. Holzner was interviewed. Between the third and fourth interview, Ms. Holzner and her partner got married and founded a new family including two more sons, who were born between then and the end of the study. Meanwhile, the family did not participate in an interview in the fourth wave, since Ms. Holzner was involved in a court case that affected Benedikt and his older siblings, but no more information was provided about its exact nature.

Ms. Holzner was on maternity leave during the last two panel waves, when they participated in the study again, and was working a couple of hours each weekend to earn some extra money. Of his own volition, Benedikt was still living apart from his family when the study ended.

5.2.9 The Kaiser Family with Their Son, Torsten

Mr. and Mrs. Kaiser have three sons together. Interviews with Torsten took place at 5, 7, 10, 12, 14 and 16. By the time of our second visit, they had divorced, and Mr. Kaiser had remarried by the third panel wave and later had a daughter. Mr. Kaiser was working as a civil servant and also gave dance lessons. Between our second and third panel waves, he completed his final secondary school examinations through the second-chance programme. The financial situation was fraught throughout the years, as the father's income was the only one, and later Mrs. Kaiser was herself the sole breadwinner. Mrs. Kaiser started working part-time, but the divorce had negative effects on her psychological well-being. Although the family owned a freehold flat, they were always at risk of poverty.

Torsten was always ambivalent about school, due to his bad grades and a lot of missed lessons because of internships, so he quitted school and focused on finding an apprenticeship. Torsten was able to get into training and moved to a boarding school during the week, which is very typical for apprentices in Austria.

5.2.10 The Landinger Family with Their Son, Timo

The Landingers are an extended family, consisting of six children, Mrs. Landinger, who did seem cognitively impaired, and Mr. Landinger, the father of the four youngest children. When the study began, Mr. Landinger was not living permanently with the rest of the family. The Landingers' flat impressed as desolate, with old and damaged furniture. The living area exhibited some neglect and grime.

Mr. Landinger is a qualified stonemason but was working in construction before the study began. By the time of the first interview, he was unemployed and remained so subsequently. At first, Mrs. Landinger was contributing to the family income through part-time work as a switchboard operator, later she was also unemployed due to health issues. The family climate was always tense, and by our third wave, Mrs. Landinger had fled to a women's shelter with three of her children following a dispute with her partner. Soon after the incident, they were reconciled and moved to another county, where they rented an old house in need of renovating and eventually got married.

The socio-economic situation of the family varied between dire and precarious throughout, especially when both parents were unable to work due to health issues. Their son, Timo, who is cognitively impaired—interviews with him took place at 6, 7, 11, 12, 15, 16 and 17—entered a supervised living facility with a socio-pedagogical focus between the fourth and fifth interviews, but later lived at home again. When the study ended, he was in a special programme in a socially inclusive workshop.

5.2.11 The Oblinger Family with Their Son, Manfred

The Oblinger family is another extended family, consisting of Mrs. Oblinger, with three children from a previous relationship, and Mr. Oblinger, with his three children. Manfred is a highly gifted boy, and our interviews with him took place at 6, 7, 11, 12, 15, 16 and 17. The two oldest children were not living at home anymore when the study began. Mrs. Oblinger has no job training and was mostly at home, doing charitable work until she suffered a stroke and other health issues and was rendered unable to work.

Mr. Oblinger was working as a technical draftsman, but, after moving to the country to get a larger flat to accommodate the large family, he had to go back to his old profession as a cook as there were no other job opportunities for him. The family received social welfare because of their precarious financial situation. By the fifth wave, the last source of income had fallen away, after Mr. Oblinger had an accident on his way back from work and contracted a serious infection following an operation. This rendered him unable to work and later led to depression. Since then, the family has been living on social welfare alone. Manfred's wish was to find a job as soon as possible to earn money and support the family. He started one training programme but quit. Later, he was able to find training as an IT-technician, which, he declared, was like a dream come true for him.

5.2.12 The Öllinger Family with Their Daughter, Viktoria

The Öllinger family has experienced a certain amount of turbulence over the years. In 2005, Ms. Öllinger divorced from her husband, the biological father of her daughter, Viktoria—interviews with her took place at 5, 7, 10, 12, 14, 15, and 16—but already had a new partner. Two years later she was alone again. She married after a short time, but got divorced again rather quickly in 2012. From then on, she has been living alone with her daughter.

Ms. Öllinger is a qualified cook but has largely been working in less skilled jobs, such as cleaner, switchboard operator or school bus driver. She has been struggling with health issues for a long time and was left unable to work after the fourth wave. She spent weeks on end in the hospital and almost died when she fell into a coma. Since then, she has been receiving a disability pension but had to file for private bankruptcy due to her strained financial situation. For financial reasons, Ms. Öllinger and her daughter moved frequently over the years. Their most recent flat was a pleasant, new one run by a co-operative on the outskirts of their town. Viktoria is planning to finish school after recently moving to a new one and wants to later work as an office clerk.

5.2.13 The Pfortner Family with Their Son, Helmut

The Pfortner family consists of the parents, who are married, their son, Helmut—interviews with him took place at 4, 6, 9, 11, 13 and 15—his older sister and the paternal grandmother who came to live with the family at the time of our the third wave. Mr. Pfortner is self-employed in the machine engineering sector, with a workshop adjacent to the family house. Mrs. Pfortner is a qualified office clerk and was working part-time in the family business. After the third panel wave, she was responsible only for the bookkeeping of the business and was working part-time as an office clerk outside of it. Through this additional income, the financial situation improved but was still close to the threshold of poverty risk. By the sixth wave, Mr. Pfortner was suffering from burnout.

The family still lives in the same large 120 sqm big house on the outskirts of their town. Between the fifth and sixth waves, they turned the upper storey into flats for the children, including a kitchen and a bathroom. Helmut, who was struggling with writing and reading in school, wanted to follow in his father's footsteps, and, after a trial session in a company, he was able to start his job training in it, as his talent became obvious. He will become a machine engineer, then, like his father.

5.2.14 The Rohringer Family with Their Daughter, Isabelle

The Rohringer family consisted of Mr. and Mrs. Rohringer and their three children when the study began. During our fourth wave, the eldest son moved out, as he was grown up. The family had been living in the same owner-occupied apartment for a couple of years before Mr. Rohringer, a qualified butcher, had to leave because of his severe problems with alcohol.

Mrs. Rohringer was a housewife at first; later she found a little work as a child minder and also as waitress; the family was financially supported by the grandparents.

By our third wave, Mrs. Rohringer had a new partner, who had his own transportation business, and she started working as a clerk in her office at home. By the end of the study, the household income was still slightly below the poverty line. The family spent most of the weekends in the new partner's flat and lived in their own apartment during the week. Isabelle—interviews with her took place at 6, 8, 11, 12, 15, 16, and 17—was almost done training to become a childcare assistant when the study ended.

5.2.15 The Scheib Family with Their Daughter, Susanne

Mrs. Scheib was a single mother when the study began. She was living together with her daughter Susanne—interviews with her took place at 7, 8, 11, 13, 16, 17 and 18—and the younger daughter in a small flat in a terrace house. Although she was working part-time as an office clerk, the family counted as very low income. By our second wave, Mrs. Scheib had got married and moved with her children to her new husband's apartment in a big city in Southern Germany. Her new husband was working full-time as a public servant. The socio-economic situation of the family has improved steadily ever since. When the study ended, Mrs. Scheib was working part-time as a sales assistant, plus a few hours for a security contractor. Susanne quit school following troubles with teachers and peers and began training as a mechanic but has been working on completing courses in German, English and Mathematics, in order to finish her secondary school education and later study (she was not clear about what) at the university.

5.2.16 The Stab Family with Their Daughter, Simone

Ms. Stab is a migrant from the South-East of the European Union and has been living in Austria for more than 20 years. When the study began, she was living together with her daughter, Simone—interviews took place at 4, 6, 10, 12, 14, 15 and 16—and her younger son, Simone's half-brother. Simone's biological father left the family when she was two years old. The family lived in a flat in the countryside, but moved after our first interview, since they could not afford the rent anymore. At the time of the third wave they moved again and remained in their new home until the end of the study.

Ms. Stab always had to work as unskilled labourer, because her general qualification for university entrance from her home country was not legally recognised in Austria. Throughout the study she was working only a few hours or part-time as a cleaner (2005, 2007, 2012, 2016), or she was unemployed (2010, 2014).

At the time of our fifth wave, she started a retraining programme to become a massage therapist, which she hoped would open up new perspectives, but without any success. Hence, the family always had to rely on social welfare to get by. Since our fifth wave, Simone's younger brother left the family during the week, moving to a socio-educational facility. Simone was attending a polytechnic secondary school when the study ended and was planning to pursue a college degree afterwards.

5.2.17 The Weiss Family with Their Son, Alfons

Ms. Weiss was a single mother when the study began. She was living in a new but plain owner-occupied flat, together with her son, Alfons—interviews with him took place at 4, 6, 9, 11, 14, 15 and 16—and his half-brother, some three years his junior. Alfons' biological father has been separated from the family since the boy was three years old and was living farther away in the south of the same state in Austria, where he and his family possessed a farm. The financial situation of Ms. Weiss and her family remained rather mysterious until our sixth wave. She always declared a low income and not much other money, forcing her to rely on presents from relatives and charitable organisations, in order to get new clothes or furniture. She also said that she was extremely economical, which enabled her to acquire the flat and pay it off bit by bit. She explained her obviously improved situation since our first wave by her being extremely frugal. In our last wave, it turned out that she had inherited some real estate in the meantime, which provided her with additional sources of income and explained her better economic status, despite her unemployment at that time. During our last wave, she and her sons sold the flat and bought a semi-detached house.

Ms. Weiss had a new partner from our third wave onward, but it remained unclear how close the relationship really was. He never moved in with the family, and Ms. Weiss never talked much about him. Alfons himself always made it clear that he'd rather be living with his father, but his mother forbade it. During our fifth wave, Ms. Weiss had taken in a foster child, but problems ensuing between her and the child soon ended the relationship.

Alfons was in training when the study ended and was living during the week in the residential hostel provided by his training company in the city.

5.2.18 The Zarbl Family with Their Son, Norbert

The Zarbl family consisted of Mr. Zarbl, Mrs. Zarbl and their two children, Norbert—interviews with him took place at 5, 7, 10, 12, 14, 15 and 16—and his younger brother. Mr. Zarbl was working in the insurance business, and Mrs. Zarbl was working part-time as a secretary. They were living in a house in the city. Despite both jobs, the family had only a very low household income. Mr. and Mrs. Zarbl separated in between our second and third waves, and Mrs. Zarbl found a new partner later on, who was working full-time. His arrival improved the socio-economic situation slightly. When the pair got married during our third wave, they moved in together in the house that Mrs. Zarbl and her ex-husband had lived in. Her new partner's children did not move in, however, since they were already grown-up. Mrs. Zarbl was later able to get more working hours, which contributed to the further improvement of the situation, and the family was no longer at risk of poverty. Norbert was visiting a secondary school when the study ended, planning to gain a general qualification for university entrance.

5.3 Conclusion

Twelve years are a long time when talking about children's development. Within the time frame of this study, the children in our sample grew up to become young adults, some of whom had already started an apprenticeship and thus made a big step towards an independent life in the future, while others were still undecided about their future paths. Their parents (above all, the mothers) also underwent many changes, in employment, in levels of relationships, work, health etc. Some changes were experienced positively and others negatively. In this sense, this chapter illustrates how dynamic the development was over this extended period, not only for the children but for the families in general.

The family descriptions above serve as a point of orientation for the following chapters and contribute to contextualising our results. In Chapter 8, we will go on to describe and interpret the situation of each family in much more detail.

Notes

1. For a description about the Austrian system for professional qualifications see the Directive 2005/36/EC of the European Parliament and of the Council of 7 September 2005 on the recognition of professional qualifications (Text with EEA relevance), *Official Journal of the European Union*, pp. L 255/70–L 255/71. Available online at: http://eur-lex.europa.eu/LEXUriServ/LexUriServ.do?uri=OJ:L:2005:255:0022:0142:EN:PDF.

2. The Fein family did not participate in the fifth interview due to psychological issues on the part of the mother and was also not available for a call-back interview. We use the information about the five interviews conducted with them.
3. The Grubert family was not available for the call-back interview.
4. The Hirtner family was part of the sample from the first wave of data collection in 2005 onwards. However, it was not possible to contact them for the second and the fifth interviews. In order to close this knowledge gap, we specifically asked them what had happened in the intervening years when we met them for the fourth and sixth interviews.

Open Access This chapter is licensed under the terms of the Creative Commons Attribution 4.0 International License (http://creativecommons.org/licenses/by/4.0/), which permits use, sharing, adaptation, distribution and reproduction in any medium or format, as long as you give appropriate credit to the original author(s) and the source, provide a link to the Creative Commons licence and indicate if changes were made.

The images or other third party material in this chapter are included in the chapter's Creative Commons licence, unless indicated otherwise in a credit line to the material. If material is not included in the chapter's Creative Commons licence and your intended use is not permitted by statutory regulation or exceeds the permitted use, you will need to obtain permission directly from the copyright holder.

CHAPTER 6

Socialisation in Different Socialisation Contexts

6.1 Introduction

In the first five chapters, we provided a general outline of the connections between Social Inequality, Childhood and the Mediachildhood (Chapter 2) and discussed the theoretical basis of an approach to socialisation (Chapter 3), which is integrated, praxeological, related to lifeworlds and freighted with methodological consequences for our longitudinal study (Chapter 4). In Chapter 5, we introduced the families of our panel in order to demonstrate how the results of the study arose. In the following chapter, we will present the main results and illustrate their provenance by recalling briefly some relevant theoretical and methodological aspects of our longitudinal study.

According to our integrative approach, as outlined in Chapter 3, socialisation is conceptualised as a contextual, interwoven process, in which the children and the subsequent adolescents constructed the way they live against the background of the specific social situation, in which they grew up, and of their psycho-social development as individuals. Following Ien Ang's understanding of contextualism, we have to analyse the entangled interplay between the different contexts that shaped the children's growing up, for instance, the family, media, peers and educational institutions. In this chapter, we will present our first analytical step, where we describe and discuss the relevance of each context, together with its reflection in the children's everyday lives. As a second step, we will focus on the direct interplay of two of these contexts, family and media, and analyse parents' practices in mediating their children's media use (see Chapter 7). Finally, by reconstructing the *options for action*, *outlines for action* and *competences for action* of the families involved, we will analyse how the different contexts are integrated into their everyday lives (see Chapter 8).

The empirical basis for this chapter is what we term the focused analysis of the data collected in twelve years (see Chapter 4). Based on the matrices, we structured thematically for each family across all waves of data collection, we identified and condensed all references to the different contexts. In the following, we will describe these condensed observations and selectively illustrate them by referring to particular children and their families and by quoting (translated) statements from the interviews. We would like to point out that the purpose of this chapter is to highlight the particularities of the families in our sample, who are, as was described in previous chapters, socially disadvantaged. Since there is no data available about a control group from different socio-economic contexts, the goal is not to present the families' particularities as phenomena that would only be found among socially disadvantaged ones. The interpretations that follow below must be seen as observations of phenomena occurring among families in our panel and are not meant to single out certain problems as exclusive among socially disadvantaged individuals. Since for example media play an important role in the life of most young people (see Common Sense Media, 2015, 2017; MPFS, 2017, pp. 6–10 and 13–15; Ofcom, 2017, pp. 21–74; see also Chapter 2), certain phenomena could also occur among non-socially disadvantaged children and adolescents, but, and this is the crucial point, in a family context that is marked by entirely different experiences, opportunities and especially economic and educational circumstances. The aim is thus to highlight the individual dealings with the respective situation of a family and a child in the family, the potential causes for certain actions and interests that were identified and to point out patterns that emerged across our sample.

In this chapter we present our observations about the social connections and social contexts that the young people in our sample experience. Due to the density of the data that was collected over such a long period of time, this has to be understood as a compact overview that builds on the interpretation of a rich stock of data from various qualitative methods. A deeper look into this data and the origin of the interpretations will be given in Chapter 8 of this book.

The chapter is structured as follows: the first sub-section focuses on media as context for the children's socialisation. After a general overview of the role of different media within young peoples' media repertoires, we will look back into the role of media extending over preschool and elementary school and into mid-childhood. Then we will analyse the adolescents' patterns of media usage in more detail. We can thus illustrate and reflect upon the interwoven processes of a dynamic media environment and of children's growing up and dealing with relevant developmental tasks in their everyday life. The next sub-section (see Section 6.3) is dedicated to the family as a context for socialisation and sets out the roles of parents and siblings as well as the overall process of *doing family*. While media and family can be regarded as the key contexts of socialisation for all the children, it became apparent that some other contexts were also very important, at least for some of the children. Section 6.4 on the role of Extra-Familial Socialisation Contexts will deal with Relatives and Friends of the Family (6.4.1), the children's and adolescents' Peers, Friends and Romantic Relationships (6.4.2), Kindergarten, Schools and Apprenticeships (6.4.3), Assisted Living Communities and Apprenticeship Hostels (6.4.4), (Sports)Clubs (6.4.5) and Politics and Society as a whole (6.4.6).

6.2 Media as a Context for Socialisation

6.2.1 *The Role of Media, Extending Over Preschool and Elementary School into Mid-Childhood*

Today's socialisation is mediatised socialisation (Paus-Hasebrink & Bichler, 2008; see also Couldry & Hepp, 2017, p. 151). This had already become obvious in the first two years of the longitudinal study—the children were five to seven years old. Media were highly relevant at kindergarten age, as well as in the first years of school.

One fundamental outcome during the whole inquiry was noting how the families were quite well equipped with media devices. Thus, the restricted socio-economic background of the families is not reflected in restricted media devices. Media were an integral part of everyday life—for the parents as well as for the children. Especially in the second wave of the survey, with the children entering elementary school, the households upgraded massively with new computer equipment. Nearly every family owned a computer with internet access; several children even got their own computers.

In the *first wave*, when the children were about five years old, their media repertoire included mostly programmes on private television channels and specifically labelled for children. Books were not very common within the families, but if there were some, they were usually linked to cross-media distribution strategies of heroes or stories that appear in different media channels, for example audio-cassettes, video games or movies. During the first wave of the survey, the computer was used for video games at most.

In the *second wave*—the children were already in school—they were highly interested in early evening programmes for general audiences from private television channels (see Paus-Hasebrink & Bichler, 2008). Books still did not find much favour, as computers gained more relevance than in the first wave. However, these devices were barely used for educational purposes, although this was the parents' primary intention when buying them. In this wave, violent computer games were part of the everyday life of some boys in the panel, for example, for Timo Landinger, Erich Grubert, Manfred Oblinger and Torsten Kaiser. This was especially the case if the families were quite stressed anyway. In the second wave in 2007, it was striking that, for most of the boys, the computer was already their favourite device, and online computer games were among their favourite media. The internet was not important at all during that time. Today, due to the rapid diffusion of tablets and smartphones, the situation would certainly be quite different among children at a comparable age.

By the same token, television played a specially important role (see Paus-Hasebrink & Bichler, 2008; see, as well, research from for example, Grüninger & Lindemann, 2000; d'Haenens, 2001; Roberts & Foehr, 2004; Rideout & Hamel, 2006; Rideout, Vandewater, & Wartella, 2003; Woodard & Gridina, 2000). We can assume that this would no longer be the situation today, when even younger children use tablets or smartphones quite early (see, for example, MPFS, 2014, pp. 5–7; Chaudron et al., 2015; Education Group, 2016; MPFS 2016, pp. 29–30; see Chapter 2). At that time, our children experienced their favourite television series, particularly those offered by private channels, as reliable companions (compare, for example, Feierabend & Scolari, 2018, pp. 169–170 and 174). They were searching for series providing orientation and stability or even a solid structure for their recreational time, which they often perceived as empty. For instance, Olivia Fein assigned her favourite cartoon characters as her "best friends". Against the background of her particularly stressful life-situation, her media use can be interpreted as flight into a media-based fantasy world. Among the boys, cartoon series and especially anime series with a strong hero like *Herkules, Dragonball (Z), Yu-Gi-Oh!, Tom and Jerry, Pokémon, Tarzan* or *One Piece* were preferred. These stories are very exciting, and their protagonists are strong and courageous, as they have to engage in fights and duels.

By contrast, the girls tended towards female protagonists engaged with everyday topics, like *Kim Possible, Bibi Blocksberg*, a highly favoured German cartoon with a strong girl in the centre of the story, or *Charmed* and *Sabrina* and, a while later, *Hannah Montana*. Besides that, they liked anthropomorphic animal figures, for example *Spongebob* or *Benjamin Blümchen*, by then a very popular cartoon series in Germany and Austria. When the girls grew older, they also liked daily soaps.

During the *third wave* of the survey—the children were about ten years old by then—the usage of computers and the internet was increasing, even though television retained its relevance. Computer games, like free browser and social games, but also online multiplayer role games—often, according to the official national classification of media content, only suitable for sixteen-, or even eighteen-, year-olds—were notably popular among the boys, for example, *Call of Duty 3 & 4* (recommend for people older than 18 years), *Super Mario, Super Mario Galaxy, Mario Kart, Animal Crossing* (versions recommended for adolescents older than 16), *Naruto, Skyrim* (for people over 18) and so on. The girls preferred so-called simulation games. It is noticeable that the children were hardly interested in social networking sites at that time. The boys, but, above all, the girls, used audio media mainly for current pop and rock music.

The relevance of Facebook, Messengers and YouTube for the eleven- to twelve-year-olds increased distinctly during the *fourth wave* of the survey. About half of the children were using such media services. Along with computer games, communicating with friends became certainly more relevant, especially among the girls. A few of the adolescents were not allowed to join Facebook at this time, others voluntarily abstained. Television maintained its status as a reliable partner in everyday life. Whether it was computers, television or internet usage, the media repertoire of the boys and girls was primarily based on entertainment. They occasionally used the internet for educational purposes, but beyond that, any search for information was rarely intentional.

As regards television, the children were now using programmes for general audiences, mainly on private channels. As they grew older, daily soaps ceased being a favourite with them. The girls mostly favoured casting shows, for example, *Deutschland sucht den Superstar*, the German version of *Pop Idol*. The boys liked international series, like *Scrubs*, *Two and a Half Men* and *How I Met Your Mother*. In Austria, all these international formats are broadcast with German dubbing. Where they did watch cartoons, the boys liked action-stories, like *Naruto*, *Superman* and so on. They preferred comedy series, reality TV, casting shows and crime series. The girls chose series with a strong girl as the focus. These findings concerning the preferred content on TV are comparable to the results of nation-wide representative studies (see, for example, Ofcom, 2017, pp. 297–298; MPFS, 2017, p. 41).

Across the first four waves of data collection, it was very noticeable that parents and their children gave quite different answers and statements on the children's most favoured media content and media protagonists, especially when the children were going to kindergarten or to school. In the first waves of research, this mostly applied to the usage of television. In this case, the parents' and the children's answers differed greatly over the programmes' transmission times and, when children grew older, over the length of their television usage as well. Most parents expressed wishful thinking by quite often naming programmes, which did not seem violent or full of strong visual effects. They were aware of the public discourse on the media usage appropriate to children and adolescents (see Chapter 7). As the boys grew older, parents mostly were concerned that boys might use pornography or hard-core media content. As for the girls, they did not mention disliked media content as often. All in all, parents ceased to care about the public debates on appropriate media content for older children.

At this point, we offer a short interim conclusion: similarly to other young people, our children assigned media different functions according to their personal needs and concerns. Some children deliberately watched television to escape from boredom and to structure their everyday lives. Furthermore, they used television and the characters shown there as an orientation and were, in fact looking for virtual mentors, usually in the form of strong characters of their own gender.

6.2.2 The Role of Media in the Phase of Adolescence

We examined the phase of adolescence during the fifth and the sixth waves of our study (2014 and 2016). During this important phase of their youth, the essential developmental tasks for our adolescents (see Havighurst, 1972; Tarrant, MacKenzie, & Hewitt, 2006), for example, developing their identity, finding the means of understanding their identity by learning to present and position themselves socially, participating in different peer groups and in society at large, and distancing themselves from their parents. In order to cope with these tasks, the adolescents developed new codes and forms of verbal expression or used other media than that used by their parents (see MPFS, 2017, pp. 32–38). As with other adolescents (see Paus-Hasebrink, Schmidt, & Hasebrink, 2011; Paus-Hasebrink, Wijnen, & Brüssel, 2011), the young people in our panel used social media applications intensively, for example message boards to test und present themselves as a form of game playing, to maintain their relationships to friends and, in a few cases, to establish their first romantic bonds. These practices can be conceptualised as advanced, media-related forms of *identity management, relationship management* and *information management* (see Paus-Hasebrink et al., 2011, p. 27):

- Identity management connotes accessing specific aspects of character, like certain experiences. Furthermore, there is a fashioning of the self, motivated by a visual presence (for example, pictures, videos) on social media.
- Relationship management is basically about every relationship, but rather more specifically about maintaining or gaining friendship.
- Information management is about selecting, channelling and filtering every kind of information, for example, research within Wikipedia.

To develop this general observation on social media use, we will now condense and interpret our data regarding the particular roles of different media for adolescents.

6.2.2.1 Smartphones as the New Access to the World

For most of our subjects, smartphones played a vital role (see, for example, Lauricella, Cingel, Blackwell, Wartella, & Conway, 2014; MPFS, 2017, pp. 13–15 and pp. 26–29; see Chapter 2). Norbert Zarbl put it the following way: "Without a smartphone, nothing will get done".[1] More than half of the adolescents in our panel favoured smartphones and, above all, WhatsApp. These results correspond with results from MPFS (2017, pp. 27–29 and 33–36) and Education Group (2016). The adolescents liked WhatsApp mostly because this service is free of charge—in contrast to texting (regarding the importance of messenger applications and more particularly of WhatsApp among adolescents, see Koch & Frees, 2017, p. 445; Ofcom, 2017, pp. 104–105).

6.2.2.2 New Audiovisual Services as Means for Interactive Entertainment
Among the adolescents of our panel, the video platform, YouTube, proved to be more important than television. As many of them described it, this media service meets their needs and interests particularly well. In this respect, a gender difference becomes apparent: while the girls within the panel chose content with a focus on beauty and styling topics, the boys were more interested in videos about computer and video games (for example, 'Let's Play'-videos). However, regular television was still important. Either it was used as a sort of secondary medium, as the adolescents were concurrently using mobile phones or playing computer games, or it was specifically used for watching entertainment shows, crime stories or sportscasts. In order to satisfy more specific individual needs and compose their own audiovisual repertoire, the adolescents used streaming services, YouTube and pay television like Sky and Sky Go, but also platforms like Burning Series, kinox.to or *Naruto*-Tube that are regarded as illegal. Concerning the diversity of streaming offerings used by adolescents, we find comparable findings in nation-wide representative studies (see MPFS, 2017, p. 42; Ofcom, 2017, pp. 29 and 74–81), though the profound insights concerning the usage of alternative applications or such that are regarded as illegal are unique results of the qualitative panel study at hand.

6.2.2.3 Print Media as Marginal Elements of Adolescents'
  Media Repertoires
Reading books, newspapers or magazines was not a habit with most adolescents in our panel, at this point we consider large differences compared to other young people of this age (see, for example, MPFS, 2017, pp. 13–14 and 18–21). A remarkable exception was Gudrun Dornbacher, who regularly read books and newspapers and also wrote her own short stories (see Chapter 8). Compared to her, only a few

adolescents mentioned print media: Mario Hirtner related how his mother sometimes used to buy a newspaper; Manfred Oblinger stated that his parents took a tabloid newspaper, but it remained unclear if the two boys were themselves interested in newspapers. Benedikt Holzner was the only one to read a newspaper in his family, while Viktoria Öllinger browsed her mother's newspapers on a regular basis. Thus, most adolescents, primarily boys, favoured online games, game consoles and a, more or less, broad variety of social media services over printed media as their individually compiled repertoires.

6.2.2.4 Media Protagonists as Guides to Desired Success and Financial Independence

Media stars, especially YouTube-Stars, were regarded as role models, and for some of the girls and boys so called influencers were highly relevant (see also Ofcom, 2017, pp. 93–94; MPFS, 2017, pp. 44–45). They were admired as examples for social advancement and for being heard by society because of their symbolic and financial success, an opinion some of the panel's adolescents stressed. The children displaying this pattern might see them as role models for financial independence and material security. Among the boys, particularly YouTubers who present games, rankings and tips for online gaming were considered popular. Some of them seemed to see different male YouTubers as reference characters, most likely because they embody success, are humorous and influential, and, consequently, famous. Some of them wished to become YouTubers themselves, like Manfred Oblinger: "This is my dream, to be a YouTuber one day" (Interview, sixth panel wave 2016).

The girls favoured popular female stars and celebrities, and especially during puberty, these female YouTubers served as role models on topics like beauty and styling and provided opportunities to deal with topics that were important to the girls.[2] In these videos, they found information on, for example, how to present themselves as girls or young women, information their mothers maybe could not, or would not, pass on to them. That some of the girls, like Olivia Fein, lack their mothers' support became clear in the interviews, in one case, Ms. Fein herself repeats her daughter's reproach after she was not able to give her a satisfying answer with regard to her beginning menstrual cycle:

> When, when she started having her period, it was pure horror. She got it in winter. She has very severe cramps and always gets mad, because she asks

me 'How was it when you got yours?' and I just told her that I never experienced pain […] and I told her how it was for me, that I can't really help her the way she needs it and she just said 'What kind of mother are you? You can't even help me as a mum!' I just told her to go and ask her grandmother. (Interview, sixth panel wave, 2016)

6.2.2.5 Social Media Practices as a Symbolic Expression of Individual Spaces

Media services like WhatsApp or Snapchat were primarily seen as a possibility to create individual spaces independent of their parents' communicative practices. Boys used these services to exchange information or videos about computer games. While joking about topics within this community, they permanently checked their position in the peer group. Girls were most likely to chat on social networking sites like Facebook or to share pictures on Instagram. WhatsApp was used for exchanging videos and especially for voice mails. In contrast to the boys, the girls used media services to communicate with their female friends, and especially their best friends, about problems. They tried to give advice, to gain acknowledgement and affirmation of their image from their friends. They used WhatsApp particularly, as it shaped their friendships with peers and communicated their emotional support during difficult times of life. Some girls used social media as a sort of public diary, within which they recorded the highlights of their everyday day life while waiting for their followers to like and acknowledge their postings. Sometimes WhatsApp or Snapchat were merely used for questions, about what to wear, for instance. However, we can conclude that social media services and applications are now a vital part of the everyday life of adolescents.

6.2.2.6 Computer Games as an Expression of Problems Within the Boys' Lifeworlds, but also as a Possibility to Gain Different Kinds of Experience

Many boys from the panel, like Timo Landinger, Manfred Oblinger, Mario Hirtner, Torsten Kaiser and Alfons Weiss, who belong to families with massive socio-emotional problems, referred overwhelmingly to first-person-shooter and battle games, like *League of Legends*, *Call of Duty*, *Grand Theft Auto (GTA)* and *World of Warcraft*. Of course, these games are very popular among boys and young men in general (see MPFS, 2017, pp. 48–51; Ofcom, 2017, pp. 108–112), what was extremely particular about these boys in our sample, however, was that they lacked a socially fulfilled life beyond the world of (online) media (on this aspect see also Li, Hietajärvi, Palonen, Salmela-Aro, & Hakkarainen, 2017). Mario Hirtner and more particularly Manfred Oblinger were exposed to a wide range of experiences playing online games. But in consequence, there are achievements which should not be ignored: The technical knowledge and the abilities mediated through online gaming, hacks, cheats and exchanges with other gamers—in their own country as well as in other countries—meant that they were able to advance to an apprenticeship within the IT industry.

Against the background of their lifeworld (see Chapter 8 for examples and more detailed elaborations), the crucial importance of computer games for these boys can be explained by the following specific functions:

- *Compensation for a lack of stimulation*: The boys used computer games because of the lack of other possibilities and to compensate the emotional or actual absence of their parents to fill their time with an activity which is particularly important to them, which they find fun and which creates a means of escape from their constrained reality. Timo Landinger is one example, he always expressed his wishes to do more things together with his family, like trips and activities on weekends, but none of the family members ever wanted to do anything like that with him, in general, he felt that no one in the family liked him:

    Interviewer: Would you like to spend more time with your mum and dad, can you talk to them about problems?
    Timo: [*No reaction, keeps playing the video game*]
    Interviewer: Or is that difficult?
    Timo: Hm…difficult.
    Interviewer: Why?
    Timo: No one talks to me, no one asks me 'What do you wanna do?' Because they don't like me.
    Interviewer: They don't like you?
    Timo: [*Nods*] I don't think they do. (Interview in 2012)

His parents saw video games as better leisure-time activities, it seemed that they enjoyed that Timo left them alone when he was in his room all day long, playing games. For Timo, as well as other boys from the sample, these games came to provide a familiar, reliable and comfortable environment that they otherwise lacked. The boys did not perceive the time spent on computer games as empty, but rather as an enrichment of their everyday lives.

- *Distinction and competition*: In their world of game playing, the boys were successful and could, therefore, gain acknowledgement. In socio-emotionally stressed families, this was the only way they got this kind of approval. Game playing provided a safe environment, where they could compete and prove themselves to other adolescents. Due to their involvement and their highly developed skills and competences, some of them were able to keep up with and even overtake their contemporary competitors.
- *Experiencing self-efficacy*: Online games provide the chance to solve individual tasks satisfactorily and to face risky challenges within an online world—all without the danger of failure in the real world.
- *Experiencing companionship*: In some cases, the adolescent boys, like Manfred Oblinger, Mario Hirtner and Torsten Kaiser, could not build stable relationships to their peers, felt themselves to be mavericks and maintained few contacts beyond their online environment. When Manfred Oblinger was younger for example, his mother did not approve of the neighbour's children (many with migration backgrounds), claiming that they were a bad influence (2005 and 2007) up to the point where Manfred would try to sneak out to see other children. In order to compensate him for the lack of social contact, Manfred's mother encouraged him to play video games and bought games for grown-ups because he was interested in them more than in children's games: "I keep saying, he needs something, since he doesn't have any friends. I can't produce a friend out of thin air if there is no one. I can't. That's why I think, just let him." (2007)

Yet, through their abilities in online game playing, Manfred and some of the other boys in the sample cooperated with other gamers and socialised within this online space. This enabled them to deal with their developmental tasks virtually. Contacts with other committed peers contained the chance to talk about technical questions as well as about new strategies to cope with the challenges of online game playing. Manfred Oblinger enjoyed helping his online companions to deal with technical problems and to find new ways of achieving their game-playing goals.

- *Dealing with frustration and aggression*: The frequent frustrations in the everyday lives of the adolescent boys often resulted in aggression, especially for those who lived in generally aggressive families. The boys could not live out their aggressions within the family, so the computer games served to vent the frustration in their lives. Timo Landinger serves as one prominent example to illustrate this. When he was still in elementary school, he always wanted to be one of the Pokémon from his favourite games, because, as he hinted at in an interview in 2007, he would hurt his family and shoot at his peers in school so that they would be afraid of him and start to respect him.

  The boys' playing especially violent computer games from a first-person-shooter perspective was generally not really approved by the parents, with exception of Timo Landinger, and during the first and second wave of the survey, Manfred Oblinger. Unlike their everyday life, the only possible negative consequences for them within this virtual world were to lose and, therefore, to be angry about that. Normally, this anger was over their own lacking competence or their bad luck. Both perspectives fed the desire to start again and to do better the next time.

Overall, we can conclude that, even during their adolescence, the boys and girls perceived relevant media content as an important—but not the only—source of information and orientation to cope with their everyday lives. So media were used after long days at school or at work to maintain the relationship with close friends or with a partner. Most of the adolescents had habitually used the media since childhood to satisfy different needs. Hence, it seemed likely that they would turn to media while going through challenging times at school or when starting their apprenticeship. With a preference for content that was entertaining, they suceeded in distracting themselves, at least short time, from their burdens of everyday living.

6.2.3 Conclusion

In terms of media content, the findings presented above show that media fulfilled different functions in the everyday life of our children. These functions are narrowly linked to their developmental tasks as well as to the various experiences the panel members underwent throughout their childhood and adolescence. When children were confronted with severe emotional experiences, for example the family being torn apart, they particularly tended to engage with certain characters within the media. In this way, they were looking for a supportive counterpart for comfort and to give them an individual sense of safety. Television was primarily a cheap, and, therefore, accessible way to spend some time together, because the families' financial problems precluded any other possibility. In general, throughout their socialisation, the media served in a variety of ways as window to the world, through which to both perceive and be perceived.

Accordingly, we noted that the media became particularly relevant in the children's lives if there were conflicts within the family. This especially happened when parents were not able to maintain certain living standards because they had to deal with their own problems and challenges in their daily routine. As a consequence, they neglected their children and could not manage to support them properly in coping with their developmental tasks. In this case, the young people preferred media content and media services, which seemed suitable for their particular situation. Hence, micro-structural factors, like age and gender, specific developmental tasks and also the children's specific *Eigensinn* (self-will), all influenced their media usage.

6.3 THE FAMILY AS SOCIALISATION CONTEXT

Our study shows that socialisation research must be family research. It indicates that the family is the primary and essential context if children's socialisation is to be sustainable. In this respect, Larson (2006) highlights the role of perceptive, supportive and caring adults in young peoples' growing up, for example, in inculcating motivation and engagement (see as well Rogers Hollifield & Jewsbury Conger, 2014). Furthermore, Notten and Kraaykamp (2009, p. 185) stress that "parental media guidance takes place less frequently in families that have experienced a divorce and in larger families". But how the parents dealt with their children and how media accompanied the individual development in children were determined by the specific interplay of the parents' *options for action*, *outlines for action* and *competences for action*. Their individual emotional patterns, like affection, or, by contrast, neglect, refusal and even aggression shaped the way the children learned how to deal with everyday challenges in life and, in this context, with available media. Over the years of our research, it became manifest that parental disinterest in their children's own concerns, anxieties and wishes, and, closely linked with this, in their media usage as well, had significant consequences for the children. In some cases, these were even traumatising experiences, as with, for example, Timo Landinger, Mario Hirtner and Alfons Weiss, all of whom had to cope with a strong sense of being alone. But we also recognised excessive control over the children's contact with media—among the Rohringer family—as a signal for the parents' lack of trust in their children. These factors interfered with the children's meeting the challenge of building their own *competences for action*. In another case, an excessive wish for closeness was experienced as terrifying by Viktoria Öllinger and became an impediment to socialisation. The example of her family is notable for the mother–daughter relationship displaying ongoing processes of "parentification", a reversal of roles involving the daughter, "taking on both emotional and functional responsibilities that typically are performed by the parent" (Engelhardt, 2012, p. 45). Viktoria cared for her ill mother and coped with all challenges of organising their everyday life. So, for Viktoria, there was not enough space to develop her own interests through using media; she suffered from an eating disorder and behavioural problems.

Even though we should not assume that there is a direct, or even causally determined, impact by the media on socialisation, it is likely that they become more important if adolescents' socialisation is shaped by a complicated family context and if the parents are not able to give their children enough attention to make them feel safe and comfortable.[3] The children in our study who experienced security and emotional closeness were less likely to be overwhelmed by the challenges of their everyday lives. This outcome applied to their dealings with developmental tasks and their coping with family structures or their media usage. These children were developing ambitious *outlines for action*, for example, concerning apprenticeships, and were establishing their *competences for action*, in contrast to the adolescents who were not comfortable within their family and hence had to deal with various tasks, including their media usage, on their own.

These circumstances were especially pronounced in families where the adolescents had brothers or sisters and were affected by their relationship to siblings. Schmidt (2014), for instance, has analysed the relevance of siblings for the social and cognitive development of children and adolescents. Feinberg, Sakuma, Hostetler and McHale (2013) have demonstrated the role of siblings for well-being, and the research by Rogers Hollifield and Jewsbury Conger (2014) has also shown the significant influence of siblings on adolescents and young adults. On media usage, it became clear to us that older siblings often acted as a guide or role model regarding the choice of media. The younger siblings would adopt the media preferred by the older ones[4] and talk more intensely and closely about media with siblings than with parents. Especially during the first waves, the younger children asked their older siblings for help. The older sisters and brothers were able to guide and support the younger siblings and were, as with Amelie Aufbauer, guided themselves not only in their own media usage but were also providers for the younger children, for example, by making breakfast, if the parents could not deal adequately with these kinds of tasks because of external pressures, as, for example in the Kaiser, Hirtner, Landinger, Oblinger and Weiss families. In the case of the Ebner family, the parents were not able to use computers; the Stab and Aufbauer families had the same problem when their children were younger, but later on the parents too showed more competence. In general, older and also younger siblings were often more familiar with the media usage of their siblings than their parents; during the interviews with Mrs. Holzner and Mrs. Weiss, the brothers were occasionally present and were better informed than the parents.

Research on the role of siblings states that the relationships between siblings are strongly shaped by how parents interact with their children. In addition to the emotional quality of the siblings' relationship, the individual nature of any child, and also the constellation of siblings (see an overview in Schmidt, 2014), as well as the parents' behaviour as educators all play an important role. We confirmed what Schmidt (2014) has summarised in her overview: "A positive parental behaviour of the parents promotes a positive behaviour in the siblings relationship". But if the parents' behaviour tended to be dismissive, as with the Landinger family, the siblings were more likely to display bad behaviour among themselves. In the Landinger family's case, a bad emotional situation impinged on the youngest brother, Timo (see case description for Timo Landinger in Chapter 5). He felt disregarded by his older siblings and reacted acutely to his parents' behaviour, particularly that of his father. Furthermore, individual discrimination against the children—a child being, generally speaking, disregarded or, by contrast, favoured—played an important role for the children. If a mother or a father favoured a child who was brought into the family with a new partner, as in the case of Benedikt Holzner or Alfons Weiss, the parents' behaviour translated into a tense but also apathetic interaction with their other children. They retained less attention than their (half-)siblings and were sometimes severely neglected. The preferred children were less notable for their media usage than their siblings, who had a fraught relationship with their parents. This was the case with the brother of Simone Stab.

Within the scope of this study, it also appeared that some parents could not avoid focusing conflicts on only one child. This might have been caused by their lack of socio-emotional capacities, sometimes accompanied by their restricted housing situation limiting the space available for parents and siblings themselves. In this particular case, temporary accommodation out of the family (see Chapters 5 and 8), or a sibling moving out, led to a less tense socio-emotional relationship in *doing family*. However, although Mrs. Stab did manage to build up an extraordinary relationship with her daughter, Simone, she could not, as a financially challenged single mother, care for her son equally. After severe conflicts because of the son's excessive game playing, Mrs. Stab decided to put him in a socio-pedagogical institution during the week. The situation within the family then eased, fewer conflicts were likely to happen, and the son himself actually coped better when he was back for weekends. Mrs. Stab struggled in her life as a single mother. She acknowledged that she was not able to care for both children equally without a partner. For the Aufbauer family, the oldest sister moving out led to a more comfortable family climate and better core relationships. Before that, the single mother could not afford an adequate flat, so the whole family suffered recurring conflicts because of the different needs of the children. The oldest sister—20 years old during the sixth wave of the survey—had a completely different daily routine to her significantly younger siblings (16-, ten- and one-year old). She was highly stressed by them when she had to deal with different tasks. Conversely, there were conflicts within the family, for example when the older sister wanted to listen to loud music, but for her younger siblings it was bedtime. After her move, the younger siblings got their own room, and the family climate improved significantly, because they had more room overall, and the younger children could live out their own wishes and ideas better.

6.4 Extra-Familial Socialisation Contexts

Besides the families, extra-familial contexts, such as kindergarten or school alongside friends and peer groups, also played a major role in the adolescents' socialisation and grew in importance over the years. In contrast to early childhood and mid-childhood, the dominance of the family decreased as the scope of the children's living environment increased and they explored new micro-systems.

6.4.1 Relatives and Friends of the Family

Relatives, and especially grandparents, played a relevant role for many families. They weren't only helping the family with a range of issues but supported them financially as well. Mrs. Weiss inherited real estate and didn't have to work anymore, as the rental income provided a living for her children and herself.

The children were often supported by their grandparents as important caregivers in their everyday life, for example, by giving the children pocket money when the parents could not afford it, as with Mrs. Aufbauer, a single parent. Occasionally, the grandparents or relatives gave presents in the form of media devices like laptops or smartphones. The grandparents, aunts and uncles not only helped to improve the financial situation of the families but also offered educational help or saw to their grandchildren's welfare while the parents were over-challenged (with respect to research on aunts, see May & Lahad, 2018). Olivia Fein identified her grandmother as an important person in her life and would even discuss puberty problems (during the fifth wave of the survey) with her. Her mother did not have either time for the concerns of her daughter or any interest in them. After Olivia in 2008 threatened to fall down the stairs in school on purpose, while behaving aggressively towards the other children, her grandmother, together with the school principal, approached the child protection services to initiate an examination of the domestic circumstances. After that, Olivia was taken into an assisted living community, where adolescents of different ages were living together and receiving therapeutic treatment. During that time, she visited her family only every second weekend. For Elisabeth Ebner, her aunt was the most important companion in her everyday life. Her parents did not have enough time because there was so much work on their farm, so Elisabeth spent a lot of time with her aunt, who became her most important confidante. In the same vein, the aunt intervened in the Pfortner family and mediated a conflict caused by the seemingly extraordinary alcohol consumption of the father. In the case of Alfons Weiss, his uncle paid for the boy's cell phone contract without his mother knowing. For Torsten Kaiser, his grandparents were very important, although his mother was concerned about the contact to the paternal grandfather, as he allowed Torsten to play games she found inappropriate.

However many families lacked any good connection to their relatives. Families with meagre resources—financially and temporally—would have particularly profited, either through the grandparents supervising their children or supporting the family through money. Some of the families were socially isolated generally, because they were not able to build up and maintain close connections to other families or relatives. Mrs. Öllinger, who grew up with foster parents, was supported by them to a certain extent, although the connection was quite loose. As the family lacked regular contact with friends and relatives, Mrs. Öllinger and her daughter were glad to find the mother's biological brother, unknown until then, during the sixth wave of survey. Mrs. Öllinger immediately contacted her brother and sister. The mother and daughter established relations at least with a sister, or respectively aunt, to the family's benefit. During her socio-economic and health crisis, every such contact made her happy.

6.4.2 Peers, Friends and Romantic Relationships

In the context of identity formation, especially in middle childhood and adolescence, peers are of prime importance, but also when it comes to questions and the need for help, peers are highly relevant (see Packer, 2017, pp. 487–493). "Considering the social relationship between child and adult to be contradictive, among their peers, the children are the creators and innovators of their own world. We may therefore regard children as mediators between different worlds" (Lillehammer, 2010, p. 10). Contacts with peers means (Youniss, 1980) that children have a particular opportunity to form relationships with other children on an equal and mutual basis, whereas their relationships to adults are characterised by an authority gradient. The interaction between children serves as an impulse to further developmental steps and to engage with the concomitant tasks. Furthermore, a child's issue with identity—potentially prevalent, according to Erikson, at any time during the developmental process—can be handled on a different, egalitarian basis during the exercise of self-perception in peer relationships. Self-perceptions can be tested; emotions can be integrated into self-awareness and self-control (cf. Krappmann, 1991, pp. 373f.). As Grundmann states: "Thus, in a group of coevals, individual interests have to be negotiated, and the skills of every individual have to be validated" (Grundmann, 2000, p. 96, translated by the authors).

It was noticeable during the first waves of the survey that the children met their friends outside of the institutional education and support facilities only infrequently, if they were not living in the same neighbourhood or the same region. One reason is that the parents did not really support their children in maintaining friendships. Sometimes, remote housing situations, due to high rents within city areas, were the main reason for the girls and boys living nearly isolated from others, apart from visiting kindergarten and school.[5] Either there were no children living in their area, or the parents forbade their children to get in contact with other girls and boys from families in any neighbourhood with a migration background (for example, Manfred Oblinger, who got violent computer games for sixteen- to eighteen-year-olds from his mother as compensation). In this context, the residential environment of the family became hugely important. The socio-economically less resourced families were often living in housing areas with a high ratio of immigrants, so to play with peers, the children were dependent on the neighbours' children. Since several parents were afraid that children with a migrant background might have a negative impact on their own children, they tried to block every kind of contact or friendship with children from their neighbourhood. Thus, these children had to suffer from a lack of contacts to peers and friends, while others, who had the opportunity to establish and maintain friendships, stressed their importance. As Benedikt Holzner memorably puts it during the second wave of the study: "Because I like them, and they can explain anything to me". Peers had been the most relevant persons to him for information and exchange about the world.

Across all our waves of enquiry, we noted the media serving as important facilitators of peer relationships. During kindergarten, the media were, as yet, barely relevant for children in their peer context. They usually used the media alone or accompanied by siblings or parents. Stories shown through media were at best re-enacted with coevals (for example, stories and actions from *Dragon Ball Z*, *Lilo and Stitch*, *Disney's Adventures of the Gummi Bears* or *Pumba Bear*). Two years later, a more collective way of using media became common, indicating that the importance of media within the peer group had risen. During the period of elementary school, the children used media—mostly computers, but also game consoles, television and radio—together with friends or classmates.

According to Reitz et al., "when boys and girls grow older their attention shifts from parents to peers, thus peers become a core influence for their development" (Reitz, Zimmermann, Hutemann, Sprecht, & Neyer, 2014, p. 281; see also Harter, 2012). Accordingly the boys of our panel mainly focused on playing computer games together, and the girls preferred to go to the movies or sometimes read some girls' magazines together. As children moved through school and later changed schools during the third and fourth wave of the survey, peers in general, and friends in particular, became more important for the adolescents. As Morgan states, "developing a meaningful sense of one's sexual orientation and identity is an important undertaking during emerging adulthood" (Morgan, 2012, p. 52). Hence, romantic partnerships also became more relevant for the adolescents. Now they were using media services like Skype, MSN, other chat services and even Facebook, to maintain their contacts.

During the last two waves of the survey, it appeared that children from families that suffered under particular socio-economic and socio-emotional challenges and had severe problems with *doing family*, were not able to utilise their increased mobility and capacity for communication. For them, there was no social security net available from relatives or friends of the families. The adolescents, mainly boys, had problems keeping up with peers in their individual development, so they often felt like mavericks in class. Either they had no friends, or just a few, with whom they shared their interests. Their friendships were primarily based around their online games. The girls did not depend on such online contacts. Viktoria Öllinger, Olivia Fein and Isabelle Rohringer had at least one good friend to talk with about their problems. Tarrant et al. (2006) point out the narrow relationship between adolescents' objective position in a peer network and indicators of social competence, including loneliness, depression, aggression and a general self-concept (Tarrant et al., 2006). Against this background, it is not surprising that adolescents, like Manfred Oblinger, Timo Landinger and Viktoria Öllinger, all of whom faced considerable challenges in their families and had difficulties dealing with restricted relationships, had not bonded with someone in a romantic relationship yet. Olivia Fein was the only one consistently seeking confirmation of her identity from males.

Other adolescents in our panel deemed face-to-face-relationships more important than mediated recreational time. They certainly used computer games and were interested in other (media-related) activities, but these were not a basis for leisure time, whereas immediate contact to friends was by far more important to them. At this time, some of these adolescents also experienced first romantic relationships, and some were able to maintain a relationship for quite a long time.

6.4.3 *Kindergarten, School and Apprenticeship*

The time in kindergarten, and later also in school, played an important role in the children's everyday lives. During the first two waves of the survey, parents delegated a great amount of responsibility for the children to kindergarten and schools. Single mothers, above all, regarded kindergarten and schools as important socialisation contexts. They expected these institutions to teach their children the skills and behaviours they were not able to teach themselves for various reasons, a lack of time being an obvious one.

Many parents stressed during the interviews that the children should be taught manners (for example, sitting still, showing respect), creative skills (handicrafts and drawing) and formal skills like maths, writing, reading, and foreign languages. According to several parents at that time, transmitting knowledge and rules of behaviour would be more efficient in kindergartens and schools than at home, like Ms. Hirtner pointed out in 2010 when asked what children can learn in school that they cannot learn at home: "Well, everything about relationships, I think they learn that better from outside of the family […]. They learn social skills, they learn how to treat others".

Particularly during the first waves of the study, but also later on, the parents looked to kindergartens and schools to teach the use of different media, what we call media competences. If the parents were assuming that their children were still too young to deal with media, they viewed schools as the most important places for their children to gain media competence later.

For several children the nursery school or elementary school teachers were initially important as well. They acted as role models for social orientation, where there was no chance to learn that within their family.

Later, we noted that children within socio-economically and socio-emotionally fraught families, like Viktoria Öllinger, but also Manfred Oblinger, tended to have equally fraught relationships to their teachers. They often could not get along with the teachers, felt misunderstood and pressured, so that several adolescents had a hard time at school. They perceived their everyday school life as a great burden while dealing with bad grades and worrying about having to resit a year. The struggles in school were often also a result of a lack of help with homework and projects at home, as well as a lack of funds to finance professional tutoring.

The adolescents—mainly boys—who got apprenticeships during the last wave of the study or the phone interview, mostly perceived this development as a positive and life-changing step towards their adulthood. Finishing compulsory school was a big relief, because the individual pressure to successfully complete school, while having to deal with personal problems within the family, was gone. Instead, they had a perspective of becoming productive within their apprenticeship. A very characteristic case in this context is Manfred Oblinger, who made an important contribution to the stressed socio-economic status of his family with the money he earned. He felt that he had no part of the family's problems anymore, but was nevertheless proud to support them. He wanted to leave the high school he attended in order to help the family financially, although it would have been an option to graduate and to pursue a college degree. Manfred suffered from losing his first apprenticeship—his position had unfortunately been terminated within the first three months. After his experience of failure, Manfred tried to cope with his disappointment by joining the online world again. He gained weight massively and showed first signs of a depression, just as his parents did. The apprenticeship in his desired branch, IT, has been a chance for him to prove his extensive knowledge and competences while feeling valuable and needed.

Other adolescents, who also got appropriate apprenticeships, felt their jobs led to strengthened *competences for action* and self-efficacy and they gained self-esteem from then on. Against this background, Mario Hirtner had to abandon his training to be an electrician because of his fear of heights, but he did receive a position within the IT sector after some preparation for it. Even the former socially isolated adolescents reported better social contacts, usually with their colleagues. They got along with them much better than with their classmates. And in addition, they declared the less influential position of their parents to be something fairly positive.

6.4.4 *Assisted Living Communities and Apprenticeship Hostels*

Moving to assisted living accommodation did play a crucial role for some of the adolescents, and especially for Benedikt Holzner. These particular children received therapeutic treatment by social educators in such accommodation and could experience a structured daily routine, which was very different from their lives with the socio-economically and socio-emotionally burdened families.

The widespread prejudice over children in such facilities suffering negative consequences could not be confirmed in our results. Much rather, the facilities had a stabilising effect on the children's lives. For Benedikt Holzner, living there led to an enduring transformation, which showed itself in his strengthened resilience by the end of the study. He chose to continue living there, although he had already started his apprenticeship and was able to earn his livelihood. Through his caregivers, Benedikt experienced the attention, affection and closeness that he missed so desperately at home. He also displayed a positive development with regard to his excessive media use. The fixed daily routine and the supervision and regulation of his media use reflect on his use of media. Just like Benedikt Holzner, Timo Landinger also felt at ease at the facility, where therapeutic treatment and support was available for his, in fact, massive psychological problems. However, his release led to a regression in his development. Timo suffered not just because of his father's controlling behaviour and the latter's claim to be the sole contact person but also because of his father's psychological and physical violence aimed at casting out what he had learned in the facility. Timo has been left alone with his problems and was looking yet again for stress relief and self-assertion in violent computer games. Our study leads us to surmise that a prolonged residence in the facility would have been good for him.

6.4.5 *(Sports) Clubs*

According to the European Commission (2011), participation in sports is a policy goal in many countries, "because sport is regarded as an important vehicle for generating all kinds of social, psychological, health and academic effects" (Pot, Verbeek, van der Zwan, & van Hilvoorde, 2016, p. 319). A lot of research has been conducted on the socio-economic differences and their effect on participation in sports activities (for example, see overview in Pot et al., 2016; see as well Dagkas &

Quarmby, 2012; Devís-Devís, Beltrán-Carrillo, & Peiró-Velert, 2013; Kraaykamp, Oldenkamp, & Breedveld, 2013). Most research shows that there are "vast differences in sport participation rates between children of lower and higher social classes" (Pot et al., 2016, p. 321) in general. Although sporting club membership is more common in higher SES groups, Pot et al. show "that if youngsters with a lower SES participate in organised sports, then the socialisation process is similar to that of youngsters with a higher SES" (Pot et al., 2016, p. 333). They conclude that parents are the key to participation in sports: "If they are able to provide a context in which sporting capital can be transmitted, chances are higher that children will (continue to) participate in sports, irrelevant of the SES of the parents. Nevertheless, differences in socio-economic contexts are very relevant when studying differences in participation rates between youngsters from lower and higher SES families" (Pot et al., 2016, p. 333). This remarkable result also correlates with the findings of the Institut für Sozialforschung und Gesellschaftspolitik (IGS) from 2011 (see Engels & Thielebein, 2011) about the relation of social class and participation in culture, education and leisure opportunities for children and adolescents, which were published in the Wealth Report of the Ministry of Work and Social Affairs of the Federal Republic of Germany. In relation to the results of the World Vision study 2010, it says: "the social background seems to be an essential factor, which is influencing the membership in a sports club. The class-specific analysis shows that only a third of the children of the lower class are active in a sports club, while it's 81% in the upper class. The authors of the World Vision Study explain that it is of high importance, with regard to drop-off in membership numbers, to make the access to these clubs as easy as possible for children of the lower class" (Engels & Thielebein, 2011, p. 11). In the case of Austria, Einböck, Proyer, and Fenninger (2015) clearly show differences between young people threatened by poverty and other children or adolescents doing activities in leisure time, including sports or being a member in a sports club. Children who are not poor or threatened by poverty do, therefore, participate more frequently in sports.

From our panel, Helmut Pfortner was the only adolescent, who practised sport intensively and was member of a sports club. His family was in better socio-economic state from the third wave of the survey onwards. Benedikt Holzner and Alfons Weiss did sports as well—Alfons was, in fact, in a sports club when he was younger—but to a lesser extent. The vast majority of the panel was scarcely interested, or not at all, in sports. Two girls, Amelie Aufbauer and Simone Stab, were active in a sports club at the beginning, but, in case of Simone Stab, she herself abandoned this activity because of a lack of time, and in the case of Amelie Aufbauer, she gave up her sports activities for lack of money. One could clearly see the relation between the socio-economic resources of their families and their activity as a club member. Amelie's and Simone's families accessed only a few socio-economic resources during the survey.

The structure of the family has been identified as another essential factor. Accordingly, for children of single parents it was less common to be active in a sports club than other children—not least, because their parent was not able to support their child, for example by driving them to the sports club or picking them up after sports events or training, because of their day-to-day duties. Because of their burdened lives, the parents themselves weren't at all, or, at best, just occasionally, active in clubs or similar facilities and hadn't been able to direct their children in this direction.

6.4.6 *Politics and Society*

The political and societal context became more relevant in the socialisation of the adolescents compared to their early and mid-childhood, but not to the same extent as was the case with aspects of their lives described above. This became apparent in the attitude of many families towards neighbours with a migration background. Some families thought that the families with a migration background, especially the families with Turkish-Muslim origins, who lived in their areas, could be a threat to their children's socialisation. This was the case for the Grubert family and the Holzner family (in the first wave of the survey), the Aufbauer family (in the second wave), the Fein family (first wave) and the Tannhaus family (who withdrew after the second wave of the survey). They feared that their children would copy bad behaviour from the neighbourhood children with a Turkish background. For this reason,[6] the parents of Manfred Oblinger did not allow him to have any contact with neighbouring children from a Turkish background at first. For some time, Manfred was convinced, despite his high-level intellect, that people with a migration background would take resources (welfare, jobs) away from families like his. He was the only adolescent interested in political topics from an early age. He has been enthusiastic about the now-deceased, populist right-wing politician, Jörg Haider. Manfred had the fantasy that Haider would close the borders for people with a migration background. The boy was strongly affected by Jörg Haider's sudden death in a car accident in the fall of 2008. He himself had planned to become a "Bundesheerlermann" [soldier of the Austrian Armed Forces, the authors] (second and fourth panel wave) to "be able to ensure order" in that role. Manfred was later very happy over Barack Obama's victory in the United States' elections, whom he saw in the position of an underdog as a black politician nevertheless displaying considerable success. During this period, Manfred fantasised of playing a similarly powerful role in his home country one day, as with Obama's presidency for the United States. Manfred had a Muslim friend for a period of time, during the fifth wave of the survey; as a result Manfred's mother builds a friendship with the boy's mother as well. During this period, so his mother, he had shown interest in Islam and he even sympathised with the "Islamic state" military for some time (fifth panel wave).

While most of the families had not shown any interest in political topics throughout the first five survey waves, apart from topics that had an immediate impact on their everyday lives, this changed in a sustained manner with the refugee crisis of 2015 and 2016, when they were confronted with the many refugees arriving in Austria. Refugees became a major topic in almost all families during the first period of the refugee crisis, and especially during the sixth wave of the survey. In order to better understand this issue, in the sixth wave of the survey we asked all families, parents and children, directly about their experiences with refugees, their attitudes and, in relation to that, the role of the media.

It stood out that those families socio-economically and/or socio-emotionally strained saw the influx of refugees as threat and competition. On the one hand, they perceived the immediate proximity of their apartments to refugee accommodation as problematic. On the other hand, many parents perceived a feeling of competition, especially because of the financial and non-cash benefits, which the refugees received from the state and which they viewed as unjust. Many families had developed a fear for their livelihoods and viewed the payments to refugees as unjustified, because, in their eyes, the latter had never to contribute anything. The families also objected that refugees "had been given so much food" that they "would just throw it away", while they themselves had to "count the money" to make ends meet. Some parents mentioned critically that some refugees would "carelessly" stroll through their residential areas and leave much garbage behind. Some families with daughters and some girls related how they feared the many young, male Muslim refugees. They told of unpleasant and negative encounters, where they felt being gazed at and harassed. Fear was also generated through the massive media coverage of the events on New Year's Eve 2015–2016 in Cologne or through the social networks, where horror stories about refugees' behaviour purported to be facts. Friends and acquaintances also contributed negative experiences with refugees.

The adolescents learned about the refugee crisis through the intensive coverage in the media, especially through social media. Some of them were even annoyed by the constant flow of refugee-related information and tried to avoid it as far as possible. Others used YouTube and some bloggers on the topic to look for orientation and guidance. In general, adolescents as well as their parents regarded media coverage on this issue as suppressing or embellishing facts, and, therefore, as not credible. As they perceived the situation, public opinion condemned critical views on refugees as "racist" or "Nazi".

In addition to the media, the adolescents were confronted with the refugee issue through heated arguments in their families, and also as a daily topic at school. Some adolescents felt emotionally assailed, because of certain arguments they had with their teachers, who tried to explain the situation of refugees, in order to reach some kind of understanding with their pupils. Some children recounted how their schools had invited refugees to tell about their own experiences and their reasons for leaving their home country. This directly opposed the opinion in their families, who spoke mostly critically and negatively of refugees.

In a few families, mainly the families Dornbacher and Pfortner, we did not register resentments against people with a migration background, either among the parents or their children. These families expressed understanding towards the situation of these refugees who were driven out of their countries. Gudrun Dornbacher even actively got involved in the refugee relief.

6.5 Conclusion

This chapter discusses the core aspects of our longitudinal study over nearly twelve years. Our goal was to demonstrate how the dynamic development of the children and their media repertoires, on the one hand, and the role of different contexts of socialisation, such as parents, siblings, relatives and friends of the family, on the other hand, contributed to the children's socialisation. We could show how parents and children acted at different phases of their lives and which media services and media content they used, in order to make sense of everyday life. It became clear what the different ways looked like by which our subjects incorporated media, "established" as well as "new" ones. In this context, we identified the children's patterns of media usage and illustrated them by characteristic examples. These patterns underline how micro-structural factors, like age and gender, the specific developmental tasks and also their specific *self-will*, had an influence on the children's media usage. Media became particularly relevant for the children's lives if there were conflicts within the family.

Beyond that we shed light on the contexts of peers, friends and romantic partners, of kindergartens, schools and apprenticeships, as well as of assisted living communities and apprenticeship hostels. We discussed also how the young people participated in (sports)clubs—if they did at all—and what relevance sports had over the twelve years of the research. It became clear that only a few children did any sports at all. We discussed the role of politics and society by focusing on the question as to how our subjects—both parents and children—dealt with neighbours from a migration background and with the refugee crisis between 2015 and 2016. Most of them were scared of these people or afraid that they would get more support from the federal government of Austria—social facilities and social services—than they themselves.

In this chapter, we have shown how different contexts become relevant in the process of socialisation. In the next chapter, we will focus on the direct interplay of two of these contexts, family and media. We will discuss this more deeply by looking into parents' mediation practices and how they can be interpreted against the background of the parents' and children's *options for action*, *outlines for action* and *competences for action*.

Notes

1. The original data is in German, all direct quotes that are used in this chapter were translated into English by the authors. In order to make the text more reader-friendly, we did not include such a reference for the individual quotes.
2. See Gebel, Schubert, Grimmeisen, and Wagner (2016). The authors also registered similar outcomes in the case of ten- to twelve-year-old YouTube users.

3. In a new survey, Festl and Gniewosz (2017) analysed the role of parental strategies of media education with reference to new and digital media services and their importance for the family climate. They distinguished the relevance of what the parents' individually thought they could do. Festl and Gniewosz allude to the formal education of mothers and fathers: "The results confirmed that mothers and fathers with higher ICT parenting competence more often co-used the internet with their child, which was found to be a resource of positive family climate. With regard to the families' education background, we found the parents' co-use of ICTs was a signification mediator for the middle- and lower-educated families, precisely for lower-educated fathers" (Festl & Gniewosz, 2017, p. 2).
4. Mario Hirtner, for example, allowed his little brother to play computer games which are actually forbidden to him. As a reward, he then demanded an Ice Tea from his brother. The siblings often met in Mario's room to watch funny YouTube videos. The little brother was one of a just a few social contacts beyond the internet.
5. See Kutscher's research (2014). She came up with similar results.
6. Gniewosz and Noack (2015, p. 1787) state that "during the past several decades, societies increasingly have become ethnically diverse. In this respect, developing attitudes toward immigrants or members of other social groups can be regarded as an important developmental task". Following this, they investigated negative aspects of intergroup attitudes, namely intolerant attitudes towards immigrants in Germany and focused on "the parent–adolescent transmission of attitudes towards immigrants between young people age 12 and 16". They summarise that "adolescents' attitudes were predicted by maternal and paternal self-reported attitudes".

References

Chaudron, S., Beutel, M. E., Černikova, M., Donoso Navarette, V., Dreier, M., Fletcher-Watson, B., ..., Wölfling K. (2015). *Young children (0–8) and digital technology: A qualitative exploratory study across seven countries. The EU Kids Online Network & Joint Research Centre*. London, UK and City of Luxembourg, Luxembourg: LSE and Publications Office of the European Union. Retrieved from http://publications.jrc.ec.europa.eu/repository/handle/JRC93239.

Common Sense Media. (2015). *Census media use by tweens and teens*. San Francisco, CA: Common Sense Media. Retrieved from https://www.commonsensemedia.org/research/the-common-sense-census-media-use-by-tweens-and-teens.

Common Sense Media. (2017). *Census media use by kids age zero to eight 2017.* San Francisco, CA: Common Sense Media. Retrieved from https://www.commonsensemedia.org/research/the-common-sense-census-media-use-by-kids-age-zero-to-eight-2017.

Couldry, N., & Hepp, A. (2017). *The mediated construction of reality.* Cambridge, UK: Polity Press.

d'Haenens, L. (2001). Old and new media: Access and ownership in the home. In S. Livingstone & M. Bovill (Eds.), *Children and their changing media environment: A European comparative study* (pp. 53–84). Mahwah, NJ: Lawrence Erlbaum Associates.

Dagkas, S., & Quarmby, T. (2012). Young people's embodiment of physical activity: The role of the 'pedagogized' family. *Sociology of Sport Journal, 29*(2), 210–226.

Devís-Devís, J., Beltrán-Carrillo, V. J., & Peiró-Velert, C. (2013). Exploring socio-ecological factors influencing active and inactive Spanish students in years 12 and 13. *Sport, Education and Society, 20*(3), 361–380.

Education Group. (2016). *5. Oö. Kinder-Medien-Studie 2016. Das Medienverhalten der 3- bis 10-Jährigen* [Children and media in Upper Austria]. Linz, Austria: Education Group.

Einböck, M., Proyer, M., & Fenninger, E. (2015). Lebensbedingungen und Sichtweisen von Kindern und Jugendlichen in und über Armut. Ergebnisse aus einer Erhebung zu den Lebenswelten und Netzwerken armutsbetroffener, armutsgefährdeter und nicht-armutsgefährdeter Kinder und Jugendlicher in zwei österreichischen Regionen [Living conditions and perspectives of children and adolescents in poverty, at risk to poverty and not at risk to poverty in two regions of Austria]. *Projektberichte der Volkshilfe Österreich.* Wien, Austria: Volkshilfe. Retrieved from https://www.volkshilfe.at/cms/download.php?downloadId=348&languageId=1.

Engelhardt, J. A. (2012). The developmental implications of parentification: Effects on childhood attachment. *Graduate Student Journal of Psychology, 14,* 45–52.

Engels, D., & Thielebein, C. (2011). *Zusammenhang von sozialer Schicht und Teilnahme an Kultur-, Bildungs- und Freizeitangeboten für Kinder und Jugendliche* [Coherences between social class and the participation in cultural, educational and recreational opportunities]. Köln, Germany: IGS Institut für Sozialforschung und Gesellschaftspolitik.

Erikson, E. H. (1950). *Childhood and society.* New York, NY: W. W. Norton.

European Commission. (2011). *Developing the European dimension in sport.* Brussels, Belgium: European Commission. Retrieved from http://eur-lex.europa.eu/LexUriServ/LexUriServ.do?uri=COM:2011:0012:FIN:en:PDF.

Feierabend, S., & Scolari, J. (2018). Was Kinder sehen. Eine Analyse der Fernsehnutzung Drei- bis 13-Jähriger 2017 [What children are watching on TV: An analysis of the TV usage of three- to 13-years-olds in 2017]. *Media Perspektiven, 48*(4), 163–175.

Feinberg, M. E., Sakuma, K.-L., Hostetler, M., & McHale, S. (2013). Enhancing sibling relationships to prevent adolescent problem behaviors: Theory, design and feasibility of siblings are special. *Evaluation and Program Planning, 36*(1), 97–106.

Festl, R., & Gniewosz, G. (2017, April 25–29). *The role of mothers' and fathers' ICT parenting for family climate*. Speech at the Annual Conference of the International Communication Association (ICA) in San Diego, CA.

Gebel, C., Schubert, G., Grimmeisen, L., & Wagner, U. (2016). "… dieser YouTuber, der hat ganz krasse Maps bei Minecraft gefunden." YouTube-Stars, Games und Kosten aus Sicht von 10- bis 12-Jährigen. Ausgewählte Ergebnisse der Monitoringstudie "Monitoring Aufwachsen zwischen Selbstbestimmung und Schutzbedarf" ["…this YouTube guy who found rad maps in Minecraft". YouTube stars, games and costs as perceived by ten- to twelve-year olds. Selected results of the monitoring-study. "Monitoring growing between self-determination and need for safety"]. *ACT ON! Short Report Nr. 3*. München, Germany: JFF. Retrieved from http://www.jff.de/jff/aktivitaeten/von-a-z/projekt/proj_titel/act-on-monitoring.

Gniewosz, B., & Noack, P. (2015). Parental influences on adolescents' negative attitudes toward immigrants. *Journal of Youth and Adolescence, 44*(9), 1787–1802.

Grundmann, M. (2000). Kindheit, Identitätsentwicklung und Generativität [Childhood, development of identity, and generativity]. In A. Lange & W. Lauterbach (Eds.), *Kinder in Familie und Gesellschaft zu Beginn des 21sten Jahrhunderts* [Children in family and society at the beginning of the 21st Century] (pp. 87–104). Stuttgart, Germany: Lucius & Lucius.

Grüninger, C., & Lindemann, F. (2000). *Vorschulkinder und Medien. Eine Untersuchung zum Medienkonsum von drei- bis sechsjährigen Kindern unter besonderer Berücksichtigung des Fernsehens* [Pre-school children and media: A study concerning media consumption among three- to six-years old children with a special focus on TV consumption]. Opladen, Germany: Leske und Budrich.

Harter, S. (2012). *The construction of the self: Developmental and sociocultural foundations* (2nd ed.). New York, NY: Guilford Press.

Havighurst, R. J. (1972). *Development tasks and education*. New York, NY: Longmans Green.

Koch, W., & Frees, B. (2017). ARD/ZDF-Onlinestudie 2017: Neun von zehn Deutschen online [ARD/ZDF-Online study 2017: Nine out of ten Germans are online]. *Media Perspektiven, 47*(9), 434–446.

Kraaykamp, G., Oldenkamp, M., & Breedveld, K. (2013). Starting a sport in the Netherlands: A life-course analysis of the effects of individual, parental and partner characteristics. *International Review for the Sociology of Sport, 48*(29), 153–170.

Krappmann, L. (1991). Sozialisation in der Gruppe der Gleichaltrigen [Socialisation among peers]. In K. Hurrelmann & D. Ulrich (Eds.), *Neues Handbuch der Sozialisationsforschung* [New handbook on socialisation research] (pp. 355–375). Weinheim, Germany and Basel, Switzerland: Beltz.

Kutscher, N. (2014). Soziale Ungleichheit [Social inequality]. In A. Tillmann, S. Fleischer, & K.-U. Hugger (Eds.), *Handbuch Kinder und Medien* [Handbook children and media] (pp. 101–112). Wiesbaden, Germany: VS Verlag für Sozialwissenschaften.

Larson, R. (2006). Positive youth development, willful adolescents, and mentoring. *Journal of Community Psychology, 34*(6), 677–689.

Lauricella, A. R., Cingel, D. P., Blackwell, C., Wartella, E., & Conway, A. (2014). The mobile generation: Youth and adolescent ownership and use of new media. *Communication Research Reports, 31*(4), 357–364.

Li, S., Hietajärvi, L., Palonen, T., Salmela-Aro, K., & Hakkarainen, K. (2017). Adolescents' social networks: Exploring different patterns of socio-digital participation. *Scandinavian Journal of Educational Research, 61*(3), 255–274.

Lillehammer, G. (2010). Introduction to socialisation: Recent research on childhood and children in the past. *AmS-Skrifter, 23,* 9–19.

May, V., & Lahad, K. (2018). The involved observer: A simmelian analysis of the boundary work of aunthood. *Sociology.* First published January 2018. https://doi.org/10.1177/0038038517746051.

Morgan, E. M. (2012). Contemporary issues in sexual orientation and identity development. *Emerging Adulthood, 1*(1), 52–66.

MPFS (Medienpädagogischer Forschungsverbund Südwest). (2014). *mini-KIM-Studie 2014. Kleinkinder und Medien* [miniKIM-Study 2014: Toddlers and the media]. Stuttgart, Germany: MPFS. Retrieved from https://www.mpfs.de/studien/minikim-studie/2014/.

MPFS (Medienpädagogischer Forschungsverbund Südwest). (2016). *KIM-Studie 2016. Kindheit, Internet, Medien. Basisstudie zum Medienumgang 6- bis 13-Jähriger in Deutschland* [KIM-Study 2016: Childhood, internet, media]. Stuttgart, Germany: MPFS. Retrieved from https://www.mpfs.de/fileadmin/files/Studien/KIM/2016/KIM_2016_Web-PDF.pdf.

MPFS (Medienpädagogischer Forschungsverbund Südwest). (2017). *JIM 2017. Jugend, Information, (Multi-)Media. Basisstudie zum Medienumgang 12- bis 19-Jähriger in Deutschland* [JIM 2017: Adolescents, information, (multi-) media]. Stuttgart, Germany: MPFS. Retrieved from. https://www.mpfs.de/fileadmin/files/Studien/JIM/2017/JIM_2017.pdf.

Notten, M., & Kraaykamp, G. (2009). Parents and the media: A study of social differentiation in parental media socialization. *Poetics, 37,* 185–200.

Ofcom. (2017). *Children and parents: Media use and attitudes report*. London, UK: Ofcom. Retrieved from https://www.ofcom.org.uk/research-and-data/media-literacy-research/childrens/children-parents-2017.

Packer, M. J. (2017). *Child development: Understanding a cultural perspective.* London, UK, Los Angeles, CA, New Dehli, India, and Singapore: Sage.

Paus-Hasebrink, I., & Bichler, M. (2008). *Mediensozialisationsforschung. Theoretische Fundierung und Fallbeispiel sozial benachteiligte Kinder* [Media socialisation research—Theoretical foundation and a case study on socially disadvantaged children]. Assisted by C. Wijnen. Innsbruck, Austria: Studienverlag.

Paus-Hasebrink, I., Schmidt, J.-H., & Hasebrink, U. (2011). Zur Erforschung der Rolle des Social Web im Alltag von Heranwachsenden [Growing up with social web]. In J.-H. Schmidt, I. Paus-Hasebrink, & U. Hasebrink (Eds.), *Heranwachsen mit dem Social Web. Zur Rolle von Web 2.0-Angeboten im Alltag von Jugendlichen und jungen Erwachsenen* [Growing up with social web: On the role of web 2.0 services in the everyday lives of adolescents and young adults] (2nd ed., pp. 13–40). Berlin, Germany: Vistas.

Paus-Hasebrink, I., Wijnen, C., & Brüssel, T. (2011). Social Web im Alltag von Jugendlichen und jungen Erwachsenen: Soziale Kontexte und Handlungstypen [Social web in adolescent's and young adult's everyday life]. Assisted by U. Viieder. In J.-H- Schmidt, I. Paus-Hasebrink, & U. Hasebrink (Eds.). *Heranwachsen mit dem Social Web. Zur Rolle von Web 2.0-Angeboten im Alltag von Jugendlichen und jungen Erwachsenen* [Growing up with social web: On the role of Web 2.0 services in the everyday lives of adolescents and young adults] (2nd ed., pp. 121–206). Berlin, Germany: Vistas.

Pot, N., Verbeek, J., van der Zwan, J., & van Hilvoorde, I. (2016). Socialisation into organised sports of young adolescents with a lower socio-economic status. *Sport, Education and Society, 21*(3), 319–338.

Reitz, A. K., Zimmermann, J., Hutemann, R., Sprecht, J., & Neyer, F. N. (2014). How peers make a difference: The role of peer groups and peer relationships in personality development. *European Journal of Personality, 28*(3), 279–288.

Rideout, V. J., & Hamel, E. (2006). *The media family: Electronic media in the lives of infants, toddlers, preschoolers and their parents*. Menlo Park, CA: The Henry J. Kaiser Family Foundation. Retrieved from https://kaiserfamilyfoundation.files.wordpress.com/2013/01/7500.pdf.

Rideout, V. J., Vandewater, E. A., & Wartella, E. A. (2003). *Zero to six: Electronic media in the lives of infants, toddlers, preschoolers and their parents*. A Kaiser Family Foundation Report. Menlo Park, CA: The Henry J. Kaiser Family Foundation. Retrieved from https://kaiserfamilyfoundation.files.wordpress.com/2013/01/zero-to-six-electronic-media-in-the-lives-of-infants-toddlers-and-preschoolers-pdf.pdf.

Roberts, D. F., & Foehr, U. G. (2004). *Kids and media in America*. Cambridge, UK: Cambridge University Press.

Rogers Hollifield, C., & Jewsbury Conger, K. (2014). The role of siblings and psychological needs in predicting life satisfaction during emerging adulthood. *Emerging Adulthood, 3*(3), 143–153.

Schmidt, C. (2014). *Die Bedeutung von Geschwistern für die soziale und kognitive Entwicklung von Kindern und Jugendlichen – Theorien und Forschungsbefunde* [The importance of siblings for the social and cognitive development of children and adolescents—Theories and outcomes]. München, Germany: ifp Staatsinstitut für Frühpädagogik. Retrieved from http://www.familienhandbuch.de/familie-leben/familienformen/geschwister/diebedeutungvongeschwisternfuerdiesozialeundkogn.php.

Tarrant, M., MacKenzie, L., & Hewitt, L. A. (2006). Friendship group identification, multidimensional self-concept, and experience of developmental tasks in adolescence. *Journal of Adolescence, 29*(4), 627–640.

Woodard, E. H., & Gridina, N. (2000). *Media in the home: The fifth annual survey of parents and children*. Washington, DC and Philadelphia, PA: The Annenberg Public Policy Center of the University of Pennsylvania. Retrieved from https://www.annenbergpublicpolicycenter.org/wp-content/uploads/survey72.pdf.

Youniss, J. (1980). *Parents and peers in social development: A Sullivan-Piaget perspective*. Chicago, IL: University of Chicago Press.

Open Access This chapter is licensed under the terms of the Creative Commons Attribution 4.0 International License (http://creativecommons.org/licenses/by/4.0/), which permits use, sharing, adaptation, distribution and reproduction in any medium or format, as long as you give appropriate credit to the original author(s) and the source, provide a link to the Creative Commons licence and indicate if changes were made.

The images or other third party material in this chapter are included in the chapter's Creative Commons licence, unless indicated otherwise in a credit line to the material. If material is not included in the chapter's Creative Commons licence and your intended use is not permitted by statutory regulation or exceeds the permitted use, you will need to obtain permission directly from the copyright holder.

CHAPTER 7

The Interplay Between Family and Media as Socialisation Contexts: Parents' Mediation Practices

7.1 Introduction

In the previous chapter, we gave an overview over relevant social contexts in the socialisation of the young people in our study. Here, we will display the context of the parents and their mediation practices against the background of their specific everyday lives. We will present their ways of parenting and their mediation of media literacy on the basis of the focused analysis (see Chapters 4 and 6; see Paus-Hasebrink, 2018a), in which we reflected on the data across all the families in our panel with respect to the three analytical concepts *option for action*, *outlines for action*, and *competences for action* (see Chapter 3; see Paus-Hasebrink, 2018b) in a condensed form. A more detailed in-depth look at these aspects will be provided in Chapter 8 of this book.

In order to show what social disadvantage in the field of mediation means, we will firstly lay out relevant aspects of social disadvantage within a mediatised landscape and the general effects of such disadvantage in everyday life (see Chapter 2). As the present chapter focuses on parents' mediation practices and how they changed over time, we secondly discuss them from two angles: one the one hand, with respect to both the children's age and their media usage and, on the other hand, by considering the changing conditions in the families' conduct of everyday life. We decided to use the term "mediation practices", as they are part of parents' overall parenting practices. Against this background, we discuss the different mediation practices we observed in the study. Finally, we will discuss and summarise our insights and outcomes relating to parents' mediation practices.

7.2 On the Role of Mediation Practices Amid Social Inequality

The unequal distribution of resources and opportunities affects family life (Jokinen & Kuronen, 2011, p. 45; see Toczydlowska & Bruckauf, 2017), as socially disadvantaged families have to face and particular challenges in their everyday lives, such as unemployment, often interlinked with health problems, and challenging socio-emotional problems (Paus-Hasebrink & Kulterer, 2014; see Chapter 2). Against the background of a rapidly changing media landscape, which can be characterised by a meta-process known as "mediatization" (Krotz & Hepp, 2013; Lunt & Livingstone, 2015), these families—like families in general—are confronted with an enormous amount of media. However, poor or socially disadvantaged youngsters (see also Laubstein, Holz, & Seddig, 2016, p. 67) display different patterns of media usage from children in better-situated families and thus confront their families with a particularly challenging task in supporting them in acquiring media competences. With the internet in particular, we have to keep in mind the relevance of a "second-level digital divide" (Hargittai, 2002), "participation divide" (Hargittai & Walejko, 2008) or "third digital divide" (see also Helsper, 2012; Ragnedda, 2017). Hence, we may view these parents and their children as experiencing a lack of options for participating in contemporary mediatised society in an appropriate and beneficial way.

The large amount of research on parental mediation has produced mediation scales, which differentiate three relevant mediation strategies. Following Valkenburg, Piotrowski, Hermanns, and de Leeuw (2013), we can distinguish between parents by the mediation strategy they prefer: The first strategy is "restrictive mediation". Parents who use this strategy, according to Valkenburg et al. (2013, p. 445), "restrict the time that their children spend with media", the second strategy is "active mediation"; this includes parents explaining media content to their children and conveying their opinions about certain media content. And the third strategy is called "co-viewing or co-use" which "refers to the extent with which parents use media together with their children, without actively engaging in discussion"

(Valkenburg et al., 2013, p. 445). Research that is focused more deeply on transactional aspects such as socio-economic and social-cultural aspects shows an interrelation between the way parents bring up their children, the mediation strategies they apply and, their socio-economic and social-cultural circumstances when managing their everyday lives. Further literature points out that more highly educated parents try to support their children by practices of "active mediation", for example, by focusing on conversation. Less educated parents apply more restrictive mediation (for example, Rothbaum, Martland, & Beswick Jannsen, 2008; Livingstone, Mascheroni, Dreier, Chaudron, & Lagae, 2015; Paus-Hasebrink, Bauwens, Dürager, & Ponte, 2013; Vekiri, 2010). These general findings seem to apply to the usage of the internet as well. As the research of the EU Kids Online network shows, special attention must be paid to socially disadvantaged children, because they are more vulnerable than other children to harm from online media. Furthermore, their parents use more restrictive measures to control their children's internet use instead of trying to actively support and facilitate a safe and satisfying way of dealing with media (Paus-Hasebrink, Ponte, Dürager, & Bauwens, 2012, p. 267).

Given our focus on how the parents approach the mediation of media literacy/competence, we decided to use the term mediation practices, as they are part of parents' overall parenting strategies. Against this background, we discuss the different mediation practices we observed. Finally, we will discuss and summarise our insights and outcomes relating to parents' mediation practices. Our focus is on parents' mediation practices and how they changed over time, on the one hand, with respect to both the children's age and their media usage and, on the other hand, due to the changing conditions in the families' everyday lives.

7.3   Selected Findings from the Longitudinal Study: From Kindergarten to Youth

At the beginning of the longitudinal study, the children were in kindergartens and television was their main media activity, whereas (picture) books, reading to children and listening to radio plays were quite rare. At this time, the parents had some general ideas about mediation practices; most of them remarked that children should not see violent content, but over time it became obvious that this opinion was clearly influenced by social desirability. It was very rare for parents to pick up media-related topics and talk to their children about them. Only when the children themselves wanted to talk about something on television, parents would respond—to the best of their knowledge. All in all, we observed a lack in parents' media competences to support their children. Only few of them were able to deal with media topics and to communicate with their children, let alone to give them background information about media contexts.

When children went to school, we observed a striking change: all the parents, without exception, upgraded their media equipment. Regardless of their financial resources, they bought computers, because they did not want their children disadvantaged. And in addition, they were afraid to lose teachers' and other parents' respect, if their children were badly equipped.

Apart from providing the equipment, most parents did not give much thought to actually teaching their children how to use the various devices in a responsible way. Mr. Boll said in 2005 that: "It [comment: talking about how to use media (devices)] is not important to me, it's too early for him anyway".[1] He, like many other parents, claimed that his children would know what was good for them and how long and how they could use media anyway, without being able to indicate where that knowledge would stem from. Teaching media competence, both in the technical as well as the social sense, was not something that many parents felt responsible for. Almost all parents of the panel assigned this task to teachers, because of either their own lack of experience and competence in using "new" media or their unwillingness to make an effort and engage with the issue, as Mr. Boll pointed out: "That's [comment: school] where they can learn more about media than you can teach them, because you're lacking the know-how".

This phenomenon held good throughout the study. As the years passed, and the children grew older, the families were still well equipped with media devices; in the third and especially the fourth wave of the survey, most households owned a desktop computer with access to the internet (see also Livingstone et al., 2015, p. 14). As the parents displayed very little knowledge of internet use and any concomitant skills, they evinced an impalpable anxiety about the risks and dangers on the internet, especially concerning the high costs involved and any virus infections. As they grew older, the children found new devices and new services, such as smartphones and, above all, the social media, increasingly important in their media repertoires. This brought new challenges in media usage and media competence with it, but the development was often only observed at a distance, with hardly any mediation on the part of the parents.

Many parents had a negative attitude towards electronic media and preferred not to look more closely into the content their children used. In some families, issues related to privacy protection were mentioned, but most of the parents did not have enough knowledge and competency to give their children advice and to mediate their internet usage.[2] Instead some of them revealed themselves as careless in using social media; for instance, putting photos of their children on social network sites like Facebook, and thus embarrassing their children. At the same time, some parents recognised that nowadays the competent use of computers and the internet has become a key qualification for the future career of their children. In these cases, the parents once again relied largely on schools to teach media literacy, especially when it came to the internet (see as well Paus-Hasebrink et al., 2012, p. 267; 2013, pp. 122–125). Beyond that, most parents adopted the position that their children were now grown up and, therefore, they could feel even less responsible than in previous years.

7.4 Practices of Parental Mediation

The parents mostly showed little competence when it came to issues of mediation, often due to their own deficient *options for action*, and their deprived social situation due to unemployment and so on, which often left them preoccupied with a lot of problems, while coping on multiple levels of everyday life with challenges, such as a lack of time for their children, a lack of leisure time for themselves, worries about the future and so on. These factors closely interacted with parents' *outlines for action*. They were often severely limited in building and organising *outlines for action* (such as dealing with media offerings and motives to use; dealing with conflicts and proximity; interacting within family, neighbourhood, peer-groups, friendships, kindergarten or class; preferences, goals, plans and motives for action in general, plans for their future in special), as they were not often able to define goals for coping with problems in everyday life. Many of them had difficulties in forming their own plans and fulfilling their wishes and desires, both as couples and as parents, and as families as well. All of our families had an ideal image of themselves and of family in general—and there was scarcely anyone for whom this did not include caring for their children per se. But the interplay between deficits in *options for action* and *outlines for actions* often induced developing or blocking adequate *competences for action* to manage the challenges of everyday life—all in all, they did not have the needed resources for supporting their children as they grew up, including their media usage in general, and even less with their internet usage. Against this background, one has to bear in mind that the parents were less educated and had little or almost no knowledge about all aspects of using the internet, whereas the technical operation of so-called "old media", such as television, was no great problem for them. Their awareness of media contents and their backgrounds meant they were not competent to support their children.

In the following, we will look deeper into the specific mediation practices identified in the families over the study's entire duration (see Chapters 5 and 8).[3]

We identified five dominant mediation practices: *laissez-faire, unmethodical restriction, arbitrary control and exploitation of dominance, amicability* and *child-centred practices*. These practices closely interacted with the parents' specific palette of *options for action, outlines for action* and *competences for action*. These practices do not always occur exclusively and separately from each other, often we could identify a mixture of practices that were used depending on the situation (also because parents were often insecure about how to react in certain situations or because they had no coherent approach to parenting), with one practice that could be seen as dominant, however, or we could observe that the dominant practice in a family changed over time.

7.4.1   Laissez-faire[4]

The majority of parents espoused laissez-fair-practices, as they did not cope well with everyday challenges and accordingly showed either little or no interest in their children's media usage, or they were even prepared to declare that children had to learn that life is, to express it informal, not good but evil. In our interviews, some mothers did say that children had to learn that life is not uniformly benevolent, but that bad things can happen as well, something they could learn best by using media, something that for example Ms. Stab believed in the first waves of the study when she used media to show her children the "harsh reality" of the world (2007). Another example is Ms. Holzner, who, in 2007, watched reality shows together with her children for educational purposes, in a way as a "worst practice"—example of what happens when children don't behave: "What we watched, what we really watched was this show 'Teenagers out of control'. On RTL [comment: a German commercial television station], because I, that was something for them, because I told them: when you keep behaving like this at home, that's where you will end up. I'll kick you out, I'm telling you, I'm not interested in this anymore, if the police starts calling every other day, because I have to come pick you up, or because you are loitering or if one of you is hiding out somewhere, I don't care for that".

Some of the parents believed that there was no need for media education or communication about media in the family after their children went to school. The opinion was that they should, by then, be old enough to at least learn about life using media in a sort of trial and error approach.

Often, different media, mostly the television, were used to keep children occupied when the parents had other things to do, as was the case in the Boll family at the beginning of the study. Since the parents were working a lot on the farm, their children were left to use media entirely unsupervised claiming that "they pretty much know" (2005) what and how long they were allowed to use media, resulting in some of the children using the television excessively even though the parents claimed that the children would spend more time outside.

Many parents gave the impression that schools are seen as better places for learning media competence. This was often implied by referring to their own limited knowledge about the matter and also because, as some parents like Mr. and Mrs. Landinger saw it, especially at the beginning of the study, children spent more time in school with their teachers than at home with the parents, thus taking themselves out of the responsibility. Interestingly, towards the end of the study, many parents complained about the poor media education classes in school or did not sign their children up for special (free) programs offered by the schools.

Single-parent families and extended families were particularly prone to this practice, in particular those living in severely deprived socio-economic constellations, without any hope that things might improve, and, in this connection, also stressed by difficult socio-emotional situations and excessive demands almost overwhelming them (see also Nikken & Opree, 2018, pp. 1844 & 1855). These families had substantial problems in coping with everyday life challenges. Single mothers espousing these practices had extreme difficulties in *doing family*, partly because of their experience of being abandoned. When life situations changed, because a new partner came into the family, and problems occurred over a child from an earlier partnership, we noted this practice again. In the cases of extended families with more than five—in some cases even up to nine or ten children—parents could not manage all the everyday tasks, so that their stressful everyday context left them no resources to support their children's growing up.

As their children grew older, other families, who had previously displayed different attitudes, also started to indicate a more laissez-faire stance towards their children's media usage. They were convinced that their children were old enough to use media without any rules or mediation from their parents.

7.4.2 Unmethodical Restriction

The practice of restrictive parental mediation includes proscriptions and limitations, in order to control their children's—often extensive—media usage. However, parents did not apply these rules consistently, and they did not monitor compliance. On the contrary, parents sometimes undermined their own regulations, either by allowing media as reward or banning it as punishment. As with laissez-faire, we observed this practice in extended and in single mother families. When the children were young, parents wanted time for housework, business or just for themselves, so they frequently used the television as a baby-sitter—often without looking at the content.

Unconsidered use of media to keep their children occupied was frequent and extensive in these families, reflecting their individual contexts and their insufficient *options for actions*. It precluded building and performing *outlines for action* among parents showing problems in coming to terms with their lives. This practice was particularly prevalent when children were younger. The studies by Valkenburg et al. (2013) and Livingstone et al. (2015) display similar results. By mid-childhood, or in adolescence, this practice had become rarer, because parents believed their children would not need mediation anyway.

7.4.3 Arbitrary Control or Exploitation of Dominance

This heading describes practices ranging from arbitrarily controlling children to dominance with a certain degree of violence—on the level, for example, fathers who physically beat their children, or exerted psychological pressure. Such parents were trying to discipline their children, in order to treat their own, rather crude, problems (see examples of the Landinger family, the Rohringer and Weiss family in Chapter 8). This practice identified dysfunctional partnerships between parents as also affecting relationships with their children. Mr. Landinger used physical violence to end unwelcome discussions with his son Timo:

> *Interviewer*: Do you talk about this with your father, or?
> *Timo*: No, because if I keep bugging him, he becomes aggressive, and I don't like that.
> *Interviewer*: What does it look like when he becomes aggressive? What does he do then?
> *Timo*: He slaps me.
> *Interviewer*: You? How do you react?
> *Timo*: I'd like to hit him back, but he is my father, so I can't do that.
> [...]
> *Interviewer*: Is it a a dab or does he really heit you hard?
> *Timo*: He hits me really hard [...] That always brings me into an angry phase." (Interview in 2014)

In some cases, parents' massive dissatisfaction over their *options for action* and their *outlines for action* led them to overestimate their *competences for action*. This, in turn, provoked negative feelings projected onto their children. These parents' arbitrary practices of control or even dominance displayed their actual lack of parenting skills. For example, Timo Landinger's father used violent computer games, rated as only for adults, to calm his son down by offering them, among his mediation practices, as reward. Mr. Landinger justified his approach (2014) because they had hardly any free time and a lot of stress and when Timo entered puberty, Mr. Landinger talked about tensions that could best be resolved if Timo stayed in his room, playing video games or watching television. If the tensions became too much, he would exert violence and humiliation to reinforce his dominance in the household.

Timo was almost addicted to video games as an avenue for coping with his own aggressions caused by his father's violence.

Mrs. Rohringer is an example for a mother who exerts an extraordinary amount of control over her daughter's media use. She works at home and thus has almost total control about what the children do after school. At age 15, her daughter was not allowed to have her Facebook account to herself, her mother had access to it on her own phone and kept following her daughter's doings. If things happened that she did not approve of, she disconnected the wifi, she also controlled her daughter's WhatsApp messages, exerting dominance by stating that "she knows I am her boss" (2014).

7.4.4 Amicability

Some parents, especially single mothers, showed a high level of amicability where they used media together with their children. However, this was, above all, a strategy for spending time with their children, and mostly not for showing active engagement or any other mediation practices. This practice is quite similar to co-viewing or co-use (see Valkenburg et al., 2013). As children, and particularly daughters, grew older, these mothers valued media usage with their children. They practiced an amicability, blurring the lines between parent–child roles, as was especially the case in the Öllinger family. These mothers, like Ms. Öllinger, had massive problems coping with limited *options for action* (in Ms. Öllingers case her illness and the inability to leave the house much, leading to massive reliance on media as entertainment and connection to the outside world) and unfulfilled *outlines for action*, especially because of loneliness and the lack of a partner to share their worries and problems. So they compensated by explicitly using media together with their daughters or using media to keep a connection to their daughters outside of the house as well, while, at the same time, almost completely disregarding their children's wishes and interests, constraining them to a certain extent. In these families, mothers did not, in fact, apply mediation practices at all and merely talked about interesting content.

7.4.5 Child-Centred Mediation Practices

We rarely observed these practices in our panel. Child-centred mediation occurred in some cases of better-*doing family*. We observed this especially in families with upgraded *options for action* and, in connection with this, settled *outlines for action*, which led to more scope for adequate *competences for action* where parents did have the resources to focus on their children's interests and needs like the Dornbacher family (see Chapter 8). This practice was rather found in nuclear families with improving finances through new employment, better-salaried jobs or a double income. A similar result concerning income features in the study from Livingstone et al. (2015, p. 10). These families succeeded in creating more relaxed environments for all family members: a better socio-economic, and hence a better socio-emotional situation, gave parents the opportunity to cope better with everyday challenges. Furthermore, where mothers married a new partner, who was better off and able to be a good and caring stepfather, improved circumstances meant *doing family* worked well.

7.5 Conclusion

Given the correlation between parents' socio-structural background and their specific ways of interacting, our long-term study showed that parents' resources shaped their competence in supporting their children (see Paus-Hasebrink et al., 2013). Based on the three central analytical concepts, *options for action, outlines for action* and *competences for action*, parents' and children's practices, including parents' mediation practices, become understandable and comprehensible as relating to the links between subjective perception, orientations driving action and everyday life practices, all against the backdrop of socio-structural conditions.

With respect to specific forms of interaction between the three analytic concepts, *options for action, outlines for actions* and *competences for action* (see Chapter 3), parents' resources dictated how they either succeeded or failed in their everyday lives. With parents' specific *options for action* in mind, the longitudinal study emphasises the importance of interaction between family members (see Goldberg, Grusec, & Jenkins, 1999), especially in parent–child relationships, where the degree of proximity, trust and reciprocity parents were able to build up with their children had relevant consequences for their parenting ability and for family communication. We observed that the parents' mediation practices via the specific ways they interacted with and monitored their children were highly relevant to the children's socialisation (Paus-Hasebrink, 2017; see as well Schofield Clark, 2013; Smetana, Robinson, & Rote, 2015). Our qualitative and long-term perspective allowed insights into the interplay of the dynamics between the children's age, the parents' individual conduct of everyday life, the context of their socio-economic and socio-emotional situation, as well as their coping practices with everyday challenges in *doing family*. Studies (for example, Van den Bulck, Custers, & Nelissen, 2016) show that the parent–child relationship is bidirectional and that children themselves also determine what pedagogical practices their parents will use, however inconsistently they may apply them (see Chapter 8).

Notes

1. The original data is in German, all direct quotes that are used in this chapter were translated into English by the authors. In order to make the text more reader-friendly we did not include such a reference for the individual quotes.
2. Festl and Gniewosz described "that the parents' co-use of ICTs was a significant mediator for the middle- and lower-educated families, precisely for lower-educated fathers" (2017, p. 2).
3. Knop, Hefner, Schmitt, and Vorderer (2015) identified similar mediation practices in their research on children's and adolescents' use of mobile phones and internet.
4. Livingstone et al. (2015, p. 10) use the term "laissez faire", in order to describe a special "mediation strategy", which can be characterised as "warm and supportive but non-demanding".

References

Festl, R., & Gniewosz, G. (2017, April 25–29). *The role of mothers' and fathers' ICT parenting for family climate*. Speech at the Annual Conference of the International Communication Association (ICA) in San Diego, CA.

Goldberg, S., Grusec, J. E., & Jenkins, J. M. (1999). Confidence in protection: Arguments for a narrow definition of attachment. *Journal of Family Psychology, 13*(4), 475–483.

Hargittai, E. (2002). Second-level digital divide: Differences in people's online skills. *First Monday, 7*(4). Retrieved from http://firstmonday.org/article/view/942/864.

Hargittai, E., & Walejko, G. (2008). The participation divide: Content creation and sharing in the digital age. *Information, Community and Society, 11*(2), 239–256.

Helsper, E. (2012). Which children are fully online? In S. Livingstone, L. Haddon, & A. Görzig (Eds.), *Children, risk and safety on the internet: Kids online in comparative perspective* (pp. 45–57). Bristol, UK: The Policy Press.

Jokinen, K., & Kuronen, M. (2011). Research on families and family policies in Europe: Major trends. In U. Uhlendorff, M. Rupp, & M. Euteneuer (Eds.), *Wellbeing of families in future Europe: Challenges for research and policy* (pp. 13–118). Dortmund, Germany: Familyplatform. Retrieved from https://eldorado.tu-dortmund.de/bitstream/2003/28914/1/WellbeingOfFamiliesInEurope.pdf.

Knop, K., Hefner, D., Schmitt, S., & Vorderer, P. (2015). *Mediatisierung mobil. Handy- und Internetnutzung von Kindern und Jugendlichen* [Mediatization mobile: Mobile phone and internet usage of children and adolescents]. Leipzig, Germany: Vistas.

Krotz, F., & Hepp, A. (2013). A concretization of mediatization: How mediatization works and why 'mediatized worlds' are a helpful concept for empirical mediatization research. *European Journal for the Philosophy of Communication, 3*(2), 37–152.

Laubstein, C., Holz, G., & Seddig, N. (2016). *Armutsfolgen für arme Kinder und Jugendliche. Erkenntnisse aus empirischen Studien in Deutschland* [Consequences of poverty for children and adolescents: Empirical evidence from research in Germany]. Gütersloh, Germany: Bertelsmann Stiftung. Retrieved from https://www.bertelsmann-stiftung.de/fileadmin/files/BSt/Publikationen/GrauePublikationen/Studie_WB_Armutsfolgen_fuer_Kinder_und_Jugendliche_2016.pdf.

Livingstone, S., Mascheroni, G., Dreier, M., Chaudron, S., & Lagae, K. (2015). How parents of little children manage digital devices at home: The role of income, education and parental style. *The EU Kids Online Network.* London, UK: LSE. Retrieved from http://www.lse.ac.uk/media@lse/research/EUKidsOnline/EUKidsIV/PDF/Parentalmediation.pdf.

Lunt, P., & Livingstone, S. (2015). Is 'mediatization' the new paradigm for our field? A commentary on Deacon and Stanyer (2014, 2015) and Hepp, Harvard and Lundby (2015). *Media, Culture and Society, 38*(3), 462–470.

Nikken, P., & Opree, S. J. (2018). Guiding Young Children's Digital Media Use: SES-Differences in Mediation Concerns and Competence. *Journal of Child and Family Studies, 27*(6), 1844–1857.

Paus-Hasebrink, I. (Ed.). (2017). *Langzeitstudie zur Rolle von Medien in der Sozialisation sozial benachteiligter Heranwachsender. Lebensphase Jugend* [Longitudinal study on the role of media within socialisation of socially disadvantaged adolescents: Phase of adolescence]. Baden-Baden, Germany: Nomos.

Paus-Hasebrink, I. (2018a). Mediation practices in socially disadvantaged families. In G. Mascheroni, C. Ponte, & A. Jorge (Eds.), *Digital parenting: The challenges for families in the digital age* (pp. 51–60). Gothenburg, Sweden: Nordicom & University of Gothenburg.

Paus-Hasebrink, I. (2018b). The role of media within children's socialization: A praxeological approach. *Communications: The European Journal of Communication Research.* Ahead of print, 17.10.2018 (pp. 1–20). DOI: https://doi.org/10.1515/commun-2018-2016.

Paus-Hasebrink, I., & Kulterer, J. (2014). Socially disadvantaged children, media and health. In C. von Feilitzen & J. Stenersen (Eds.), *Risks and rights: Young people, media and health—The international clearinghouse on children, youth & media yearbook* (pp. 33–44). Gothenburg, Sweden: Nordicom.

Paus-Hasebrink, I., Bauwens, J., Dürager, A. E., & Ponte, C. (2013). Exploring types of parent–child relationship and internet use across Europe. *Journal of Children and Media—JOCAM, 7*(1), 114–132.

Paus-Hasebrink, I., Ponte, C., Dürager, A. E., & Bauwens, J. (2012). Understanding digital inequality: The interplay between parental socialization and children's development. In S. Livingstone, L. Haddon, & A. Görzig

(Eds.), *Children, risk and safety on the internet: Research and policy challenges in comparative perspective* (pp. 257–271). Bristol, UK: Policy Press.

Ragnedda, M. (2017). *The third digital divide: A Weberian approach to digital inequalities*. London, UK and New York, NY: Routledge.

Rothbaum, F., Martland, N., & Beswick Jannsen, J. (2008). Parents' reliance on the web to find information about children and socio-economic differences in use, skills and satisfaction. *Journal of Applied Developmental Psychology, 29*(2), 118–128.

Schofield Clark, L. (2013). *The parent app: Understanding families in the digital age*. Oxford, UK: University Press.

Smetana, J. G., Robinson, J., & Rote, W. (2015). Socialization in adolescence. In J. E. Grusec & P. D. Hastings (Eds.), *Handbook of socialization: Theory and research* (2nd ed., pp. 60–84). New York, NY: Guilford Press.

Toczydlowska, E., & Bruckauf, Z. (2017). *Growing inequality and unequal opportunities in rich countries: Social and economic policy unit* (Innocenti Research Briefs No. 16). Florence, Italy: UNICEF Office of Research—Innocenti. Retrieved from https://www.unicef-irc.org/publications/918-growing-inequality-and-unequal-opportunities-in-rich-countries.html.

Valkenburg, P. M., Piotrowski, J. T., Hermanns, J., & de Leeuw, R. (2013). Developing and validating the perceived: Parental media mediation scale—A self-determination perspective. *Human Communication Research, 39*(4), 445–469.

Van den Bulck, J., Custers, K., & Nelissen, S. (2016). The child-effect in the new media environment: Challenges and opportunities for communication research. *Journal of Children and Media—JOCAM, 10*(1), 30–38.

Vekiri, I. (2010). Socioeconomic differences in elementary students' ICT beliefs and out-of-school experiences. *Computers & Education, 54*(4), 941–950.

Open Access This chapter is licensed under the terms of the Creative Commons Attribution 4.0 International License (http://creativecommons.org/licenses/by/4.0/), which permits use, sharing, adaptation, distribution and reproduction in any medium or format, as long as you give appropriate credit to the original author(s) and the source, provide a link to the Creative Commons licence and indicate if changes were made.

The images or other third party material in this chapter are included in the chapter's Creative Commons licence, unless indicated otherwise in a credit line to the material. If material is not included in the chapter's Creative Commons licence and your intended use is not permitted by statutory regulation or exceeds the permitted use, you will need to obtain permission directly from the copyright holder.

CHAPTER 8

The Typology of Socially Disadvantaged Families

8.1 Introduction

The previous two chapters looked at some of the core aspects of our longitudinal study, as observed from the children's development, their media repertoires and the different contexts of socialisation that play a role in their lives, and they considered the mediation strategies that we identified from our panel.

The study's data shows one thing very clearly: the children in the sample grew up in very dynamic and heterogeneous contexts. Each family displayed patterns of factors unique to it and shaping the everyday life experiences of all its members, and especially the children's. The specific interplay of individual key factors in a family influenced the socialisation of the children. The influence of different factors varied for each family: for some, one particular financial situation was more challenging than it was for others; different families coped with available resources in very different ways, for some, the climate between family members put a strain on their everyday lives and weighed on them more heavily than the financial deprivation.

Our discovery of the similarities in, and differences between, the respective family lives (*doing family*) of our subjects was the starting point for developing a typology of the families in the sample. We followed Kluge's (2000) approach to the construction of qualitative types (see Chapter 4), beginning by identifying the main dimensions available for characterising the families. Building on the results of the first four waves, we identified the following: the socio-economic situation of the family (e.g., their finances, employment and their standard of living), the socio-emotional climate (e.g., the relationship between family members, the observable conduct of family members with regard to each other and so on) and the identifiable coping strategies (how each family was able to deal with everyday challenges resulting from social disadvantage).

We first developed our typology in 2014 (see Paus-Hasebrink & Kulterer, 2014, p. 239), after four waves of data collection (2005, 2007, 2010, 2012). On the study's completion, after two more waves of data collection (2014, 2016), we revised and improved our typology in 2017 (see Fig. 8.1). The dimensions used for the identification and description of the types remained largely the same, but were in some cases renamed to provide a better understanding of their meaning. Due to various changes that the families themselves underwent between both waves, some families were moved from one type to another (e.g., because their financial situation had improved or because the family climate became more relaxed, or because their situation took a turn for the worse) and ultimately, one of the previous five types was merged with another already existing one (Type 1 and Type 2) since the differentiation

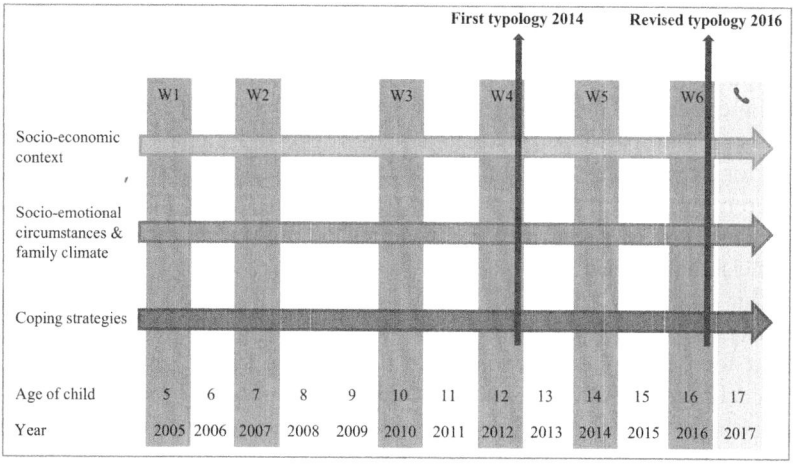

Fig. 8.1 First typology 2014 and revised typology 2016

between both had become less distinct as the remaining families of previous Type 2 had experienced an aggravation of their problems. These changes resulted in four family types, as shown in the matrix below (see Fig. 8.2). This shows how the various dimensions combine to illustrate the different family types.

The following portrayal of the family types views each family as a whole, together with its development over the years, but it focuses on the most recent data from the last two waves of data collection. At the core of the analysis and description of the types are the three analytical concepts: *options for action*, *outlines for action* and *competences for action* (see Chapter 3). Our portrayal of the types aims at highlighting the interplay of these three concepts against the background of the challenges confronting parents and children—the life tasks confronting the parents and developmental tasks (Havighurst, 1972) confronting the children—and their strategies of socialisation and of parenting, as well as their accompanying media use. We stress that these concepts were not identified independently and then analysed with regard to how they relate to each other, as the families' individual natures and the nature of their relationships are much more complicated. Not all factors can be defined by simply looking at their objective manifestations, but they

Characteristics \ Family type	Type 1	Type 2	Type 3	Type 4
Socio-economic background	Very strained	Not strained anymore/hardly strained	Strained	Not strained anymore
Socio-emotional circumstances and family climate	Very strained	Very strained	Less strained	Not strained
Coping strategies	Unable to cope	Unable to cope	Fairly competent	Fairly competent

Fig. 8.2 Four family types—typology 2016

also have to be analysed for each individual's subjective perception of their situation—very similar circumstances on the objective level do not automatically mean the same thing for different individuals and have the same consequences for them.

To demonstrate what is meant by that, we have chosen one case to describe in more detail. It represents each of the family types and provides a deeper insight into lifeworld of the respective child and its family, and displays with the different combinations of characteristics, and the individual interplay of these characteristics designating the family as belonging to this type. This form of in-depth analysis allows for a better understanding of the processes of socialisation the children undergo throughout the years and what role media play in this context.

The other families within the same type will be dealt with in less detail, while still addressing the relevant issues.[1]

8.2 The Families of Type 1

Massive Socio-Economic Problems as the Result of Multiple Forms of Deprivation: The Families Overwhelmed in All Respects. (Landinger, Oblinger, Fein, Öllinger)

The families of Type 1 are either large families (with more than five children[2]) or single-parent families. All of them struggled with everyday life challenges throughout the duration of the study, so that their respective circumstances remained, comparatively, the most critical right up to the end of the research.

These families experienced deprivation on various levels: on the one hand, they experienced massive socio-economic deprivation while, on the other hand, psychological and physical problems additionally burdened the family situation, often leading to parental unemployment or contributing to developmental problems in the children. All of these families continued to suffer under their situation right up to the end of the study.

A precarious financial situation was often mirrored in the living situations. Either the families lived in rather small and/or old apartments or older houses, some in remote, rural areas with weak infrastructure where rents are lower and job opportunities scarce, or in deprived and less popular areas in cities. For the adolescents, this meant fewer choices over schools, job training and education programmes, thus limiting their perspectives for the future, as well as often restricting their latitude for spending time outside of the family home.

At the end of the study it became clear that the parents of these families would probably not be able to improve their situation because they were overburdened by the challenges posed by the limited *options for actions*. At least one of the children from the Type 1 families, Manfred Oblinger, found a promising future perspective in training to become an IT technician. The future of Timo Landinger and Olivia Fein, who were both participating in special programmes to help unemployed teenagers integrate into the job market, was still rather unclear at the end of the study. Viktoria Öllinger had aspirations to finish school, maybe go abroad, and then later find a job in public service, but it still remained to be seen whether her endeavours would be successful.

With regard to the parenting strategies of the Type 1 families, we can say that most of them had a sense of responsibility for the development of their children and for their opportunities in life, but some of them, like the Fein and Landinger families, clearly saw their children as an additional burden and maintained a rather distanced relationship with them. In this context, the media were seen as welcome "tranquillisers", especially in the early years, and as ways to keep the children occupied without too much effort. They often reflected on this issue, but it was clear that the gap between the parents' ideals, between their *outlines for actions* ("wanting") and their actual *competences for actions* (actually "doing"), was often too big. This became evident in many aspects of the way they lived and, in the ways, they dealt with their life tasks, with parenting and media education figuring among these.

8.2.1 *The Case of Timo Landinger and His Family*

8.2.1.1 Situation and Climate of Relationships Within the Family
Timo (17 years old in 2016) was the youngest child in a large family that suffered from severe deprivation on multiple levels throughout the study. The family consisted of Mr. Landinger and his wife (between the last two interview waves, they got married after having a relationship for 28 years) and six children; Mr. Landinger was the biological father of the four youngest siblings. The family situation had been marked by instability, conflict and violence throughout the years.

Timo's situation within this family was especially depressing, as, from an outside perspective, his world seemed rather constrained and bleak. The crisis in the family escalated at one point between the first and second waves of data collection, driving Timo's mother and the younger children into a women's shelter. The parents reconciled and moved to another county, but the situation did not improve for Timo. He remained psychologically impaired, and his needs were mostly neglected by his parents, who were initially too preoccupied with financial issues, and later with health-related ones (psychological as well as physical). Both parents were permanently unemployed and did not seem eager to actually find a job but tried to get as much welfare money as possible. Through online research, Mr. Landinger diagnosed himself with 62 diseases and sought to have them acknowledged in order to receive more money.

The housing situation mirrored the precarious financial situation of the family. At first, it was living in a crowded apartment and later moved into a house in a remote, rural region of Austria—we could not ascertain how the family was able to finance this purchase. The house needed renovating and the family put some effort into improving its state, with some success. The interior of the house was messy and anything but clean. The living area was crammed with objects, and everything smelled of stale cigarette smoke (both parents were heavy smokers). The exception was Timo's room, where he seemed to try to bring some feeling of order and control into his life by keeping it tidy.

The adjacent building on the family's property remained rather desolate, and its function was unclear right up to the end of our study. It was used for storage, but also for hobbies, and it included a bathtub and warm running water.

All the problems burdening the parents during the study meant that their constant struggle impinged directly on the children, with violence often used as the parents' main response to conflicts. All this contributed to rather cold relationships, with hardly any affection between the family members, and Timo clearly suffered from this lack of warmth and affection, stating in one of the interviews that he had the feeling that no one liked him, not even the cat.

The climate within the family was, furthermore, marked by the very dominant father, who seemed to derive his self-esteem solely from his sway over the family. In order to maintain his dominant position, he used psychological humiliation, as well as physical punishment. Mr. Landinger expected subordination from the other family members and did not hesitate to enforce his will, although he denied any use of violence. His son's statements, and his wife's behaviour clearly suggested otherwise. Mrs. Landinger was clearly marked by her relationship to her husband, as she seemed timid and jumpy in his presence and had only very limited *options for actions*. She also seemed to be psychologically impaired and was in therapy in a special facility during the last years of the study. She seemed to have prematurely aged and apparently had no significant influence on the family's life.

Timo's cognitive and emotional-affective development had suffered under the multiple problems the family experienced, as well as from the lack of support within it. He was diagnosed with ADHD and other mental deficits and needed special care, which could not be provided by his parents. He did not receive adequate treatment and help, despite being home-schooled for some time, was then admitted to a psychiatric clinic after a situation in primary school escalated and was finally placed in a specialised socio-pedagogical living facility and school where he lived during the week. He completed his years of compulsory schooling in this facility and moved back into his parents' house permanently between our fifth and sixth waves. He showed progress in his development during the time he spent in the facility, did not have to rely on a number of different medications anymore and clearly profited from the stable routine, the therapeutic exercises and strict guidelines for media use and from the contact with other children of his age. However, returning home landed him back in his confined micro-cosmos, where he spent his days with computer games and working with a special programme aimed at enhancing his chances for job training but without producing any results by the end of the study.

Timo remained slow to develop and had severe problems with writing, as his network map shows (see Fig. 8.3).[3]

It cost Timo no little effort to produce the map, which is full of mistakes, like the "E" used instead of a "3" in "PS3" (PlayStation 3), as well as spelling mistakes.

Mr. Landinger openly stated that he wanted to undo what the school/facility taught his son, so that Timo would be socialised as Mr. Landinger saw fit. Timo had no friends and no social contacts outside of the family anymore. He had one friend, but Timo's father saw him as a threat to his dominance in the family and so drove him away. Violence and demonstrations of power were seemingly the only *competences for action* that Mr. Landinger knew.

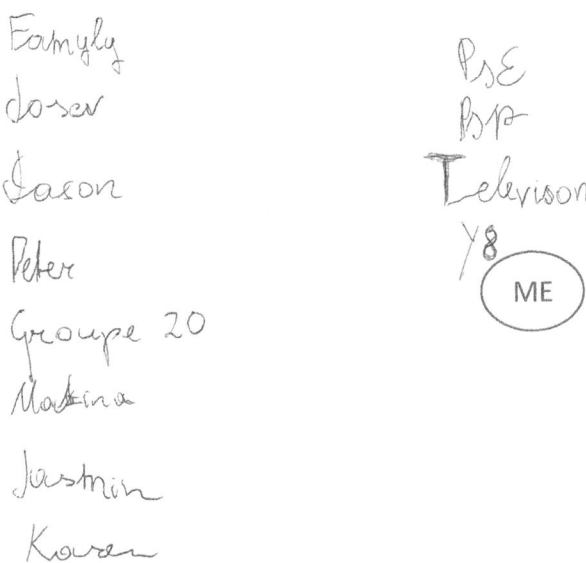

Fig. 8.3 Network map by Timo Landinger in 2016 (Tracing based on the original, translated and anonymised by the authors)

Much like his mother, Timo appeared to have resigned himself to his fate, as he made no attempt to break free of the situation or to change anything. His options were very limited, and he simply lacked the perspective and the *outlines for actions*, as well as the competences, to see any perspective beyond his world. Timo's father actively restricted his son's options—although they were already limited due to the family's situation—probably because he feared outside interference threatening his dominant position. Timo was apparently very intimidated and said at one point that he would like to hit his father back, but conceded that he could not, as his father was, after all, just that.

8.2.1.2 Media
Against this background, the media played a crucial role in Timo's life from early childhood on. They were his constant companions when he was, more or less, left alone by his family. The Landingers did not pursue much in the way of leisure time activities and spent most of their

time confined to their home. When Timo was older and living in the assisted-living facility during the week, he often expressed interest in pursuing activities like visiting a farm or, when he was at home, learning how to make bread, but his parents always discouraged him, arguing that the weekdays were so exhausting due to commuting to therapy and to Timo's school, that the family needed time to rest on weekends. So, Timo was left to pursue his media consumption as a way of keeping him occupied.

Since the beginning of the study, the media had served as a platform to engage in fantasies of power, which helped Timo to cope with the lack of power he experienced in everyday life. In our second wave, Timo declared he wanted to be a Pokémon, so that he could scare his family and the children in school.

First television, and later computer games, provided an opportunity to experience some form of self-efficacy. Fighting, proving himself and a sense of achievement were his primary motives for media use, especially with regard to computer games. His fascination with violent (and age-inappropriate) video games and media content, especially with anything related to the topics of war, death and violence, persisted over the entire period.

The media not only became the primary leisure time activity for Timo, but they were also a way to cope with his aggression and give his everyday routine a structure. His parents did not restrict this media use in any significant ways, except for prohibiting the use of the internet, because they did not think that Timo had the ability to use it. We consider it probable that their real motivation was that his access to the internet would mean they would have to try to exercise some sort of control and mediation in order to avoid risky/harmful situations. Accordingly, Timo had a mobile phone from 2014 onwards, but it was an obsolete model with no internet connection.

Timo had free access to different game consoles (PlayStation 2 and 3 as well as a PSP) and a large number of video games. The two pictures[4] that Timo took of his favourite place in his room during the last panel wave show 33 video games (most of all fighting games), which represented only part of his game collection.

Mr. Landinger said in 2012 that video games were his son's world, one that he did not want to deprive him off, since, in his opinion, Timo found his own identity and more self-esteem in playing these games, even if he lost a hundred times. At this point, it has to be said that Timo was not actually good at playing these games. On a couple of occasions, he played games during or after the interviews, providing the interviewers an insight into his limited abilities to process the action and to master the game challenges. The picture of his favourite media place in his room from 2014 shows the screen of his television displaying the menu of a game he was about to play also during the interview.

In 2016, Timo himself claimed to be "addicted" to video games. On weekends he often seemed to be playing games for 12 hours straight, and during the week it was the first thing he did after coming home from his job training—something that both his own statements and his parents' statements underline. In his last interview, Timo said: "I only dream about games, games, games". Timo's parents emphasised the role that video games play in calming Timo down. In 2016, the parents claimed that, if it were not for the games, there would have been no respite from the stress with their son.

The parents' own range of media was not much broader either. The most important medium in the house was the TV. Mr. Landinger was always eager to emphasise his dedication to information programmes—he was definitely interested in various subjects and had a vast factual knowledge, but tended to conflate topics and arguments, leaving his own utterances hard to understand for outsiders. In general, it appeared that the entertainment programmes of various private broadcasting stations dominated the family's media use.

Mr. Landinger used the computer and the internet from time to time to do research or to file papers for authorities online. Books were almost non-existent in the household, and the family did not take a newspaper, but only occasionally read free local papers, while Mrs. Landinger read magazines mostly related to hobbies, such as crocheting.

Throughout the study, Mr. and Mrs. Landinger tended to a positive opinion of the media. They valued them highly for their relaxing effect and for the opportunity they provided to recover from a stressful everyday life, but hardly ever evinced any form of critical analysis. In some interviews, these parents indicated some awareness of popular public discourses on the risks of media use, especially the risks from online exposure or those associated with violent content and its effect on a child's psyche. However, their own approach to their son's media education and their rules for media usage indicate that these statements most likely deferred to social desirability. Consequently, their uncritical approach to the media precluded any form of media literacy.

8.2.1.3 Parenting and Role of Socialisation Contexts

The overall approach to parenting in the Landinger family can only be described as non-existent or, at least, amorphous and inconsistent. The parents displayed a mixture of the mediation practices we identified as unmethodical restriction and arbitrary control/exploitation of dominance (see Chapter 7). Throughout the years, there were few clear rules, and those there were (e.g., that Timo was not allowed to use the internet), were mostly not explained to him, let alone consequently enforced. Rather than monitoring Timo's media usage and discussing it with him, the parents set arbitrary restrictions. In order to assert his ideas of proper behaviour, Mr. Landinger did not shy away from physical violence, which, as he argued, was preferable to psychological violence, something he viewed as torture. When Timo was still living in the socio-pedagogical facility, his parents had even refused to do any kind of parenting at all, because they had felt that their son had to follow too many rules in the facility anyway, so they wanted to leave him alone on the weekends to relax.

All in all, it became clear over the years that Timo's parents were unwilling to deal with their responsibilities as parents in general, and with issues of media literacy in particular. As our study indicates, their parenting style—if that is even the right word to use—builds on unmethodical restrictions rather than mediation and on enforcing their ideas of dominance through violence.

For a short period, Timo was able to experience other forms a socialisation from outside of his family, which helped to widen his perspective, only to be reduced again after moving back home to his family, where his father limited his contact with people outside of the family to a bare minimum.

In the light of all this, Timo's future remained unclear. When the study ended, he still had no job prospects and hardly any friends and social contacts. During the final phone call marking the end of the study, Timo appeared apathetic and devoid of any emotion.

8.2.2 Other Families of Type 1

8.2.2.1 The Oblinger Family
This family consisted of Mr. and Mrs. Oblinger and their six children. The oldest three stem from Mrs. Oblinger's first marriage and had

already moved out by the time the study began. However, they continued to live close-by, except for the oldest son, who lived in a neighbouring region. Manfred was the oldest of the remaining siblings and impressed as highly talented.

Throughout the study, this family was overwhelmed, both by their poor financial situation and by multiple strokes of fate, especially regarding the parents' health.

The family lives in a fairly remote and mountainous area, with poor access to public transport. They moved there, shortly before the study began, to acquire an affordable home for the large family. Mr. Oblinger had to give up his job, because there were no openings for a technical draftsman in this region, and he became a cook instead—the region's tourism creates a demand for this occupation. Although prospects in the area were limited, especially with regard to education and jobs, and although the family had to sacrifice a lot when they moved there, they remained content with their housing situation throughout the study.

Mrs. Oblinger was never employed during the study, and during its last years she suffered a stroke, becoming unable to work due to the ensuing depression. Before our sixth wave, her husband suffered a knee injury coming home from work at a skiing hut. An operation resulted in a chronic infection, rendering him also unable to work and later leading to depression. So the family had to struggle with even fewer resources and was living on the bare minimum of social welfare. This situation put a strain on the climate within the family and became their dominant concern.

As a child, Manfred experienced this growing lack of resources from an early age, and it always preoccupied him. He always talked about how he wanted to earn a lot of money when he was a grown-up and that he wanted to save it. The little money he received, he hid away without spending it, presumably being content with simply possessing it. When Manfred was younger, he always feared that immigrant families could take even more resources away from him and his family through their claims on social welfare. Later on, he also voiced concerns about refugees, who did not work and received social welfare money as well. Mrs. Oblinger was, on the one hand, very engaged in helping others—although she had to cease her voluntary activities at a local food bank and as a paramedic due to her own health issues—and felt sorry for asylum seekers who had lost everything. On the other hand, she had always voiced some concerns and shown traces of hostility towards foreigners.

It was only during the last waves of data collection that she seemed to have changed her views slightly, as she talked a lot about close friends, who were immigrants from Eastern Europe and who had become very important to both Mrs. Oblinger and Manfred.

When Manfred started elementary school, a test showed that he was highly talented and intellectually highly gifted. This resulted in him being bored in school and becoming an outsider because of his intellectual abilities and his personal interests—in contrast to his peers, he was interested in politics and other serious topics. Due to the weak infrastructure where the Oblingers lived, a lack of resources on the side of the family, and a lack of adequate support programmes in the region, Manfred's cognitive abilities were hardly stimulated. Manfred was, therefore, not able to develop competencies for actions commensurate with his intellect.

It became clear throughout all waves of data collection that Manfred's parents were overchallenged with raising their kids generally, and especially with their media education (the parents showed laissez-faire practices or sometimes even unmethodical restriction, see Chapter 7). At the same time, Manfred and his siblings had access to plenty of media to compensate for other shortcomings. This soon led to excessive media use, especially with Manfred, who developed a special liking for violent video games. These games challenged him intellectually and cognitively, and he was soon able to master difficult levels, thus boosting his self-esteem. His mother provided these games because she felt sorry for her son, who was an outsider with hardly any social contacts, as she would not let him play with children with migrant backgrounds in their neighbourhood. This led Manfred to start playing shooter games at the early age of six. Right up to the end of the study, Manfred remained very much into video games and found it easier to make friends online through various games than through any social contacts in his immediate surroundings. At the same time, he developed remarkable skills in programming and in using various tools to advance his game playing.

Manfred managed to find a place for training as an industrial management assistant—despite his intellectual abilities, he did not want to continue going to school or to pursue studies at a university, he wanted much rather to earn his own money as soon as possible—but he gave it up after only two months. After this, he became fully absorbed in his world of online game playing, until he managed to find a new training position in his desired profession of IT technician. When we last called

Manfred, he seemed very enthusiastic about this position and it looked very promising. His self-taught abilities in using computer technology had finally transformed into a job opportunity. This job training now offered him a way to support his parents financially, to have money of his own and to realise his *outlines for actions*, while at the same time trying to better the situation of his family.

8.2.3   The Fein Family

At the end of the study, the Fein family consisted of Ms. Fein, her daughter Olivia, the younger son and the youngest daughter. The family was initially living in an apartment on the outskirts of their local town, an area with many immigrants and people with migrant background. Between our second and fourth data collection waves, Ms. Fein had a new partner with his own business. She also moved to another county, and both factors led to an overall improvement of her socio-economic situation although Ms. Fein herself had been unemployed throughout the whole study. After separating from her partner, who was also the father of the youngest daughter, she experienced a severe worsening of her situation. She was diagnosed with epilepsy and depression, was granted an early pension at age 33 and remained in treatment for her psychological problems. By the end of the study, she had a new, considerably older partner, with whom she had a less formal relationship.

During our second wave, Olivia, the oldest daughter, had troubles adjusting to her new surroundings. At one point, she threatened to commit suicide and was committed to a supervised living facility after her grandmother intervened. This seemed to have a positive effect in the beginning, but Olivia continued to display behavioural problems, such as masturbating in front of others (by that time she was ten years old). Olivia had always been affected by the problems and strains in her family, because the family climate was always problematic, even during periods of relative financial stability.

At the beginning of the study, Ms. Fein practised unmethodical mediation, but later she displayed total lassez-faire, was seemingly resigned to her fate and unable to take on any responsibilities. As a consequence, she was rather distanced from her children, had little interest in them and remained preoccupied with her own problems. Olivia characterised her mother as "cold-hearted" in one of our last waves and was longing for a trustworthy confidant. The relationship between Ms. Fein and her daughter Olivia was obviously damaged by the time that Olivia had spent in the supervised living facility. Both expressed feelings of estrangement after Olivia was allowed to return home. The relationship deteriorated further after a supposed incident between Olivia and her mother's ex-partner—in the last interview Ms. Fein indicated that her ex-partner was not allowed to see their daughter, Olivia's youngest half-sister, after a court-mandated visiting ban. The exact reason remains unclear, although the case had overtones of sexual abuse.

Olivia had reacted to the strained climate in her family and the alienation from her mother by displaying an overwhelming wish for attention. Her media usage indicates how her psychological insecurity made her seek images of an idyllic world. For a long time, she admired *Hannah Montana*, the star of the TV series with the same name. Subsequently, she became very interested in gossip about stars, and especially royal families, which served her as fantasies of consumption and wealth. Her desires were reflected in her *outlines for actions*, like, for example, marrying early and having a family, an expression of her longing for safety and comfort and a way for her to realise *competences for actions*. Social media served as a way for her to channel her feelings and to present herself as a sexually attractive young woman; she tried to attract attention via various social media channels, like Instagram and Facebook.

Ms. Fein seemed overchallenged by her socio-economic situation, and, above all, by her socio-emotional state, throughout the study. She had always been trying to find personal happiness with new partners as outlets for her sexuality—something that Olivia always noticed and was bothered by—as well as the prospect of more financial stability. However, all attempts failed. Sexuality and the longing for financial stability became the dominant themes in the family.

8.2.3.1 The Öllinger Family
The Öllinger family consisted of Ms. Öllinger, a single mother, and her only child, Viktoria. Ms. Öllinger was in poor health during most of the study, meaning she was unable to work. She experienced a number of misfortunes, ranging from three miscarriages, to complications after an operation, resulting in a coma and almost in death, to back problems, epilepsy and depression. By the end of the study, Ms. Öllinger had to spend most of her days at home, often in bed and unable to participate in social activities.

The situation of mother and daughter became worse over the years, with the socio-economic situation collapsing after Ms. Öllinger found out that her ex-partner had used her name to amass debts online without her knowledge. Being unable to pay the debts off, Ms. Öllinger had to file for personal bankruptcy. By our last wave, she had finally been granted a disability pension, which enabled her to "get by". Divorced twice, Ms. Öllinger was living alone with her daughter for the last years of the study. As she grew up with foster parents, she did not have a strong and reliable support network. This family's *options, outlines and competences for actions* had become extremely limited by the complex dynamic that had evolved over the years.

Despite the generally strained situation, mother and daughter were very happy with their apartment, a fairly new one on the outskirts of a bigger town, which they were able to finance with the help of housing benefits. Apart from the good housing situation, the family struggled with their financial problems and the resulting social exclusion. Due to her mother's illnesses, Viktoria was forced to take on a lot of responsibilities at an early age, a burden which left its marks on the young woman. She demanded a lot of herself, while her mother suffered from fear of loss and consequently clung to her daughter. This dynamic led to a form of reversed roles in the fifth and sixth waves of data collection. The fear of loss became a dominant theme in the family: Ms. Öllinger was afraid of letting her daughter grow up and become independent, as she might leave her on her own. Viktoria was afraid that her mother could die, that she might not be strong enough to support her and she did not want to leave and disappoint her, while at the same time dreaming of going abroad and having new experiences. The pressure and the burden may well have caused the stomach aches Viktoria developed and her early signs of anorexia. Viktoria had been adjusting her *options for actions* to accommodate her mother, not just as far as her behaviour and duties were concerned, but also regarding her media use. She shared her Facebook account with her mother, watched the TV shows the latter liked, while Ms. Öllinger herself kept in touch with Viktoria through WhatsApp as soon as Viktoria left the apartment to go to school. Ms. Öllinger's mediation practices were dominated by amicability (see Chapter 7). At the same time, the social media helped Viktoria to engage in friendships. She communicated with her best friend through WhatsApp, where they sent each other pictures of their outfits, thus giving her the chance to be a "normal" teenager. This form of media usage provided a form of independence for Viktoria, which she was otherwise unable to obtain. Viktoria remained torn right up to the end of the study, as she tried to show her mother that she had not grown up yet (by, e.g., running around naked and showing her still girlish body or cuddling with her mother) but she longed for a life of her own, without the limitations she had been experiencing over the years.

8.3   THE FAMILIES OF TYPE 2

Families No Longer, or to a Lesser Degree, Strained Socio-Economically but still with Problematic Socio-Emotional Relationship Structures. (Holzner, Weiss, Rohringer, Hirtner)

The families of Type 2 were characterised by new family constellations and new experiences of separation. As a result, the climate in these families was very strained, and their *doing family* affected.

In contrast to the families of Type 1 above, these families had seen an improvement in their socio-economic situation towards the end of the study (waves five and six), but the relationships among the family members had largely remained problematic or worsened. The family members were, by and large, overwhelmed by this situation. Mrs. Holzner, for example, had married a new husband, and this led to an improvement of her financial situation due to his stable and fairly well-paid job. She even started a new family, with two more sons, but the relationship to her "old" nuclear family, especially to her son, Benedikt, remained strained. Ms. Weiss, on the other hand, inherited real estate and managed to improve her financial situation through renting it out, but her relationship to son, Alfons, remained unchanged. Neither the newly married Mrs. Holzner nor Ms. Weiss, who had been separated from Alfons' father for all of the study, seemed interested in their sons and in maintaining a relationship with them, so that relations were inevitably strained. The Rohringer family and the Hirtner family also improved their socio-economic situations, although not to the extent of the Weiss and Holzner families. However, climate within their family was similarly strained. Relations among the Hirtners, their *doing family*, was considerably affected by Ms. Hirtner's separating from her partner, thus destabilising the network within the family.

All four families of this type showed signs of overextension in their coping strategies, as their everyday lives as nuclear families mirrored their strained socio-emotional circumstances. This overextension was also visible in the parenting and in the parents' approaches to regulating media use and educating their children about it, both functions characterised by a lack of interest.

It is noteworthy that three of the four families of this type consisted of single mothers with their children (Weiss, Hirtner, Rohringer). Before she remarried and had two more children with her new husband, Mrs. Holzner had also long been a single mother; her son, Benedikt, and his siblings had lived in supervised living facilities since wave three.

8.3.1 The Case of Benedikt Holzner and His Family

8.3.1.1 Situation and Climate of Relationships Within the Family

The life of Benedikt (16 years old in 2016) and his family had been marked by considerable turbulence over the years. It was particularly affected by a court-mandated removal of the children into supervised living facilities between waves two and three.

When the study began, Mrs. Holzner and her three children, Benedikt being the youngest, were living as lodgers in a terraced house in a rundown neighbourhood. The family disliked the neighbours, and especially the prevalence of immigrants and people with migration backgrounds, but they were, nonetheless, content with the location and the opportunities available for the children.

The whole family suffered from the violence of Mrs. Holzner's ex-partner, and she was struggling to get by with the social welfare money she received as a single mother. Benedikt was particularly traumatised by previous physical abuse, had trouble concentrating on anything, was diagnosed with ADHD and suffered from uncontrollable fits of rage. When he was in treatment as a five-year-old, his therapist certified that Benedikt had the developmental level of a three-year-old. This deficit became also clear to us in our first interview with the young boy. His family was not able to provide the help or stability necessary for him to cope with his traumatisation. During this time, Mrs. Holzner had very few *options for actions* and consequently hardly any *outlines for actions.*

Shortly after our second interview in 2007, Benedikt and his siblings were placed in special supervised living facilities after the child protection services intervened. Accordingly, our next interview only involved Mrs. Holzner, since Benedikt could not be reached in the facility.

In 2012, we could not interview them at all, because Mrs. Holzner had remarried and changed her name, which made it hard to contact her. Subsequently, she did not want to participate due to an ongoing court case affecting her and her children, refusing any explanation. Our next interview then took place in 2014. In the meantime, her older children continued living apart from her in various facilities, and Mrs. Holzner started a new family with her husband. She was living together with him and their son in the apartment that her husband had previously bought together with his ex-partner. Between the last two waves of data collection, they had another son together.

By that time, Benedikt's older brother and older sister had moved back to the city to pursue job training, but they were still living in supervised living communities for adolescents. Benedikt's school and living situation remained somewhat unclear, as his mother was always referring to a supervised living facility, while the boy himself talked about a boarding school that he was attending—which was actually the case. Mrs. Holzner had never visited her son at the facility or seen his school (she was not even sure about the exact location). She hardly showed any interest in any aspect of his life, even going so far as to disparage and mock him. While she always used to describe him as lazy, unmotivated, unkempt and so on, our interviews with the boy himself, showed him to be, on the contrary, very resourceful and proactive in his education and later search for job training. At the same time, his mother never bothered to get in touch with the school or the carers in the living facility, presumably thinking that everything was in order as long as no one called her. She also stated that she did not think very highly of the carers and made especially derogatory remarks about the female carers.

It became very clear during our last interviews that Mrs. Holzner was not interested in Benedikt and his life—disinterest can be seen as the main characteristic and attitude in the family. She was consequently hardly able to provide any information about him, his interests, his media use, his future plans or even his relationship to his biological father, her ex-partner. Mrs. Holzner seemed solely focused on her new family, putting all her energy into it, whereas Bendedikt was seen rather more as a visitor, looking in on his half-siblings at weekends now and then.

While the relationship between Benedikt and his mother was troubled, he always maintained a close relationship with his older siblings, as well as later with the younger ones too. His older siblings are his central reference persons, and he called them his family, assigning a place close to him in his network map (Fig. 8.4). At the end of the study, Benedikt also talked about his girlfriend, who was living nearby and whose family had shown kindness in accepting him.

Benedikt's plan was to finish compulsory education—he had to repeat a school year after changing from an academic secondary school to one with a focus on information technologies—and to start job training as soon as possible in order to become independent and to earn his own money. He succeeded in securing the desired job training and organised everything by himself. His *outlines for actions* were very clear and straightforward in this regard, and he appeared very grown-up and focused during the last interview. With Benedikt, it seemed that the treatment and therapy he received over the years, combined with a positive learning environment in his living facility, led to a general improvement of his development, there being no trace of his former developmental deficits by the end of the study.

It was always clear that Benedikt felt comfortable in his new living situation and that he profited immensely from the intervention in his previously troubled circumstances. The facility provided him with the stability and the available reference persons he was lacking at home, and he seems to have built his whole life around this facility and the school,

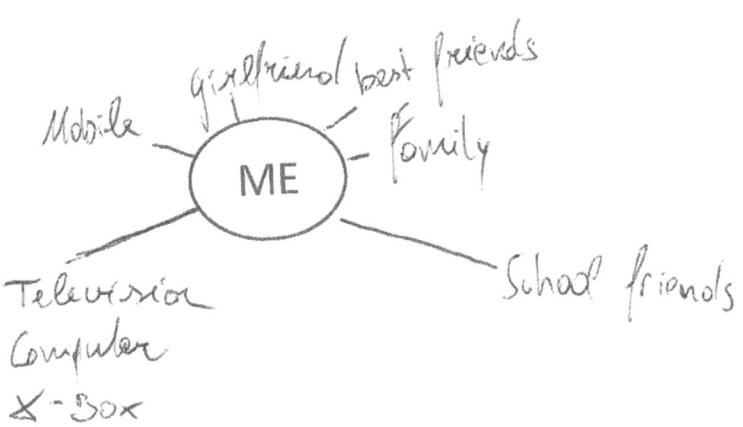

Fig. 8.4 Network map by Benedikt Holzner in 2016 (Tracing based on the original, translated and anonymised by the authors)

indeed considering it his "home". Our impression was confirmed by Mrs. Holzner's phone call at the end of 2016, explaining that she had basically lost contact with her son after the last interview. Benedikt himself could not be reached for a last short interview. While we cannot posit a causal link between his development and the intervention in his family, Benedikt was, in fact, the only child from one of the very strained families in the panel, who appeared notably confident, balanced and self-possessed by the end of the study. Given that he was one of the most serious cases when the study began, his development can be seen as the exception among our subjects.

8.3.1.2 Media
Benedikt used the media intensively as a child. They were his main source of information, his companions and often his only leisure time activity. When the study began, Benedikt spent most of the day in kindergarten, but he and his siblings were watching TV before they left and re-commenced this activity as soon as they returned home in the afternoon. They often watched until 9 p.m., even longer on weekends. Benedikt himself claimed in 2007 that he was "always" watching TV. He owned a broad range of merchandise articles and referred to his DVDs, CDs, the TV and video games as his "favourite things in life". His mother showed laissez-faire practices because of the everyday demands on her; she accordingly expected that kindergarten and school or media would teach mediation practices (see Chapter 7).

All this changed drastically when Benedikt moved to the supervised living facility. Due to the missing information from 2010 and 2012, and because Mrs. Holzner was, for the most part, unable to provide any information about her son's media use, apart from the fact that she thought he was "addicted to media" (2012), his actual use could only be reconstructed through later interviews, but it became clear that it was meticulously controlled and regulated in the facility. At the same time, it provided a lot of mediation, which found expression in Benedikt's very reflected and critical media use by the end of the study. It was true that the media still played an important role in his life, but in a very different way and on a different level from when the study began.

Like most teenagers in the panel, Benedikt became very interested in various social media services, like YouTube, WhatsApp, Instagram and

Snapchat—but he did not use Facebook. He also used online and computer games, like *Age of War* and *GTA*, and favoured television shows on commercial channels, but he was also very much into sports broadcasts and documentaries. His access to game playing consoles was still restricted by the rules of the living facility, and there were limits on internet access. In our last interview, Benedikt claimed that his smartphone was his most important media device, because it enabled him to contact his friends; the aspect of communication was very important to him. In 2016, when asked to take a picture of his favourite "media place", he took one of his smartphone. As he spent only very limited time at his mother's place, the smartphone was his most valuable media device, enabling him to use his favourite services and content wherever he went.

At the same time, he often handed his phone over to the caretakers when he wanted to concentrate on his homework. He liked to upload "selfies" on apps like Snapchat but appeared to consider carefully what he exactly wanted to post, and what not, and between the last two interviews he had deleted his Instagram account. In addition, Benedikt was interested in the news and used push-services on his smartphone to receive updates.

Mrs. Holzner's media use was mostly dominated by the radio and her smartphone. She usually watched television together with her husband. She claimed not to read anything, because reading affected her like a sleeping pill. Although the media have always played a central role in Mrs. Holzner's everyday life, her opinion about their actual relevance varied from wave to wave. In the beginning, she thought that the media were very relevant, but next time she denied them any relevance, only to change her opinion again at the end of the study.

8.3.1.3 *Parenting and Role of Socialisation Contexts*

The deprivation that Mrs. Holzner experienced at the beginning of the study translated directly into her *options* and *outlines for actions*, something particularly apparent in her parenting strategies. Being overwhelmed by the challenges she had to face as a single mother living on social welfare money, Mrs. Holzner delegated child-rearing and parenting to others, like the kindergarten, later the school, but also to the media. At the beginning of the study, Mrs. Holzner specially tried to mask her disinterest in parenting and in her children, as well as her inability to meet her own parenting goals, by presenting that as a deliberately chosen parenting style—she was always keen to display a supposedly laid back and open approach to parenting and child-raising, when she was in reality overwhelmed by the demands of raising three children on her own, while at the same time coping with other everyday challenges. Her situation often led to aggression towards the children, a lack of self-control and a neglect of the children for days. In our interviews, she declared that she left the children to fend for themselves so that they would become autonomous and self-reliable. She was never a fan of clear rules and claimed that anything forbidden was even more appealing for children, so she did not bother to set any rules or restrictions, for example, regarding the duration of television use. It seemed that Mrs. Holzner was glad that her children were occupied with the media, so that she did not have to put too much energy into entertaining them herself, as evidenced by their television watching. The issue of parenting and media education was later taken off her hands entirely when her children were removed by the child protection services.

Only after he moved to the supervised living facility, was Benedikt's media use monitored and regulated—not just in terms of duration, but also in terms of content. Benedikt reported that he enjoyed the clear rules and the fact that there was always someone available to answer his questions over media use or media content. Mrs. Holzner was, in fact, never available for discussions about media-related questions, even when Benedikt directly asked, and her new husband counted as an expert only on the technical aspects of media use. In our last interview, Mrs. Holzner said that she would not discuss media-related questions, because, in her opinion, Benedikt ought to gather his own experiences, and it was not her business to run after him. To her mind, this was an important part of letting go and of letting children grow up.

Discussions on media-related topics, but also on politics, only happened in the living facility. Benedikt enjoyed them, and it became clear in our interviews that he tended to reflect critically on the media and news coverage about, for example, refugees, where he distinguished perceptively between more and less reliable sources.

With Benedikt, it was clear that other socialisation contexts played much more crucial roles in his development than did his family after he was taken away from home. While the media were a central influence in the boy's socialisation during the first years of the study, they were later replaced by the carers and also the teachers in school as primary agents of socialisation. They had been very positively influential in Benedikt's development. There was a brief phase between our last interviews where

Benedikt felt too much pressure in his school, so he decided to switch to another, a move which helped him to become more relaxed and motivated again.

Benedikt's siblings, and especially his friends, are also very important to him and act as other relevant contexts of socialisation. For example, his idea of applying for job training as a cable-car engineer was inspired by one of his friends.

Overall, it can be said that Benedikt was able to acquire resilience and that his *options for actions*, but especially his *outlines for actions* and the competences to put them into practice changed considerably under the influence of different surroundings and contexts of socialisation over the years.

8.3.2 Other Families of Type 2

8.3.2.1 The Weiss Family

The family consisted of Ms. Weiss, a single mother, her son, Alfons, and his younger half-brother. Ms. Weiss had a relationship with a new partner during the second half of the study, but it remained unclear how serious the relationship ultimately was. Alfons had been living separated from his biological father since before the study began, a situation that he was constantly struggling with.

Between the fourth and the fifth waves, Ms. Weiss inherited real estate from her father and was thus able to improve her financial situation. At the end of the study, she claimed that she did not have to work anymore, since she was able to live from the money she received from renting apartments out. Ms. Weiss had always been a very economical person. When she was about 20 years old she took out a loan to buy the family's apartment, where they lived during the first five waves. This apartment had increased in value over almost 20 years and was sold in order to acquire a nearby semi-detached house. Throughout the study, Ms. Weiss was preoccupied with money. She always worried about not having enough and tried to downplay her financial situation. In this context, she never seemed to carry out her *outlines for actions* to her full satisfaction. It appeared that she was constantly thinking of new ways of getting additional money, for example, taking in a foster child, with the additional welfare payments that brought. It was also possible that her decision not to let Alfons live with his father, a wish he openly expressed over and over again, might also have had something to do with alimony and child support payments. She was, for example, afraid what the refugee crisis and the asylum seekers might cost her as a tax-payer and worried that the welfare system—that she made use of herself between the last waves—might suffer.

Throughout the years, Alfons made no secret of the fact that he would rather have lived with his biological father, who lived in a mountain region and had a farm. He visited his father on some weekends and during parts of the summer holidays, but constantly suffered from their separation, so that it seemed his mother was trying to get back at her ex-partner through their son. We often had the impression that Ms. Weiss was venting her anger at her ex-partner on Alfons as well. It was clear that she favoured her younger son, of whom she always spoke in a very positive way. In fact, it sometimes seemed that she was trying to steer the interviews away from Alfons towards her younger son, about whom she liked talking. Alfons did not really lack anything, as his mother made sure that he was well dressed, had everything he needed and helped him to participate in leisure time activities and selected clubs, but her interest did not seem to run much deeper than catering to basic needs. The relationship between Alfons and his mother and between Alfons and his half-brother thus remained problematic throughout the study. In this context, the media played an important role for Alfons at an early age. He found orientation and diversion in them, while, at the same time, Ms. Weiss openly stated that she was not really interested in her son's media use and showed laissez-fair practices in monitoring it (see Chapter 7). Thus, she did not make any attempts at guiding his media use or inculcating any media literacy. In her opinion, schools were responsible for teaching these skills. When she used media together with her children, Alfons was often excluded, whereas his younger brother was always there.

All in all, Alfons' wishes and feelings were of no great interest to his mother, at least not if he did not do everything the way she wanted him to. Alfons' *outlines for actions* and *competences for actions* had been hindered through the bad climate in the family. By way of coping, he started to withdraw himself from it and, for example, concealed any money he got from his father, or did not mention the new smartphone that his uncle gave him.

By the end of the study, Alfons had started job training in the nearby city, where he lived in a boarding school. With this step away from his home, Alfons had access to new and self-determined *outlines for actions* and was able to develop *competences for actions*, but he, all the same, seemed to be uncomfortable with his situation.

8.3.2.2 The Rohringer Family

The Rohringer family consists of Mrs. Rohringer, her oldest son from her first marriage (who had already moved out), her daughter, Isabelle, and the youngest son. The family lived in the same apartment in the countryside throughout the study. Mrs. Rohringer separated from her partner, the father of Isabelle and her younger brother, between our first and second interviews. He was an alcoholic, a problem which burdened Isabelle particularly.

By the third wave, Mrs. Rohringer had a new partner, a business owner who employed her in his transportation business, leading to an improvement in the family's socio-economic situation. Although the new partner was also able to bring more stability to the family, the socio-emotional situation remained strained, especially with regard to Isabelle, who suffered under her father's drunken phone calls or his cancelling of meetings. Isabelle appeared traumatised by her parents' separation and had to undergo therapy to cope with her problems In addition, Isabelle was struggling in school because of her dyslexia, which remained a problem right up to the end of the study. The problems of her children (be it Isabelle's dyslexia, or other issues in school), in combination with the separation, seemed to overwhelm Mrs. Rohringer, and she tried to maintain control over the situation by seeking to exert control over her children, yet she never communicated clear rules but set them randomly as she saw fit.

According to Mrs. Rohringer, the media had no major significance for Isabelle in the first three waves, especially since the latter had problems concentrating on anything for any length of time. From what Isabelle said herself, it seemed that she was a rather frequent media user, after all, and also possessed a broad range of merchandise products that were very important to her. As she grew older, German reality shows became her favoured television content. These were referred to as "trash TV" in the sixth wave by both mother and daughter, but nevertheless they were very important to the girl. Indisputably number one media device for Isabelle in the sixth wave was her smartphone for communicating with friends or for social media, like Facebook and Snapchat.

Although the relationship between Isabelle and her mother was initially good, and Mrs. Rohringer acted as an important pillar for Isabelle, they started to argue more often towards the end of the study, especially because Mrs. Rohringer's urge to control her daughter meant she disregarded her private sphere, displaying arbitrary control more than ever and exploiting her dominance (see Chapter 7). A particular dispute centred on the mother's apparently random, but actually comprehensive, monitoring of Isabelle's short text messages and WhatsApp-messages. The girl began to suffer under her mother's dominance, while she herself often seemed to lack drive and motivation, as well as any clear idea of her future. By the end of the study, Isabelle was wanting to move out, yet she herself did not seem able to develop any *outlines for actions* she could actually implement. For Isabelle, the media became important tools for keeping in touch with friends and for entertainment purposes. She enjoyed various fictional television series as well as "reality" shows, something her mother approved of, regarding them as valuable lessons about life.

8.3.2.3 The Hirtner Family
The financial situation of the Hirtner family was very precarious at the beginning of the study, as Mrs. Hirtner and her then partner were both unemployed. Mrs. Hirtner's son, Mario, regarded her partner as his father, although they were not biologically related. However, that was something he only learnt when the partner and his mother broke up after the fifth wave. Mrs. Hirtner found a new partner between the fifth and sixth waves. The financial situation of this newly-formed family improved during the study, especially since Mrs. Hirtner was working full-time at its end. The Hirtners lived in the same apartment throughout and were mostly content with the housing situation and the neighbourhood. It was only in the sixth wave that Mrs. Hirtner complained about refugees being housed near the apartment. In fact, she had been robbed right in front of the entrance to their block and afterwards did not feel safe anymore.

Mrs. Hirtner and Mario's biological father had been separated for a long time when the study began, and there was no contact between Mario and his father, since he did not even know that he existed. The only father Mario knew as a child, his mother's then partner, did not keep in touch with Mario after he left, but Mario did quickly accept his mother's new partner as a close person of reference.

Mario always had a very close relationship with his mother and could also do what he wanted when using the media. His mother was not interested in this activity at all and displayed a laissez-faire approach to it (see Chapter 7). But the relationship became more and more distanced after our fifth interview. Mrs. Hirtner felt unable to cope with her son's need for closeness. Especially during the last interview, it became obvious that Mrs. Hirtner had an alcohol problem. She seemed to be drinking quite frequently, neglecting her son and even becoming aggressive towards him. This led to Mario withdrawing from his family and focusing on video games. His mother was not able to help and comfort him when Mario had to quit his job training because of his fear of heights, she even began to put pressure on him and make fun of him, which led to his further withdrawal. In response, Mario redirected his *outlines for actions* and tried to "function" the way his mother wanted him to. This socio-emotional burden had an effect both on the climate within the family and on Mario's everyday life. He even withdrew from his friends and dived into his world of video games, where the social contacts he made replaced his previous relationships. At the same time, he was able to acquire many technical competencies through his interest in game playing and was in the end able to secure some new job training in the IT sector. This meant a chance for him to become more independent, but it was still obvious that the strained situation at home continued to trouble him.

Mrs. Hirtner was meanwhile suffering under the feeling that she had failed in realising her personal *outlines for actions*. In the light of these circumstances, *doing family* among the Hirtners was marked by an overall inability to cope with relationships and challenges.

8.4 THE FAMILIES OF TYPE 3

The Families Strained Socio-Economically, but Stable Socio-Emotionally and Relatively Competent. (Stab, Aufbauer, Boll, Ebner, Kaiser)

The strained socio-economic status of these nuclear families did not change, but they were able to improve their socio-emotional situation over the years. Although they experienced socio-economic restrictions, they appeared to be much less strained in coping with everyday life and *doing family* when compared to the families of Type 1 and Type 2. They became more and more successful in handling life under their existing conditions, and, although their *options for actions* were experienced as limited, they managed to compensate for the strains imposed through stable and strong relationships.

These families were mostly satisfied with their situation in life: a clear distinction from the Type 1 and Type 2 families. The Stab, Kaiser and Ebner families from Type 3 had managed to cope with their aggravated conditions very well from the beginning of the study onwards. The Boll and Aufbauer families, on the other hand, were able to stabilise their socio-emotional structures over the last two waves and subsequently managed to cope with their everyday lives fairly competently. The families of Type 3, and especially the mothers, were striving for harmony and an open approach to parenting that is focused on a lot of mediation. By the end of the study, the children who were our subjects, Amelie Aufbauer, Gregor Boll, Elisabeth Ebner, Torsten Kaiser and Simone Stab, felt very comfortable and secure in their families. Some of the siblings in some families did experience troubles at different times, but, all in all, the families, as such, were able to manage these situations and to find solutions together.

8.4.1 The Case of Simone Stab and Her Family

8.4.1.1 The Situation and Climate Within the Family

Ms. Stab was an immigrant from Eastern Europe, who had been living in Austria for about 20 years when the study began. Simone (15 years, 2016) was her oldest daughter and there was a younger son, Simone's half-brother. The family lived in the countryside throughout the study, but they moved twice on financial grounds. The family was mostly very satisfied with their housing, although, in the last interview Ms. Stab did state that she was somewhat dissatisfied with their apartment, because it had become both too expensive and too small for the family. There were also conflicts with the block's janitor, who made a lot of noise when working around the house. At the end of the study, Simone declared herself very satisfied with the apartment and with her own room, especially because of the "Indian, Buddhist and Native American flair" they had created, and which Simone's room also featured (including peacock feathers and a Buddha tapestry on the wall and a three-part dreamcatcher hanging from the ceiling).

Simone's younger half-brother was not living with the family during the week anymore after moving into a supervised living facility following conflicts in the family.

The financial situation of Ms. Stab and her family was rather strained throughout the study. Her university entrance qualifications from her country of origin were not officially accepted in Austria, and, as an immigrant from Eastern Europe with imperfect German, she faced difficulties on the job market, forcing her to work part-time as unskilled labour and sometimes be unemployed between jobs. An attempt to set up her own business following training as a masseuse had not been successfully realised by the time the study ended. Her part-time employment as a waitress and masseuse did not alleviate the financial situation of the family much. What was clear throughout the study was her unceasing will to provide for her children and to make a good life within her limited possibilities. The children never lacked the basics, but extraordinary costs, like car repairs, particularly challenged the family. Through all these challenges, Ms. Stab always kept a positive outlook on life, tried to appreciate what she had in life and to make the best of every situation without complaining or blaming others. The only thing she kept hoping for was a steady partner and step-father for her children. Unfortunately, she did not appear to meet any suitable candidates, so that her relationships were never successful.

As a single mother—Simone's father had left her when the girl was two years old—Ms. Stab was always struggling to make a living, which meant that she often had to leave her children with others, or in daycare, a fact that she declared she deeply regretted, because she regarded them as her absolute priority and felt she had not supported them sufficiently. However, Simone declared in her interviews that her mother had indeed tried to support them in many other ways. Her relationship with her was clearly very close and built on trust, with Simone saying explicitly that she had "the best mother".

The contact with Simone's father had continued to varying degrees. Only after her father remarried did she experience some problems maintaining the contact, since her father's new wife seemed to be jealous and was trying to undermine his involvement with Simone. In the last phone interview, Simone said that the contact between them has improved again after her father divorced his wife.

Simone's everyday life was rather busy. She had many hobbies and also took part in club activities, especially around the fifth wave, like soccer, karate and volleyball, and she was learning to play the guitar. After changing schools between the fifth and sixth interviews, there was not much time left to pursue those hobbies or to meet with friends. During the sixth wave, she was attending a polytechnic secondary school, allowing her to focus on sculpting, which she enjoyed. She was set on finishing school at university entrance level and going to college afterwards. But before starting college she was planning on travelling, maybe as part of a work-and-travel programme. It was obvious that Simone wanted to do whatever she could to escape the restrictions of social disadvantage in her own life. Her *outlines for actions* and her attempts to acquire the necessary competences were firmly directed towards this goal. She did not want to get diverted, not even by friends or a boyfriend, despite the fact that friendships were in general very important to her.

The family situation was overshadowed by problems with Ms. Stab's son during the last two waves. His computer game usage had escalated, and Ms. Stab felt that her son was lacking a father figure. On her own, she was not able to help him get out of this situation, although she tried hard to. There were also many disputes between Simone and her brother, and in the end Ms. Stab decided to get help from outside. Her son moved to a socio-educational living facility, where he was living during the week and in which he received counselling. The situation improved and the relationships between both mother and son and brother and sister seemed to have recovered.

8.4.1.2 Media
Simone's media equipment can be best described as modest and functional. She had always had access to basic devices, like a laptop or a phone, but usually they were not the most modern or most expensive ones. For example, her father bought her laptop during the fourth wave because she needed it for school. She was still using it up to the end of the study, when it was supposedly not suitable for her computer-aided classes, as it was already outdated. When the study began, Simone favoured the television and related to characters like Mowgli from the *Jungle Book* or Peter Parker from *Spiderman*, which mirrored her experiences of loss and loneliness, with her father being absent and her mother having to work. Money and upward social mobility were topics that interested her and influenced her choice of media content, so that she favoured *Hannah Montana* or various casting shows. Later, she developed more interest in sitcoms or crime series, while still liking casting shows.

Simone had never been much of a reader, unlike her mother, who often talked about books on topics such as psychology, philosophy and religion. Sometimes, Simone would look into magazines for teenagers, but apart from that, reading was not important to her. In our sixth interview, she mentioned a book about the Dalai Lama; this apparently was the first book to interest her.

From the fourth wave onwards, Simone's most important media device was the smartphone. Towards the end of the study, it became even more important, as it helped her to stay in touch with her friends, even though she did not have much time to meet them because of her workload in the new school. It was also important for her as a way to listen to music (from the time she gets up until she goes to bed, so she said) and to take pictures. Photography is one of her hobbies, and the phone helps her to share the pictures she takes on social media. The smartphone became her constant companion.

She had been using social media intensively since 2014, especially Facebook, Instagram and Snapchat. Her list of some 2000 friends on Facebook was quite big at that time, and even after a "clearing out", there were still 1600 left by the end of the study. But she did not share pictures on Facebook, only on Instagram, where she had stricter privacy settings.

YouTube also became more relevant to her towards the end of the study and supplanted other social media platforms. She listened to music on the platform but also followed news and items from YouTubers.

Ms. Stab's media use is, in fact, quite easy to assess. She used the internet to manage her bank account and to upload documents—for example, from the state employment agency—and she sometimes used YouTube. Earlier in the study, she used online dating platforms for a while, in the hope of finding a new partner, but ceased these activities after a couple of unsatisfactory dating experiences (one of the respondents was, e.g., an alcoholic). However, it does seem that, apart from books and the phone, the media have always played more of a subordinate role in her life. Growing up in Eastern Europe without electricity and, hence, without the media probably meant she could more easily function without the latter. She was very critical towards the media, although she is also aware of their services and did acknowledge making use of them herself. In the early years of the study, Ms. Stab had felt the need to protect her children from the harsh reality shown on the news, but later she changed her opinion. She had no tolerance for pornographic and especially violent media content, and often argued with her son, who was obsessed with violent video games. Her critical opinion was reinforced by her son's situation towards the end of the study, although she also said that it was necessary to stay up to date with developments.

Although her children became more skilled with the use of media, as she said in our fifth interview, Ms. Stab always tried to teach them awareness of the inherent risks and dangers and tried to share her own experiences with them. Simone was also able to learn from mistakes, as with one particularly high phone bill. That problem was solved together with her mother, and Simone was from then on alert to such dangers. Whenever Ms. Stab encountered a topic or a situation that she felt not competent enough to solve, she got help from someone more knowledgeable. Her attempts to raise her children to be critical and to question things was mirrored in Simone's media use. She expressed her scepticism over online content clearly and did not believe everything she saw. She also knew how to get help with problems beyond her abilities.

8.4.1.3 Parenting and Socialisation Contexts
Ms. Stab had one clear goal in her parenting: she wanted to raise children with independent personalities capable of standing up for themselves. As far as Simone was concerned, Ms. Stab was satisfied with her development, although she admitted to mistakes. With her son, she felt less successful and attributed that, to some extent, to the detrimental lack of a father figure. Despite the problems with him, Ms. Stab never gave up on her son, and their relationship did seem to improve.

Simone mirrored the positive attitude of her mother and seemed very independent, grown-up and wise for her age, something her mother attributed to Simone having to take on responsibility for herself very early in life, while her mother was absent at work. Our impression at the end of the study indicated that Simone was well-equipped with the important abilities for managing her own life. Ms. Stab was always keen to teach her children her values, like honesty, solidarity, frugality and her beliefs in God and altruism. Simone reflected this attitude in one of our interviews, where she said that she did not have any particular wishes, but that she was hoping for a better and more peaceful world, in which it was possible "to pet lions" (2010). Ms. Stab's parenting style was marked by much mediation and attempts to teach her children necessary skills as best as she could. One example is the way she always included

Simone when she was dealing with online-banking, so that the girl could see and learn how this works. Here, Ms. Stab combined amicability and child-centred mediation practices (see Chapter 7).

Ms. Stab was highly critical of herself and of her own actions. She was convinced that, like most parents, she also made mistakes while raising her children, but we were persuaded that she always tried to do her best and to do it in a loving way.

Our interviews with Simone and her mother were remarkable in the context of the panel. Hardly any other interviews with parents and children showed views corresponding as much as theirs did. Of course, Simone became more independent as she grew older and did not share everything with her mother anymore, but, all in all, it was always clear that her mother remained her closest reference person, on whom she knew she could always rely. Hence, she also drew her mother in close proximity to her in her network map (Fig. 8.5). In our last phone interview Simone said that she sees herself as "a solid and mature person".

Friends were always very important to Simone, and she had a group of close friends, with one best friend whom she had known for years, and she had a boyfriend for two years, However, contact with her friends dropped off after Simone changed to a new school, which took up a lot of her time and energy.

For Simone, her family was always the primary context of socialisation. Even with growing independence, and the growing importance of friends, her family was for her the safe haven to which she could return and on which she could rely.

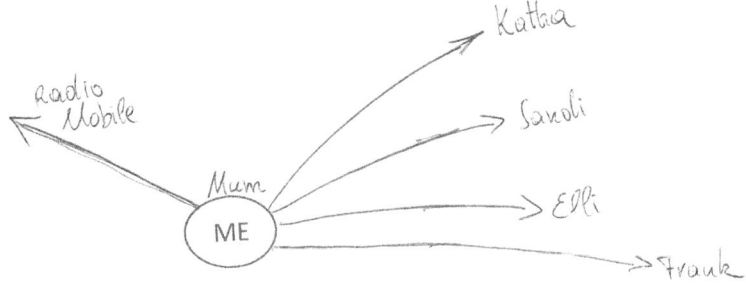

Fig. 8.5 Network map by Simone Stab in 2016 (Tracing based on the original, translated and anonymised by the authors)

8.4.2 The Other Families of Type 3

8.4.2.1 The Aufbauer Family

This family was one of those severely challenged financially when the study began. By the end, the situation had improved somewhat, but Ms. Aufbauer, a very intelligent and seemingly well-read woman, had most of the time been supported by social welfare and the childcare allowance. She had four children, all from different fathers, and described herself as a single mother by choice, having no interest in any man in her life. The family situation could be described as turbulent, with a baby always needing care, so that the older children usually had to look after themselves.

In addition, the family displayed Ms. Aufbauer's permanent urge to change things. They moved a lot during the study, that itself being also a way of receiving new housing benefits, once the one for the old apartment had ended. Amelie, one of the daughters, even called herself a "moving expert", although the many school changes and the need to find new friends seemed to burden her. By the end of the study, Ms. Aufbauer appeared to have found some balance in her life, as the climate within the family was good, and previous conflicts between the siblings as between mother and children had mostly been resolved. This improvement was due in part to the oldest daughter moving out of the apartment, thus removing some of the tension, as the apartment had become too small for so many people. The constant proximity to each other had triggered conflicts between the grown-up, older daughter and the rest of the family. Only Amelie was, apparently, somewhat disappointed when her sister, her close friend and reference person, moved out and left her behind.

The relationship between Ms. Aufbauer and Amelie improved considerably after the mother supported her daughter during a difficult time following a problematic relationship and break-up. Amelie had a partner who tried to take possession of her and who wanted to control her. Her mother stood by her and finally helped her to break free. Amelie is a very pretty and very intelligent, confident young woman, but when it came to men and relationships, she seemed to lose her confidence and became insecure. She tried to master this problem through self-help books and was thus able to independently strengthen her *competences for actions* and set herself new *outlines for actions.*

The dire socio-economic situation of the family, and the limitations that Amelie experienced through it, left their marks. Amelie was dreaming of a better future with financial independence. Her media-use mirrored her fantasies of consumption and her desire to acquire luxury goods. Various German reality shows addressing these topics were among her particular favourites (e.g., a show called *Shopping Queen*, where women get a certain amount of money to spend on an outfit) and even served to develop fantasies about her own future: one example involved becoming a real estate agent. She also liked to pick content that dealt with finding one's own way and becoming famous. Together with her mother, she liked to watch the well-known series, *Sex and the City*, treating it as a mother-daughter viewing ritual. While this particular practice may be classified as amicability (see Chapter 7), Ms. Aufbauer's dominant media practice was characterised by laissez-faire (see Chapter 7). For Amelie, the media always represented a constant in her otherwise very unstable circumstances. Their importance for her over during the study could well be described as tremendous.

In order to earn a lot of money later on, she was looking for well-paid business sectors. At one point, she was—inspired by her favourite television show—dreaming of becoming a real estate agent, especially for Russian clients. Later, she was planning to pursue a career in business administration or to study economics, and during our last phone interview, she was contemplating studying medicine. Their permanently straitened circumstances always marked the whole family's *outlines for actions*, but they stood out in Amelie's particular *outlines for actions*, with her striving for financial security, strength and resilience.

8.4.2.2 The Boll Family
The story of the Boll family was one marked by various misfortunes, from which the family was, however, always able to recover. When the study began, Mrs. Boll had a husband and a large family of nine children, a tenth child had already moved out. They were living on a farm and managed to get by on what the farm provided and through additional sources of income, like Mrs. Boll's dog breeding business. The farm was isolated in the countryside, meaning that Gregor and his siblings did not have many social contacts, and the media were often used to compensate, or to keep the children occupied. Despite this, the media did not, for a long time, play a big role in the life of Gregor and his siblings. Compared to other children in the sample, they spent a lot of time outside, playing on the farm and playing with each other. When they used television, the viewing was often actually initiated by the parents.

Overall, the family situation was fine, and the family members seemed quite happy. Then Mrs. Boll was diagnosed with cancer, had to undergo treatment. While in chemotherapy, she found out that her husband had had an affair with the children's elementary school teacher. She filed for divorce, moved out of the house and later moved back to her old home in Northern Germany, taking the younger children with her. Contact between her and her ex-husband was basically non-existent by the end of the study, and it is clear that she was never able to forgive him for his behaviour, being deeply shocked by the events, as she believed they led a happy life together.

Mrs. Boll had to get by on few financial resources, since alimony payments were either infrequent or did not come at all. However, she did not want to sue her ex-husband and found other ways to manage everyday expenses. The region she had moved to was one with very low prices for houses, so she was able to buy a cheap, old house with the help of friends. After some time, she was also able to restart her dog breeding business, which provided an important source of income, so that, together with her invalid's pension and a pension from one of her previous employers, the situation was stable.

What remained of the large family bonded closely after the misfortunes, and it was clear throughout the last years of the study that Mrs. Boll had managed to slowly expand the limited *options for actions* for herself and her children, thus expanding their horizons. With the exception of Gregor's older sister, who displayed very problematic behaviour for some time after the move, all the children managed to become independent and to find work near their mother, whom they now in turn wanted to support. After a certain adjustment period, Gregor seemed to settle into his new surroundings and had hardly any contact with his father anymore. He took his mother's side and could not understand his father's actions. The relationship to his older siblings in Austria was very good, and they were very close and important persons of reference.

After he moved to Germany, the social media began to play an important role in Gregor's life, since they provided a way to stay in touch with friends and family from back home. Ever since the move, we could characterise Gregor's motives for media usage as communication and participation in group communication (including his family, his school friends and a group that always met in the local pub) (see Fig. 8.6). Finding information and entertainment were other motives as well.

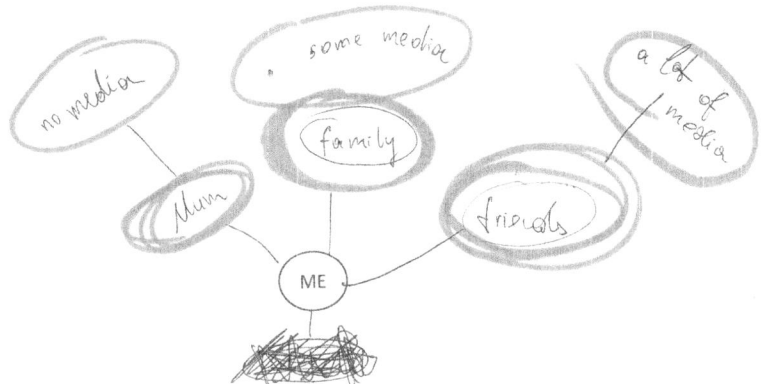

Fig. 8.6 Network map by Gregor Boll in 2016 (Tracing based on the original, translated and anonymised by the authors)

Gregor and his older twin brothers like using the media (e.g., computer games) together in the brothers' apartment. By the end of the study, it seemed that Gregor was using many more media devices and services than before moving to Germany. His parents had no time to monitor their children anyway, but evinced laissez-faire practices (see Chapter 7). However, it never appeared that Gregor was using the media entirely uncritically.

In this context, Gregor was able to develop his own perspectives and to acquire the necessary *competences for action*. His *outlines for actions* always included supporting his mother, something he did not see as clashing with his wish for independence.

8.4.2.3 The Ebner Family
The Ebner family, consisting of Mr. and Mrs. Ebner and their two children, suffered under limited socio-economic circumstances throughout our entire study. Mr. Ebner was working on the small farm where he and his family lived. At the beginning, the family was living in an old farm house without heating and suffering consequent problems with mould. They even led to the Ebner's son developing asthma. Later, they were able to move into a newer house next to the old one and viewed this change as a tremendous improvement of their situation. Although the location of the farm is somewhat remote, the family felt comfortable

there. In contrast to the socio-economic, the socio-emotional situation of the family and the climate within the family were very good during the entire study. The parents' relationship worked well, and they got married after initially living together. The children had a good relationship with their parents especially in the case of Elisabeth, who was very close to her mother. She said that her mother was her most important person of reference and also her role model. Elisabeth and her brother had a very close relationship right through the study, obviously being extremely fond of each other and never really arguing about anything. Although the parents had to work hard to make a living, it was important to them to engage in many family activities and to spend as much time together as possible.

Compared to the other families when the study began, the Ebners possessed only a very limited range of media devices. They constantly acquired more and updated them as the study progressed, but they mostly used the media for practical reasons. They did not have very much importance for Elisabeth when she was younger, yet, from the fifth wave onwards, she did claim that she would be "screwed" without media, especially without her smartphone, which crucially served to stay in touch with friends and family, and to organise her everyday life. Until the fourth wave, Elisabeth was not very tech-/computer-savvy and needed her brother's help to switch on the computer, but from then onwards, her skills improved greatly: she could navigate the internet and was even writing on a manga story in a fan forum online. Communication about the media, and forms of mediation, happened within the family throughout the study, while the parents did their best to inform their children about possible dangers, or they discussed interesting content together. All in all, Elisabeth's parents could be said to have shown a sort of child-centred mediation (see Chapter 7).

Despite the limited *options for actions*, all members of the family were able to direct their *outlines for actions* towards the family. As a result, the climate of relationships within it was intact and very stable throughout the years, providing a good basis for Elisabeth and her brother to cope with their developmental tasks and to develop their own *competences for action*. We consider that Mr. and Mrs. Ebner tried to be role models for their children and to guide them as they grew up, while at the same time leaving them their free space to explore their options. For the Ebners, an open form of communication was clearly the key to their parenting strategy. As a result, we always observed that Elisabeth did very well in her life, with strong ties to her family, a solid circle of friends and training to become a florist, a profession she had been dreaming about for a long time. At the end of the study, Elisabeth seemed fairly capable of developing her own *outlines for actions*, as well as being well able to shape her future life for herself.

8.4.2.4 The Kaiser Family

The Kaiser family consisted of Mrs. Kaiser—a single mother after the divorce from her husband between the third and the fourth waves—her son, Torsten, and his two younger brothers. She was working part-time before she developed psychological problems during the sixth wave. She had, in fact, already had a long period of hospital treatment during the fifth wave. Mrs. Kaiser still lived in the owner-occupied flat that she and her ex-husband had bought together and was, by and large, satisfied with her living situation.

Her ex-husband remarried after their divorce and fathered a daughter. In contrast to other families of this type, the contact between Mr. Kaiser and his children, as well as his ex-wife, remained fairly good. Torsten was especially close to him and loved his half-sister dearly. His important reference persons were his grandparents, who offered him much support. Conflicts between Mrs. Kaiser and Torsten occurred during the fifth wave, when Torsten was trying to gain more independence. His mother always remained anxious to maintain a good relationship with her kids, even when her mental health issues began. From the beginning of the study, through the divorce and until the end, the family was always able to solve problems together very competently, and the family ties remained strong. Yet Mrs. Kaiser and her younger children experienced Torsten's moving out as a welcome relief, because the apartment had become very crowded as the children grew older. Torsten was able to get into job training, and because of limited space at home, he had to live in a hostel during the week. This was something Torsten actually experienced as a relief.

The family had always been very well-equipped with media, and Torsten himself had been an avid media user for some time. His mother, therefore, monitored her son relatively strictly, but not methodically, whereas his father allowed him to play undeniably violent computer games. During the third and fourth waves, his mother said that he would watch television or play video games all day long if allowed to. During the sixth wave, after moving out during the week to stay at his employer's hostel, he did not have to stick to his mother's rules anymore and seemed to spend most of his leisure time with media. At the same time, he occasionally misplaced his phone, not finding it for days. Yet he seemed critical in his media use, was interested in media production, knew a lot about privacy settings on social media and had only 23 friends on it, mostly close friends and family, when the study ended.

Mrs. Kaiser tried to keep an open relationship with her children, in the hope they would not keep secrets from her. These attempts met some resistance, when Torsten started to play online video games intensively and was spending his whole leisure time with game playing. In order to minimise the potential risks to her son, she installed a filter software without informing him about it, meaning she had decided to enforce a particular restriction (see Chapter 7). In general, the climate in the family remained very good, as Torsten, despite conflicts with his mother, lovingly looked after his younger brothers and cared about them. His mother supported him, and, as he grew out of puberty, Torsten did seem to rely on her and to realise that his mother cared about him.

Despite their limited *options for actions*, the Kaiser family was able to cope with their everyday life and its various challenges in a very competent way through mutual support and communication.

8.5 THE FAMILIES OF TYPE 4

Families in Socio-Economic Circumstances No Longer Strained and with Unproblematic Socio-Emotional Relationship Structures: The Competent Social Climbers. (Grubert, Scheib, Pfortner, Dornbacher and Zarbl)

Type 4 consists mostly of families who had been living together in the same constellation for some time during the study. These families can be described as "social climbers" because they experienced a significant improvement in their socio-economic situation for various reasons, like marriage, new jobs, an additional income or a pay raise. Some of the families already had a good and solid socio-emotional relationship structure at the beginning, while others experienced a considerable improvement, often as a result of better socio-economic circumstances. All the families made a stable and solid impression by the end of the study and were able to cope with everyday life challenges quite competently. Once having moved up socially, the families were eager to secure their position and to stabilise the situation for themselves. Since they did not want to endanger their new status, their *outlines for actions* were focused on maintaining the good climate among them, in order to also secure the improved situation for their children.

The parents of the Type 4 families were characterised by a very devoted attitude towards their children and their needs, as well as interacting respectfully with them. After they largely shed the burden of financial troubles, these parents were able to focus their attention on their children rather than on finances, health issues, broken relationships or unattainable *outlines for actions*. Through their improved resources (of money as well as time), these parents had more leeway in raising their children in greater comfort and closer relationships. Parenting strategies based on child-centred mediation rather than unmethodical restriction gave the children freedom to develop their individual "*Eigen-Sinn*" (*selfwill*). This became obvious in the *outlines for actions* and the acquisition of *competences for action*, like more self-esteem and clearer goals in pursuing their own professional career paths.

8.5.1 The Case of Erich Grubert and His Family

8.5.1.1 Situation and Climate of Relationships Within the Family

When the study began, Erich (17 years old in 2016) and his single mother were living in a fairly deprived neighbourhood. Ms. Grubert was reluctant to let her son play outside and avoided contact with other residents and children. As a result, Erich spent most of his leisure time inside their apartment and used the media to relieve his boredom. He was slightly obese, hyperactive and could not concentrate on anything.

The situation of the family improved, however, when Ms. Grubert was able to increase her working hours and, in addition, find a new partner during the second wave. A newly-formed family resulted and moved to a bigger apartment in a nicer neighbourhood, remaining in this constellation until the end of the study.

These events marked a significant change in the life of the family. From then on, they experienced much more stability and were able to gradually improve their overall situation, financially level as well as regards relationships. The changes also affected Erich, whose small social circle began to widen, as his mother no longer had reservations regarding the neighbours' children. Over the years, Erich's health also improved, with any problems slowly subsiding.

Although Erich and his stepfather did not share many interests at the beginning, and the stepfather's ideas of masculinity and leisure time activities were not always in line with Erich's, the boy accepted him in his father role. They had a fairly good relationship, sometimes even sharing an interest in repairing motorcycles together. For these reasons, we proceed by referring to Ms. Grubert and her new partner as "parents".

Throughout the study, there was hardly any doubt that Erich had a close relationship with his mother. Her statements and his statements usually matched, with the exception of smaller secrets, like his first girlfriend, which Erich kept from her as he grew older, apparently not yet being willing to share them. But Erich never left any doubt about how important his family was to him. Even as a teenager, he said that he would take them with him to a desert island, while the importance of his family is underlined in his network map, where his family is drawn very close to him (see Fig. 8.7).

The financial situation of the family improved still further between the fourth and fifth waves. Ms. Grubert's partner, an IT technician, got a new job with a new employer, which meant a higher income and no more night shifts. This left him more leisure time to spend with

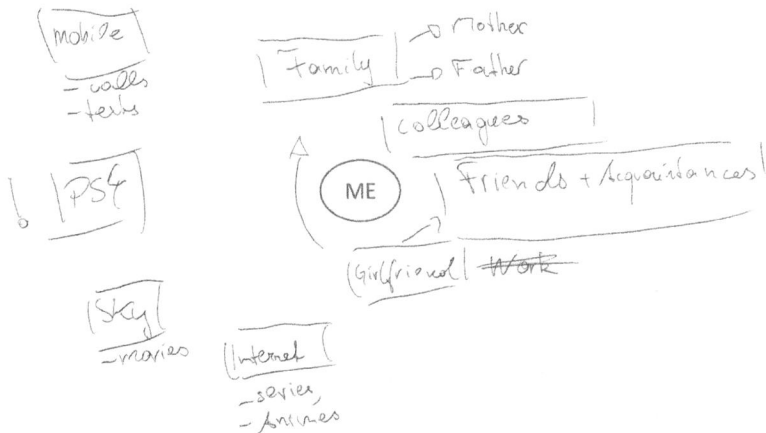

Fig. 8.7 Network map by Erich Grubert in 2016 (Tracing based on the original, translated and anonymised by the authors)

the family. Erich had also started job training to become a cook, which he enjoyed a lot, not least because he was now earning his first salary. He said that he enjoyed the concomitant freedom and independence. He offered to contribute a part of his salary to pay the rent, but his mother declined it.

This big step in Erich's life also had an influence on his daily routine, his leisure time activities, his circle of friends and especially also on his media usage. He slowly replaced the previously important school friends by friends he made at work. As Erich himself attested, the time he spent together with his colleagues during and often after work too became more important for him, so that only one long-time friend, whom he had known since moving to the new neighbourhood, was still close to him. Along with new friends, a new girlfriend also claimed his attention and leisure time.

Working usually from noon until half-past-nine or ten in the evening and having few free weekends limited the time available for the previously dominant video games. Similarly, activities together with the family also became fewer, as did Erich's involvement with the boy scouts. Instead, Erich now enjoyed the occasional night out with colleagues or his girlfriend.

The only negative development Erich experienced during the last years of the study was the complete loss of contact with his biological father. Contact had never been good, but he did hear from his father, at least from time to time. To compensate, Erich found support from his stepfather and the latter's parents.

With a stable relationship network and a lot of mutual trust within the family, the Gruberts were always able to cope with problems and challenges competently. During the last year of school, Erich was struggling with the demands and the stress, which sometimes clouded relations, but he and his parents were usually able to resolve these issues together. By the end of the study, Erich has directed his *outlines for actions* towards finishing his job training and entering another programme to become a butcher, which would enhance his later job opportunities and his income.

The parents were content with their overall situation, especially since Erich's job contributed to a better climate in the family and an even closer relationship between them, after the stresses of school were over. They were considering a house in the suburbs, while Ms. Grubert was acquiring some unspecified further education.

8.5.1.2 Media

As of the second wave, the family was always well-equipped with media, which can be attributed to the step-father's profession as an IT technician. The devices usually reflected state-of-the-art technology, although Erich's mother was the least interested among them in the latest models of smartphone or the like. Erich liked to update his media equipment, especially after beginning to earn his own money, when he started to buy additional devices. He was very proud of his favourite spot in his room, where he had his own flat screen TV, various consoles and a selection of video games.

The picture he took also shows Erich's hookah (an instrument for smoking flavoured tobacco, with origins in India that has become increasingly popular among young people in Austria in the last years), something that he was also very proud of. Brands were important to Erich when buying equipment. His parents declared that he was very selective and had a clear idea of what he wanted, where he wanted to obtain it, and where he could get the best price.

Erich's media-related interests did not change much throughout the study, but the intensity of his which media use changed over the years. During the first wave, his media usage was highly intensive due to a lack of other leisure time activities, so that the media served as a means to compensate for the limited social contacts with peers. Erich expressed an early interest in content focusing on natural science and fantasy. Anime, for example, remained a central interest of his throughout the study.

A decrease in Erich's media usage, following the changes he underwent between the first and second waves, lowered its intensity for some time, until video games gained importance between the fourth and fifth waves. By that time, the media had begun to serve as a release for school stress. They became a focal point during his youth and adolescence. During the third wave, Erich explained that his favourite object in his room was his PlayStation 3. He later acquired a PlayStation 4 (PS4), which was so important to him that he marked it with an exclamation mark in his network map from the last wave (see Fig. 8.7).

Erich's interest in video games gave him extensive knowledge of gaming vocabulary and strategies and a liking for complex and intricate games. He was familiar with cheats and managed to master the game, *Skyrim*, within just two weeks. This particular game had previously caused a conflict between Erich and his mother during the fourth wave, since Ms. Grubert did not approve of the game and refused to buy it for her son. Erich knew the game through one of his friends and, although he recognised that there was a lot of blood and violence in it, he claimed that he only wanted to play it for the storyline. When our interviewer asked whether he liked blood being everywhere, he responded: "No, actually I only play it because of the story, it's good quality, that's why I play it. I don't care, if it was up to me, it could be without the bloodshed at all!"

Playing complex video games presented a challenge for Erich and helped him experience self-efficacy. His mother assumed that he was suffering from low self-esteem after being mobbed in school because of his weight, so that being successful at video games restored some of his self-esteem.

Apart from anime and video games, the internet, social media, together with the smartphone as a device that bundles all these services, gained importance during the last two waves. Erich was mainly an observer and hardly ever active on platforms like Facebook. Unlike other children in the sample, he had only about 80 friends, but knew all of them personally.

Once Erich started his job training, he had less time for media, so the intensity of use reduced, and Erich's parents claimed that he became much more responsible with the media. He used his smartphone less in the end, since it was forbidden at his workplace, which influenced his media usage in another way as well: Erich began listening to the radio a lot, as it was always on in the restaurant kitchen. It became his most important source of information, especially during the refugee crisis in 2015/2016.

The Gruberts' family activities also included using the media together throughout the study. Usually the television had been the focus of their media usage in common, as when watching crime series together. This activity had declined due to Erich's new daily routine, but the occasional television evening together still took place.

Overall, media were very important to the Grubert family. Due to the stepfather's profession, the media also had a high practical value, given that the family's income was mostly based on working with them. The media were constant companions and were used in many different ways for entertainment and for convenience in sourcing information. As Erich's mother pointed out in the last interview, they could not imagine life without them.

Information about, for example, sport events played a crucial role. Particularly notable throughout the study was the family's large collection of books, in addition to the various electronic devices.

Ms. Grubert collected various books about pets and animals in general, and used them as sources for advice on the family's number of pets throughout the years (cats, snakes, a dog, a hamster).

Nevertheless, the generally positive attitude towards the media did not mean that all content was viewed uncritically by Erich's parents. Ms. Grubert did not care for violence and pornography, as in her refusal to buy *Skyrim* for Erich, but she said that she later gave in because in her opinion refusing would ultimately only make it more desirable to him.

8.5.1.3 Parenting and Role of Socialisation Contexts

The parenting strategies in the Grubert family were mostly based on a form of child-centred mediation, especially with regard to media literacy. The expert in the family was Erich's stepfather, at least as far as the technological aspects of media usage went. He was the one with an eye to filter software, who took care to teach Erich an awareness of privacy issues. Talking about media content or issues related to the potential risks of media usage had been happening from the second wave on. As a result, Erich appeared to be a fairly aware media user.

At the beginning of the study, Ms. Grubert told us that she strictly controlled her son's media usage, but the details of her actual practices indicated that these actually tended to laissez-faire. She often emphasised later on that she did not approve of punishment or restrictions as educational tools, but, if anything, she used praise as an incentive for the "right" behaviour. She put a lot of trust into her son and in his ability to tell right from wrong.

In Erich's case, the crucial role of a family's dynamics for the development of a child became very clear. His youth was marked by two fundamental changes, with far-reaching effects on his family's situation and on himself. The first big change was his mother's new partner, who slowly became accepted as a father figure. The relationship with his mother endured, and thus Erich experienced a form of stability and support that he was lacking when the study began. Although the interests of stepfather and stepson didn't always match, Erich gained new and different experiences and could also explore new possibilities for his leisure time.

The second big change occurred via Erich's job training, which had an impact on his daily routine, his social circle and also on his media usage. As opposed to school, which Erich sometimes experienced as a chaotic and restrictive socialisation context, his work provided opportunities for new *outlines for actions*. The new school that he attended as part of his training was much more to his liking, and he got better grades, had a good relationship with his teachers and actually enjoyed it overall.

Working together with people of different backgrounds and ethnicities seemed to broaden his horizon, causing him to talk about issues of immigrants and the refugee crisis in a very reflected and less negative way. He perceived the change of his social circle through the new school and the workplace as a positive development, because he had suffered from bullying in his old school, where brands and clothing were a big issue.

Concurrently with the job training, Erich's relationship with his parents had also changed. He still saw them as important reference bullying persons, but at the same time he enjoyed his growing independence and in turn, his parents respected their son's maturing, not seeing themselves as educators anymore. Ms. Grubert felt that the time of actual "parenting" was over, and that they were more supporters and encouragers.

8.5.2   The Other Families of Type 4

8.5.2.1 The Scheib Family

Much like the Grubert family, the Scheib family was in a very precarious situation when the study began. Mrs. Scheib was a single mother with two daughters, and the family lived in a very small, crowded apartment. She and her daughters had to make ends meet with what she earned from working 15 hours a week and received in alimony payments. Their situation changed radically when Mrs. Scheib met her prospective husband between the first and second waves. They moved to a large city in the south of Germany and into a bigger apartment in a very nice neighbourhood. As a consequence, Mrs. Scheib and her daughters experienced a massive increase in their *options for actions*, especially since the opportunities for the children in the neat, affluent surroundings, together with their better financial situation meant new possibilities for shaping their leisure time activities.

Susanne, the older of the two siblings, at first struggled with the move, because she had to leave all her friends from kindergarten behind. Among other things, she tried to use the media to compensate, but she was able to make new friends as well, which reduced the relevance of the media. Throughout the study, Susanne and her sister were in touch with their biological father back in Austria, and that also enabled her to stay in touch with other relatives in her old home-town. The only person

Susanne did not get along with was the father's new girlfriend, whom he had met before the sixth wave, but his daughter's relationship with him seemed not to suffer from this.

After these life-changing events, Susanne's situation was marked by stability, and her stepfather became an important person of reference for her. Her mother remained a central reference person as well, with their relationship seeming fairly balanced and trusting, but it was somewhat shaken when Susanne apparently suffered a personal crisis shortly before the sixth wave. She quit school, although previous interviews had always shown her to be a good student with very good grades, who liked going to school. Puberty and the developmental tasks linked to it apparently put a strain on her, which was expressed in a sudden and strong wish for independence. In the last interview, Susanne mentioned that her views and her parents' views had drifted apart by that time. She turned to an intensive use of the media, and her mother reported about up to seven hours of watching television a day. The media had gained much relevance overall, with, in particular, her smartphone becoming a focal point of her media use, especially for managing contacts and using social media. Prior to this, Susanne always displayed a very moderate use of the media, and they had played more of a subordinate role in her life between the first and fourth waves. Mrs. Scheib presented herself as rather critical of the media (and especially the mainstream media) and saw risks, but she also emphasised the benefits of the media use at various points. However, the family's range of media devices was comparatively small, especially when the study began.

When the study ended, Susanne was 18 years old and appeared to have overcome her crisis. She caught up on her school education and was aiming to earn her secondary school certificate and to continue to a higher secondary vocational school. In the meantime, the television had lost its relevance almost completely, while only the smartphone remained important for managing social contacts. As an almost grown-up, Susanne was now focusing more on her friends and considered them to be a very important part of her life.

Susanne and her family have always been competent at dealing with everyday life challenges—a central characteristic of the Type 4 families—and so they were also able to resolve Susanne's crisis and to help her find her own way to future independence.

8.5.2.2 The Pfortner Family

In contrast to the Scheib and Grubert families, the Pfortners' economic situation did not improve because of a new partner, but because of an increase in the parents' financial resources. This led to better *options for actions* for the family, consisting of the son, Helmut, a daughter older than him, Mrs. Pfortner and her husband, the father of both children. The family had been living in a house adjacent to Mr. Pfortner's workshop. On its own, the father's business was not doing well enough to support the family adequately, and between the second and third waves, Mrs. Pfortner took up another part-time job outside of the family business. This led to an improvement in the overall situation. Slowly but steadily, the business seems to have done slightly better as well, but the income continued to fluctuate, so Mr. Pfortner was thinking about expanding to make more money. By the end of the study, the family was able to renovate and extend the upper storey of the house, with an apartment for each of the children. The previously precarious and rather insecure financial situation had improved a lot over the years, and had actually disappeared by the end of the study. Helmut had suffered from their strained circumstances at the beginning, but his situation also improved along with the family's fortunes. He was even able to catch up on his school education, after being diagnosed with a limited degree of ability at the beginning of the study and having to stay in kindergarten for another year.

The socio-emotional circumstances in the family were mostly very stable throughout the study. Helmut has always had a close relationship with his father, who was hoping that his son would take over the family business at some point. Helmut was especially close to his mother in a supportive and trusting relationship, which persisted as Helmut grew older. He confided in her when he had problems, helped her out wherever he could and talked about what was going on in his life. The wider family ties appeared very strong, with his relationship to the older sister being very good, as was his contact with other relatives, like grandparents, and particularly with one aunt.

There was one conflict that shook the family during the fourth wave. It involved a fight between the parents resulting from an incident with alcohol (which was not further elaborated on). Helmut's aunt was able to mediate in this dispute, and after it was resolved, there was no more mention of conflicts or alcohol-related problems, so it was presumably a one-time incident.

Despite his very close relationship with his whole family, Helmut started to develop a more independent life towards the end of the study and began to focus on his friends and his sporting activities—Helmut has been an active wrestler for many years and is one of only few children in the panel who participated in an organised sports club activity—so that his training and competitions took up most of his leisure time. By the end of the study, he also mentions a girlfriend, who equally required a lot of attention.

Helmut was able to enter job training to become a machine-tool technician and was, thus, on track to follow in his father's footsteps. Mrs. Pfortner was very proud of her son's development and emphasised how mature, independent and autonomous her son had become.

Throughout the study, Helmut had always been a rather intensive media user, especially at the beginning, when he used the television a lot, but the focus of his media use shifted as he grew older. Especially the smartphone became more and more relevant, mostly to communicate with peers. He started to choose the media content he was using more deliberately as well and, because of his job training and his sporting activities, he did not have much time left to use the media in his leisure time. Mrs. Pfortner was very happy about this development, as she has always been critical of his media use, although she considered the media in general important.

The stability that his family provided was clearly reinforced by more financial security, and, in turn, contributed to Helmut's development. The family had always been competent at dealing with every day-life challenges and found ways to cope with problems together.

8.5.2.3 The Dornbacher Family
The situation of the Dornbacher family, consisting of Mr. and Mrs. Dornbacher and their two daughters, had been greatly influenced by changing employment in the course of the study. The family only displayed a few specific characteristics of a social disadvantage because they were living in an owner-occupied apartment in the countryside and expected to pay it off in a few years. However, the financial situation was difficult when Mr. Dornbacher was on parental leave and his wife was working 15 hours a week in an office. The father changed jobs frequently in the years following his paternity leave, and their situation was sometimes more, sometimes less strained, as was the climate among them. But throughout the years and all the developments, the parents

always made sure that they supported their children by inculcating a feeling of support and security. The fourth wave saw a big change for the family, when Mr. Dornbacher was able to get a fairly well-paid, full-time job nearby and the financial situation became notably better.

The relationship between the parents and the children could be best described as amicable, the father was a good interlocutor, especially for his daughter, Gudrun, and they would often discuss books in general, as well as philosophy. The harmonious situation also large to other relatives. Gudrun and her sister were very close to their grandparents and their various aunts and uncles. Parenting was mostly based on child-centred mediation and had a strong focus on furthering the children, no matter what the financial situation looked like.

The improved financial situation, and the better *options for actions* related to it, became visible in Gudrun's *outlines for actions* after the fourth wave—she was able to visit a private Montessori secondary school and was focusing on passing the admission test for the academy of music to study the flute (recorder/English flute) and become a music teacher. Music had been a hobby of hers for a long time, and her parents always did their best to support her in this endeavour. Like many other children in the panel, Gudrun liked watching television—especially during a period in the fourth panel wave when she had had trouble finding friends and so had used media content for orientation and coming to terms with topics that preoccupied her. Later, the smartphone became more important, but Gudrun had been an avid reader as well and actively wrote stories herself, even publishing some of them online. Her passion for books was also something that stood out in the panel and was something that her parents had passed on to her, being avid readers themselves. Her creativity and her ability to express herself were mirrored in Gudrun's network maps, which were always very elaborate. Her network map from 2014 shows how much thought she put into arranging the people who were important to her in carefully designated circles around her, thus visualising the proximity (see Fig. 8.8).

The map displays many friends, both boys and girls, some of whom had been her close friends for years (e.g., since primary school), as well as her close relatives, with whom she shares her inner circle.

8.5.2.4 The Zarbl Family

Similar to the Scheib family, the Zarbl family experienced a social elevation when Mrs. Zarbl acquired a new partner and later married him. In

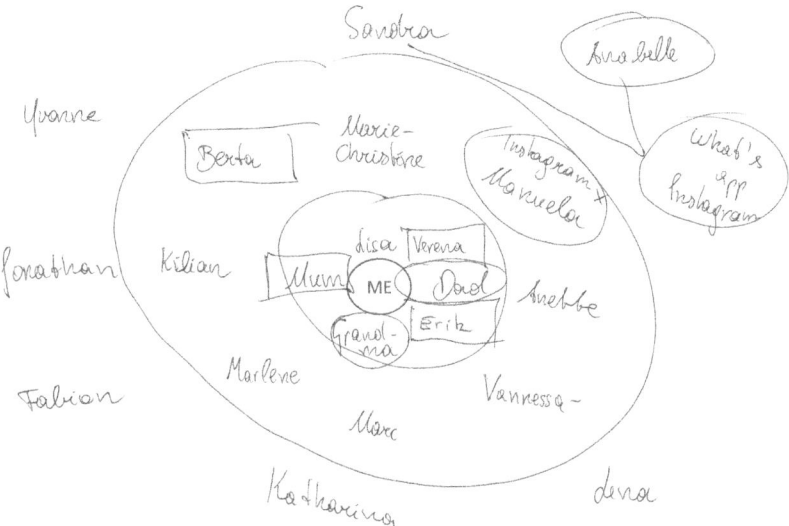

Fig. 8.8 Network map by Gudrun Dornbacher in 2014 (Tracing based on the original, translated and anonymised by the authors)

the first wave, the family still consisted of Mrs. Zarbl, her son, Norbert, his younger brother and the biological father of the two boys. The climate in the family was very strained at that time due to the parents' conflicted relationship. As a result, the relationship between Norbert and his mother was problematic. Norbert was watching a lot of television, but rather aimlessly, while his parents often used television as a "babysitter" to keep him occupied while they were struggling with their stressful relationship and overall situation. Mrs. Zarbl and her partner separated before the second wave, leaving Mrs. Zarbl short of money. However, the family's socio-emotional circumstances improved, with regard to the ex-partner too, as the separation had taken a lot of pressure off both parents. By the third wave, Mrs. Zarbl had a new partner, who brought financial stability back into the family. Subsequently, Mrs. Zarbl increased her working hours, which contributed to the further improvement of the socio-economic situation and its increasing stability. Norbert and his biological father kept in touch throughout the study, although, due to time constraints, contact reduced when Norbert started his job training. His stepfather became an important reference person as well.

Mrs. Zarbl's new partner and husband brought two kids of his own into the family, but they were already grown-up and independent and, thus, did not move in along with him. We registered only minor conflicts, one of which was, in fact, media related, when, during the fourth wave, Norbert's biological father and his stepfather differed about the action movies Norbert was not allowed to watch at home, but which his father allowed him to watch at his place. Mrs. Zarbl tried to control Norbert's media usage—to his annoyance—but she could not manage this consistently. Apart from that, Norbert's relationship with his mother improved tremendously during the study and became much more balanced. But Norbert continued to be generally introverted, although, as he grew older, he started to be more independent and spend more and more time with his friends. Communication with his friends was a priority, which is why his smartphone was so relevant to him. He also continued to like various video games, like *Call-of-Duty*. Norbert had very elaborate media equipment in his room, clearly designed to make the most of his gaming experience, as a picture of his favourite spot for media use shows that he took in 2014: A centrally arranged flat screen TV is framed with a powerful sound system, different game consoles, receiver and a stereo system are at Norbert's disposal.

When the study ended, Norbert seemed fairly competent at managing his life and future perspectives, something that he learned from his mother and his family, both parties proving to be fairly competent at dealing with life challenges over the years of the study.

8.6 Conclusion

The typology presented in this chapter clearly demonstrates that children and their families operate within an individual framework, where the family develops ways of coping or fails to cope. This chapter helps to understand how many of the researched families, especially from Type 1 and Type 2, were often overstrained in multiple ways and experienced different forms of deprivation on many levels. The families differ greatly from each other as far as their *options for action*, their *outlines for action* and their *competences for action* are concerned.

While the Type 1 families suffer from severe socio-economic problems, experienced as multiple deprivation—they are overall rather overwhelmed by their situation/unable to cope—the Type 2 families do not experience socio-economic problems anymore or only to a very small extent compared to the beginning of the study in 2005, but their situation is very strained because of severe problems on the socio-emotional level that did not resolve when the financial situation improved—especially with regard to the relationships between parents and children. As a consequence, the Type 1 families are characterised by very limited *options for actions*, especially on the parents' part, since the socio-economic resources are very scarce and the worry about making ends meet overshadows the families' everyday life. Many of the parents and children belonging to this type began to develop health issues during the study, and these dominated the everyday life and the relationship structures within the families, burdening and problematising their *doing family* even more. In the light of the limited *options for action*, the *outlines for action* often appear limited as well, and everyday challenges—like supporting the family, buying clothes, parenting and so on—meet with a lack of *competences for action*. This constellation leads to a feeling of overextension; some even fail altogether at coping with their everyday challenges. All the children who experienced this particular constellation suffer from the conditions in the family and experience hardly any support, or none at all, in fulfilling their own developmental tasks. Depending on their cognitive abilities and their self-will, they were, like Timo Landinger, either not able to develop their own *outlines for action* and to build *competences for action*, or only to a limited extent, as Manfred Oblinger was doing by the time the study ended. What stands out about the Type 1 families is how they differ from those of Type 3 and Type 4 in a fundamental sense: having no security network among relatives or friends.

Among the adolescents, it was mainly the boys who had problems keeping up with peers in terms of their individual development, so that they often turned into mavericks at their schools. Either they had no friends or very few to share their interests. Their friendships were primarily based around their online games. Considering the fact that, as we pointed out in Chapter 3, there is a correlation between the relationships among family members, the ways in which family members interact with each other, and the children's ability to form relationships later in life, romantic as well as with peers, it is not surprising that the adolescents of Type 1 had not formed romantic relationships during the time of the study.

The situation of the Type 2 families is, as was already described, different in its interplay of *options for action*, *outlines for action* and *competences for action*, as applied to the individual family members. The *options for action* improved over the time of the study for all the families of this type—mostly single mothers at the beginning—through marriage, but also through inheritances. These families experienced increased financial resources, but their problematic socio-emotional relationship structures remained unimproved and they continued to have problems and struggle with overextension within the nuclear family right up to the end of the study. The mothers of this type were often disinterested in their children and left them mostly to fend for themselves, something also mirrored in their parenting strategies and media education.

When they were no longer single, some mothers directed their *outlines for action* fully towards their new partners and new children and used their *competences for actions* to tackle challenges that they met there, whereas the "old" children became less relevant, to the disadvantage of the latter. Usually, they received hardly any support from their family with their own developmental tasks and did not feel at home in their own families. Benedikt Holzner is a very special case in this context, as we showed, since he was able to overcome the traumatic experiences from his early childhood and his mother's disinterest and neglect through moving into an assisted-living facility, where he was able to develop resilience and independence.

The Type 3 families show entirely different characteristics again. They are faced with socio-economic problems, but their socio-emotional situation is quite stable and their relationships among family members are fairly strong, which helps them to better cope with challenging everyday situations. These families experienced deprivation on the socio-economic level from beginning right up to the end of the study, limiting their *options for action* massively (similar to the Type 1 families); but, in contrast to those from Type 1, the parents (mostly single mothers), directed a great deal of their energy, their *outlines for action* and their *competence s for action* towards securing a harmonious family life, as is obvious from their approach to parenting They practised mediation, communication and trust, even though they could not always manage this consistently. These parents supported their children in dealing with their developmental tasks as best as they could under the given circumstances and within the restrictions of the socio-economic situation, so that the children appeared fairly competent at mastering their own lives by the time the study ended.

Lastly, we presented the Type 4 families, who can be characterised as "the social climbers", since they experienced an improving socio-economic situation throughout the study and did not show any problems on the socio-emotional level (anymore) either. The improvement happened through new and/or better jobs or more work hours and new partnerships. Their *options for action* improved along with the increasing financial resources. These families were mostly fairly stable at the beginning, but the socio-economic improvement further contributed to stabilising them. Their children profit from the increasing resources and the growing stability, since they experience a lot of support from their parents, whose *outlines for action* are clearly directed towards the children, helping them in their development and enabling them to develop their own *outlines for action* and acquire the necessary *competences* to realise them. It is evident that the children profit from this support network in their socialisation. The *doing family* and the parenting in these families is again marked by child-centred mediation and a much less laissez-faire approach or an unmethodical, restrictive one, as compared to the families of Types 1 and 2.

Based on the presented results, it can be established that the socio-economic frame does shape everyday life of the families, but the socio-emotional circumstances in the nuclear relationship structures are decisive when it comes to coping with everyday challenges.

The individual interplay of *options for action, outlines for action* and *competences for action* of the parents in particular, but also of the children as they grow older, form the foundation of the actual everyday life in a family, as well as their *doing family*. It also shapes *how* successful the children were in dealing with and using media in the process of their socialisation. Although it is not possible to infer a typology of media usage, it becomes clear against the background of the presented data, that media usage and what is often deemed a "bad" form of media usage can become symptomatic for other things going wrong in a child's life. In this context, an interesting finding is that the adolescents of Type 4, but also of Type 3, value face-to-face-relationships as more than mediated recreational time. They do indeed use computer games and are interested in other (media-related) activities, but these are not a basis determining their recreational time. Instead, it is the immediate contact with friends that is by far more important to them.

With regard to media usage or patterns of media use, it became clear that we could not identify type-specific patterns of media usage, especially not to the extent that such patterns would have been stable across the types throughout the study. However, we could show that the overextension and inability to cope that some families, especially Type 1 and Type 2 families, experience, expand into all areas of everyday life, especially in the ways family members treat each other, interact with each other, in how parents are willing and able to pay attention to the needs of their children and to help them come to terms with their lives. This circumstance even expands to and influences the ways in which children broadly use the media, how they handle media technology and how media literacy is mediated within the family. Some of the families, who experienced an improvement of their situation (economically or emotionally, or both), often mirror this in their stronger orientation towards their children and a more devoted attitude towards parenting, which again is also mirrored in their mediation strategies regarding media literacy, as we were able to show in Chapter 7.

In conclusion, we can say that the typology presented in this chapter draws attention to how the dynamics, both with and without the media, of family life and socialisation develop. The typology can be understood as a step—and one underpinned empirically by our research—towards a better understanding of how to systematically help families find (better) ways of coping and, regarding the use of media, develop specific media literacy concepts in order to enable a participatory response in children.

Notes

1. The original data is in German, all direct quotes that are used in this chapter were translated into English by the authors. In order to make the text more reader-friendly we did not include such a reference for the individual quotes.
2. Large families are defined as families with three or more children (Statistik Austria, 2017, p. 3); since larger families are particularly at risk of poverty, we were specifically looking for families with more than three children.
3. In order to illustrate the children's network map in an international context we decided to create a new version that keeps the style of writing, the visual elements. The terms that have been mentioned were translated and positioned at the same place as in the original map. Spelling mistakes in the original version are indicated by analogue mistakes.
4. Due to copyright reasons the pictures taken by the adolescents cannot be printed. They include visible third-party content like, for example, brands, logos and game visuals. Therefore, the text offers a description to better understand the settings instead of showing the pictures.

References

Havighurst, R. J. (1972). *Developmental tasks and education* (3rd ed.). New York, NY: McKay.

Kluge, S. (2000). Empirisch begründete Typenbildung in der qualitativen Sozialforschung [Empirically based typification in qualitative social research]. *Forum: Qualitative Social Research/Qualitative Sozialforschung, 1*(1). Retrieved from http://www.qualitative-research.net/index.php/fqs/article/view/1124.

Paus-Hasebrink, I., & Kulterer, J. (2014). *Praxeologische Mediensozialisationsforschung. Langzeitstudie zu sozial benachteiligten Heranwachsenden* [Praxeological media socialisation research: A longitudinal study regarding socially disadvantaged adolescents]. Assisted by P. Sinner. Baden-Baden, Germany: Nomos.

Statistik Austria. (2017). *Statistics Brief Armut* [Poverty]. Wien, Austria: Statistik Austria. Retrieved from http://www.statistik-austria.at/wcm/idc/idcplg?IdcService=GET_PDF_FILE&RevisionSelectionMethod=LatestReleased&dDocName=114988.

Open Access This chapter is licensed under the terms of the Creative Commons Attribution 4.0 International License (http://creativecommons.org/licenses/by/4.0/), which permits use, sharing, adaptation, distribution and reproduction in any medium or format, as long as you give appropriate credit to the original author(s) and the source, provide a link to the Creative Commons licence and indicate if changes were made.

The images or other third party material in this chapter are included in the chapter's Creative Commons licence, unless indicated otherwise in a credit line to the material. If material is not included in the chapter's Creative Commons licence and your intended use is not permitted by statutory regulation or exceeds the permitted use, you will need to obtain permission directly from the copyright holder.

CHAPTER 9

Discussion and Conclusion

9.1 THE OBJECTIVES OF THIS LONGITUDINAL STUDY

This book presents our longitudinal study, as conducted in Austria over nearly twelve years, from 2005 until 2017. Our core question focused on the role of media within the socialisation of children, who subsequently became adolescents and grew up in families exhibiting various degrees of social disadvantage. The study followed them from five, or respectively six, years of age up to the last stage of adolescence, and into young adulthood.

Even in a comparatively rich country such as Austria (see Chapter 2), the living conditions of socially disadvantaged young people are particularly demanding. They are often strongly affected by a lack of health (see Kuntz, Waldhauer, Zeiher, Finger, & Lampert, 2018) and by a limited access to education services and, linked to this, with a low level of participation in society. These challenges are intensified by the progressive transformation of the means of communication. As changing media environments are deeply integrated in a constantly changing society, where they act as a trigger for various processes of social change (see Carpentier, Schrøder, & Hallett, 2014; Hepp & Hasebrink, 2014; Lundby, 2014), transformative processes become highly relevant in individuals' everyday lives—and, therefore, for socialisation processes as well. To define the role of the media in the overall context of complex and diverse socialisation processes, a theoretically and methodologically coherent concept is needed. It helps to understand the individual perspective of human beings, as well as the overall aspects of their conduct of everyday life contexts. Despite several heterogeneous approaches from different scientific disciplines, be that sociology, psychology or other disciplines, there is a consensus among modern socialisation researchers, which spotlights the individual perspectives of different actors as the essential aspect of this academic field. Socialisation researchers now link both psychological and sociological elements and conceptualise socialisation as a "bidirectional process" (Smetana, Robinson, & Rote, 2015, p. 60) and, in this sense, as an "interactive process" (Hurrelmann & Bauer, 2015, p. 146), which is created, influenced and modified by the individual (Hurrelmann & Bauer, 2015; see Hurrelmann, Grundmann, & Walper, 2008, p. 17; for an overview about development of socialisation theories, see Prout, 2008; see Chapter 3). But we still know little about *how* these processes proceed within the development of an individual's socialisation. This is, above all, the case, because children are actually growing up in *interlinked contexts*, which are, for their part, saturated by the media. Proceeding from Ien Ang's understanding of contextualism, it seemed to us necessary to identify the relevant contexts shaping the structure of a child's everyday life (Ang, 2006, p. 69). This step was indispensable, in order to show *how* the interaction takes place in the process of young people's socialisation and to illustrate *how* the transfer from social contexts into personal characteristics, and vice versa, takes place.

For our longitudinal study on the role of media within the socialisation of socially disadvantaged adolescents in Austria, we developed a praxeological and integrative approach to (media) socialisation research, which aims to clarify the practical meaning of the individual (media) practices for children and their parents within a family context. This concept espouses a research design both theoretically and methodologically apposite and coherent, one capable of shedding light on the role of the media within the overall context of complex and manifold socialisation processes.

We explore how and why children and adolescents within socially disadvantaged families use different media services for guidance in their everyday lives and to help them to deal with their developmental tasks within their relevant contexts of growing up. To this end, it is necessary to examine not only the adolescents themselves but also their respective lives within their respective families, peer groups and other socialisation contexts, for example, in their schools. It is precisely in these contexts that they gain experience, including how to deal with different media contents and media devices. Against this background, then, young people build their specific media repertoires. Our study investigates these factors, so that we also consider it a contribution to the entire field of family research.

The core of the study lies in the question as to how children and adolescents and their parents, or respectively relatives, like stepfathers or partners of the mothers, deal with media within their socially disadvantaged families and how they use these media services to cope with the challenges of their everyday lives. A longitudinal study is ideal for examining these parameters because long-term communication processes proceed in various ways and change fundamentally in structure and function over time. A qualitative approach seems particularly suitable and enables a focus on the complex processes of building individual orientation which is shaped by conditions for the conduct of everyday life that are socially unequal and structurally distributed (Weiß, 1997, p. 246; see Chapter 3). Such an approach enables to grasp the individual understanding of their specific milieus, but also to pay attention to the common understanding about the ways of living together within their specific milieu (see Weiß, 1997, p. 259). In order to meet these requirements adequately, we focused on our carefully chosen sample and we decided to forego the implementation of a second panel with families who are not socially disadvantaged as a comparison group. At this point, our aim was to accompany our families for such a long time as possible in order to analyse the processes of growing up, the complexity of socialisation, the related dynamics and the cross-linked interplay of relevant social contexts at the best. This concept made it possible to record even the small but subtle differences and to describe the distinctions between the individual families in respect to the process of socialisation and growing up in miscellaneous socially disadvantaged surroundings.

Our study's core is a qualitative longitudinal survey accompanying the children within their families, from kindergarten until adolescence and emerging adulthood (by the end of the study, the adolescents were 16–18 years old). Additionally, we conducted a literature analysis for twelve years, concentrating on national and international research within the scope of this project (see Chapter 2). On the one hand, it framed the project, as our analysis and discussion had, perforce, to deal not only with other qualitative studies but also with quantitative studies, in order to better frame our results against the backdrop of broader findings. On the other hand, we conducted the literature review not only for internal purposes, but also for the public consumption. To this end, we made the results of the literature review publicly available as a separate publication on our project website (https://www.uni-salzburg.at/mediensozialisation). We developed our theoretical framework further by paying attention to special aspects, like the phase of adolescence as one with particular challenges (see Chapters 3 and 6). This is central to our book, because of processes inherent in it, like "sense making" and "self-making" (Arnett, 1995; see also Arnett, 2007).

9.2 THE THEORETICAL FRAMEWORK

At the heart of the praxeological perspective on socialisation processes lies the question about the subjective meaning of the (media) practices displayed by individuals and groups in their *Lebenswelt* (lifeworld) (see Chapter 3). Our focus is on individuals within their everyday lives, in their specific social space actually or symbolically available to them and where they deploy their various forms of "capital" (see Bourdieu, 1986) to make sense of their everyday lives. In this process, media services of all kinds play a substantial role. In private or professional everyday lives, specific social connections determine individuals' range of options to develop their identities, to gain *competences for action* and then to act in differing everyday situations.

We observed individuals' orientation patterns and—partly media-based—sense-making practices, but we did not consider their media usage either from a "subjective" or from an "objective" perspective. Much rather, our study follows Bourdieu's concept of "practical sense", his "praxeology" as developed in "Theory of Practice" (1977). The aim is to understand how the individual can act and does actually act in his or her lifeworld. This lifeworld reaches out beyond the individual. Hence further social contexts relating to the social milieu have to be investigated as well, as it is in them that the individual's ambitions and resources become active and specific patterns of action are "in place" and socially adequate (see Weiß, 2000, p. 47, translated by the authors). While aspiring to make their life meaningful, individuals tend to use media throughout their lives. It is especially against the background of ongoing mediatization processes that the media become signally important. Using a praxeological perspective, socialisation processes, and the role of the media within them, can be examined. Furthermore, we can demonstrate which media services are relevant among an individual's media repertoires and at which stages, during a life-long process of socialisation, these specific services become important for coping with everyday life.

Nevertheless, we need to consider additional facts concerning media usage: on the one hand, the media usage of individuals is determined by the basic structure governing their response to challenges in life. But on the other hand, media usage depends on the specific ways media contents are offered, meaning that only services actually accessible can be used.

We can identify practices of everyday life in terms of the practical, respectively everyday-practical, sense of purpose of every family member, and such findings are of particular importance in praxeologically conceptualised (media) socialisation research. On the one hand, we observe how these practices are developed by the children and adolescents and their siblings, but on the other hand, we also observe how they were developed by the parents too. The following analytical concept enables us to reconstruct the further development in the practices of all of our subjects. It is based on three analytic concepts (see Chapter 3):

- *Options for action* are, on the one hand, related to an individual's specific socio-structural conditions and, on the other, to the socio-structural aspects of society as a whole and to its political, economic, cultural and media contexts. Options for action designate the objective characteristics of an individual's social conditions, which are shaped by the rules of the social field(s) in which he/she operates. Options for action represent an ordered array of possible (and impossible) actions.
- *Outlines for action* are related to subjective perceptions of social conditions and represent the ways in which the subject transforms the characteristics of his/her situation, viewed objectively, into a subjective guide for action. These outlines reflect what makes sense to the subject and indicate the viewpoints from which he/she structures his/her perceptions and interpretations of the world. Thus, all of the families' goals and plans, or those of the individuals, are closely tied to a subjective perception of the social milieu.
- *Competences for action* are related to the resources at the individual's disposal to accomplish the above outlines for action. As Bourdieu maintains, these competences characterise the material, cultural and

social resources available to an individual and serve as cognitive or motivational prerequisites for his/her actions, including the use of the media. These competences are reflected in the realisation of the individual's outlines for action.

Based on the *options for action*, *outlines for action* and *competences for action*, it is theoretically and empirically possible to understand the connection between a social milieu and the subjective structure of making sense of one's own life. Our approach to young people's socialisation, as presented in this book, provides answers through a combined analysis of both the subjective and structural components of practice. It focuses on the lifeworld of a child, and of the subsequent adolescent, within their family, where they conduct their everyday life and where, starting in early childhood, media activity is given its meaning. This approach helps in examining the everyday structures of a child's or adolescent's life, as shaped by the family's social situation, in order to describe the "arrangements" for everyday life and the process of *doing family*. It is through these arrangements that practices, including media practices, are formed and media actions gain structure and meaning. This approach makes it possible to reconstruct the transfer process, namely, how socio-structural conditions transfer onto an individual's subjective perception and (media-related) actions and how this perception leads to an independent orientation towards the world. Following this approach, it is possible not only to look superficially at how children and adolescents deal with media, but also to investigate how they subjectively make sense of the media as a source for coping with their developmental tasks. This acquires special attention to the structures of their everyday life, namely their socio-economic aspects as access to certain media, but also the general availability of media contents in the specific area of living. Against this background, media usage can be read as a practice within a socially constructed everyday life and, hence, as a form of observable practical ability.

9.3 On the Longitudinal Study and Its Process

Our study on the role of the media within the socialisation of socially disadvantaged adolescents in Austria started in 2005 and accompanied the growing-up of selected children, respectively teenagers, within their families until the end of 2016 and the beginning of 2017. To grasp complex processes like this analytically, and in order to operationalise them empirically, it is necessary to develop a rich design (see Chapter 4) that covers different levels of socialisation associated with the micro-, meso- and macro-processes of growing up. Thus, individual biographical changes and changes within the socialisation contexts display forms of social coherence. The families, which are significantly important for the socialisation of the adolescents, form a salient example.

We based the longitudinal study's methodology, therefore, on triangulation (Patton, 2002, p. 563; Paus-Hasebrink, Prochazka, & Sinner, 2013, p. 23), enabling it to analyse and describe the interaction between development-psychological processes of growing up—children coping with their developmental tasks, as well as parents coping with their life tasks—and socio-economical (for example, unemployment or a new job, a better or worse financial situation) or socio-emotional factors of a family (for example, divorce of the parents, severe misfortunes within the family). Furthermore, specific wishes and interests come to light and demonstrate how socialisation is accomplished and how media are relevant during this process.

At the macro-level, there are socio-structural factors, like the income and the educational qualifications of the parents which determine their social milieu. In other words, the way of life of a family is crucially shaped by its social status. The following aspects stand out: the constantly changing, interdependently existing and, in an general sense, relevant socio-structural factors of the country, such as its political, economic and cultural contexts, its media system, including a vast amount of technical and, therefore, societal change in media infrastructure, the structure of the educational system, the overall economic situation of the country, the labour market, matters linked to family issues (for example, maternity leave and family support), together with the laws governing them, and the availability of kindergartens and schools, as well as recreational facilities for children, adolescents and families. These factors have a definite impact on the life of the families and, therefore, frame their way of life. Socio-structural conditions define the field in which children and their parents and siblings live and where a child moves around and learns to deal with its relevant developmental tasks and life challenges. These conditions determine the specific and milieu-dependent situation a child grows up in. They affect socialisation in a crucial way because they form testing grounds for individual identity. But quite often these conditions fundamentally restrict the given spaces.

Within the meso-level, the question arises about the social resources a family can deploy to ensure socio-structural support. On this level, certain relationship structures between parents and their children and siblings, but also between relatives like grandparents, aunts and uncles, are responsible for the basic family climate. In this context, it is also important to determine the parental life tasks (what is important for mothers and fathers? Do they live within a family, or are they separated and, for example, in a new romantic relationship?) as well as the life tasks of the siblings. So, it becomes vital to examine the educational resources of the parents and, therefore, the way, they and the siblings deal with media services. The amount of media equipment as hardware, the place where it is available and in which (social) contexts it can be used, are also important variables. As a part of a social network, the parents' friends, neighbours and, with increasing age, their own friends and peers gain more and more importance for the children. These outcomes are similar to the previous findings from studies conducted during the childhood and youth of subjects (Paus-Hasebrink & Bichler, 2008; Paus-Hasebrink & Kulterer, 2014). Children are companions for each other (see Krappmann, 1991, p. 362) and during their socialisation, with whom they are interacting is crucially important. They do share particular interests with friends, and they may be supported and recognised within a peer group, but also rejected. These conditions have a significant impact on the way children organise their everyday lives, how they develop their social relationships and thereby become self-confident. A specific lifestyle within a family and the social network among siblings and with parents form the basis for children's dealing with the media.

The micro-level connotes the child itself. Here, the main focus of the overall research project covers aspects like age and gender, hence the specific developmental tasks and the specific media usage concomitant with them. The relevant factors on the micro-level also affect the meso-level, like the family's way of living together. One aspect should not be underestimated in its effect on the overall climate in the family, namely a child's capacity for dealing with those developmental tasks arising, for example, from a change of school or from being a part of relevant social contexts (for example, being accepted within their peer group or in different social groups in general). However, the lifestyle of the family has a greater impact when children are growing up, and they—to differing degrees depending on age and development—do reciprocally shape the way of living within their family, while, on the other hand, also being extensively dependent on their social environment. The specific way of living within the family frames the way a child grows up and deals with the media, indicating, in turn, the role the media play in the child's socialisation.

Our study comprised six waves of interviews (2005, 2007, 2010, 2012, 2014, 2016 and additionally a final telephone call back survey at the end of 2016 and the beginning of 2017). We traced media socialisation processes, and especially the individual changes in adolescents' socialisation, as this was affected by a dynamically changing media environment significant for both individuals and society. Over the nearly twelve years, we, therefore, covered every important stage from kindergarten to late adolescence in the lives of the children and adolescents.

To apply our central concepts *options for action*, *outlines for action* and the closely related *competences for action*, we developed the following research approaches. We defined the *options for action* of a family, and particularly of our subject, the child growing up within this family, and we identified the socio-structural factors for social disadvantage, adopting the layer model of social inequality (see Hradil, 1999; Hradil & Masson, 2008). A standardised questionnaire was used in every wave of the survey, in order to gather basic information about the *options for action* (income, educational level, housing situation and so on). With help of observation protocols, the interviewers registered information about the families' homes and neighbourhoods, as well as about the media equipment available. These observations also helped to describe the configuration of family life, the *doing family* (see Jurczyk, Lange, & Thiessen, 2014; Morgan, 2011). They functioned as a link to the examination of the *outlines for action*, such as the adolescents' goals and plans and those of the parents, all of which are closely related to the individuals' perceptions of the social milieu. The basis for this research step was in the interviews with the chosen children, and with the adolescents subsequently, and with one or both of their parents or guardians. The interviews also helped to record the perceived *competences for action* of the young people and their parents, as they formed their own concepts, and then traced what the adolescents thought of their parents, and vice versa.

The guided in-depth interviews were the core of this study. To cope with the nature of a mediatised society and with the adolescents' new stage in life, we modified and enhanced our methodological approach during the fifth (2014) and sixth (2016) waves of the survey. The theoretical foundation was redrawn, so that new research results were forthcoming. Following the methodical approach of *thinking aloud* (Bilandzic, 2005, pp. 362–364; 2017, pp. 407–408) we sought discussion of the adolescents' social networks profiles as a response to the much greater importance of social network sites. To investigate the increasingly differentiated relationships in the adolescents' everyday life, we had them draw "network maps" (Hepp & Düvel, 2010, p. 271) to visualise their media and information repertoires. The third methodological approach addressed the overall trend towards personal media equipment in our subjects' own bedrooms. Inspired by the concept of "bedroom culture" (see Bovill & Livingstone, 2001, p. 3), we took photographs, together with the adolescents, to show their rooms and their favourite places for media use. These photographs allowed insights in the specific construction of the young peoples' personal living environments, which are the central spaces for developing an individual identity and, as such, acutely influenced by media services and contents.

The collected material was regularly evaluated after every wave using a sensitively aligned repertoire of different methodologies to analyse the data while consistently comparing them with the past outcomes of the study. In all cases, the evaluation and interpretation were guided by the three theoretical concepts: the *options for action*, *outlines of action* and *competences for action* of the adolescents and their parents. A survey of these concepts allowed especially meaningful indicators to emerge from during the last step of the evaluation, which can be summed up by three dimensions: socio-economic conditions, socio-emotional relationship structures (*doing family*) and strategies of the family to cope with everyday life. These three dimensions enabled us to construct a typology for denoting the differences between our individual families.

9.4 THE SCOPE OF THIS STUDY

Highly ambitious and informative longitudinal studies are rare in communication research. Special economic and organisational challenges have to be managed, while the survey and its evaluation are both elaborate undertakings, because of the great amount of data collected. The extended duration and procedure of the research necessitate particular forms of reflexivity and explication. The theoretical-methodological viewpoint has to be integrated into a transparent and comprehensible research frame to achieve high-quality results when considering structures of meaning like the (re)construction of media practices. Both the quantitative research paradigm, as well as the qualitative, indicate that the value of a study depends not only on the method of collecting data. Qualitative analyses need intersubjective traceability together with coherent data evaluation (see Chapter 4). The interactive theoretical and methodological design of this study—both parts were updated as the children were growing up to adolescence and their everyday lives were becoming more and more mediatised—offers a reliable basis for a transparent way of examining the research topic.

We aimed to pursue the structures of meaning and, therefore, the subjective distribution in the ways the children and their parents constructed them. This was linked with the goal of detecting coherences and registering the complex interplay of the various factors shaping the life of the socially disadvantaged families, thus tracing the children's overall development and their socialisation. Many aspects of this study may well link to the international research on socially disadvantaged families and their ways of dealing with media services, but we have not concentrated on identifying "typical" patterns for the process of growing up in socially disadvantaged families and comparing them with non-disadvantaged families. Any such question requires, of course, a different research design. What we regard as committed social research makes it important to direct attention towards the actual needs of socially disadvantaged adolescents. Furthermore, our study shows how socialisation is understood *as a process* and to find out which aspects interact in what ways during young people's socialisation as they grow up.

9.5 THE PARTICULAR CHALLENGES OF A LONGITUDINAL STUDY

To understand the role the media play during children's development as individuals, means understanding how their social contexts are designed. Most important here are their social contexts, like family and the children' management of everyday life. Gaining any insight requires a longitudinal perspective, because it is only possible in this way to experience how media usage and preferred ways of shaping everyday life are linked. In this case, social research is intended as family research, but with specific reference to the child and its individual conditions and issues. Hence, a qualitative approach is necessary to derive any more profoundly coherent results from the research topic.

The collection and evaluation of qualitative longitudinal data inevitably become a major challenge for researchers. Making the qualitative data from a panel of subjects over twelve years as intersubjectively traceable as possible for its readers requires a triangulation-based, mutually monitoring and permanently updated methodological design. But this was not the only challenge to be overcome, given that the research team had to confront several internal and external problems. The simple recruiting and maintaining of the panel was quite an extensive effort. A distinct tenacity was required to contact the adolescents and families every two years and to convince them to remain part of the panel—telephone numbers and email addresses were changed, correspondence was often ignored. Several relocations and changes within family-constellations brought further problems. And in addition, the team of researchers brought its own challenges, where the duration of the project involved various personnel turnovers by dint of, for example, limited-term appointments, changes in personal circumstance and student assistants graduating. Hence, the people involved had changing subjective perspectives and individual ways of working. All of this had consequences for the strategies during the evaluation process and the comparability of results, which is indisputably the central quality factor for a longitudinal study! In this respect, it required considerable efforts to maintain a traceable and transparent, well-documented and comprehensible work and thus meet the needs of empirical social research.

Within the longitudinal study on socially disadvantaged adolescents, different measures were deployed. With the aid of a certain degree of standardisation, even in the qualitative research, the high level of comparability was secured. Coding schemes were changed quite sensitively, thematically structured matrices with given categories. We took care to maintain the meticulous and multiply-secured documentation of these procedures. Any standards, like rules of transcription and anonymisation, as well as the description of the codes, were strictly documented, so that our approach is continuously traceable over several years. A highly important step to support these standards involved workshops on interviewing and coding conducted by experienced researchers, who were familiar with the all the facts established by the research as well as the atmosphere within the families. These workshops were repeated immediately before every wave and included every aspect of the research project. Interim reports and summaries were sent to the sponsor of the study, the Jubiläumsfonds der Oesterreichischen Nationalbank [Anniversary Fund of the Austrian National Bank], but work on several books and chapters proceeded concurrently and was also helpful in maintaining continuity and serving as a basis for further waves.

To continue a longitudinal study over several years means always having to be prepared for new challenges within the research process, requiring solutions aimed at resolving basic research questions—in retrospect, that is one fundamental finding. Every new wave of the survey, and occasionally even the evaluation, is a balancing act between continuity and change. Besides that, it is important during such a long research project to constantly bear in mind the ethical question regarding the teams' responsibility towards the families of the panel. These questions became still more important when interventions in family structures seemed to be necessary, due to responsibility reasons as engaged social scientists. These particular matters require a careful, sensitive and responsible treatment and resolution—in some circumstances with the help of qualified psychologists who showed the research team options and possibilities for affected families/family members (of course this happened anonymously and information was forwarded to the people affected as a suggestion for help). The aspect of intervention during the process of conducting qualitative research does not happen frequently and it is hardly ever documented in publications. Notwithstanding, we are convinced that engaged social scientists are ethically bound to intervene in a well-considered way if necessary. In accordance with the aim of traceability and for reasons of transparency such actions are obligated to be documented. Although interventions are infrequent, this aspect of social science is being examined in the literature. A best practice research guide from the EU Kids Online-Network (see Lobe, Livingstone, Ólafsson, & Simões, 2008, p. 57) raises questions concerning children at risk, problematic situations during the process of research and possible ways of acting; Furthermore, the respective section includes experience reports of David Finkelhor, Sonia Livingstone and Ingrid Paus-Hasebrink who describe practical examples from their research and give advice on how to manage such difficult and complex situations in real-world.

9.6 The Media and Socio-Pedagogical and Political Consequences

The development of everyday competences for dealing appropriately with the media counts today as an important and socio-politically necessary goal for children and their parents. In order to familiarise adolescents with responsible, but also independent, ways of dealing with the media, it is essential to widen their analytical perspectives. Research does not simply examine children and their media-pedagogic practices in kindergartens, schools and youth facilities, but responds to parents and their media practices as well. Here, the outcomes of this longitudinal study show conclusively that socially disadvantaged parents often lack appropriate competences. This result corresponds with other findings showing how less educated parents apply more restrictive ways of mediation (for example, Livingstone, Mascheroni, Dreier, Chaudron, & Lagae, 2015; Paus-Hasebrink, Bauwens, Dürager, & Ponte, 2013; Rothbaum, Martland, & Beswick Jannsen, 2008; Vekiri, 2010). It follows, then, that supportive and educational concepts are needed to reach parents with less formal education or respectively, suffering social disadvantage, with a view to encouraging and guiding them in matters of media education (see Aufenanger, 2004; Lampert, 2013; Wagner, Gebel, & Lampert, 2013; see also Baudouin et al. 2015; Dinh, Farrugia, O'Neill, Vandoninck, & Velicu, 2016; O'Neill, Staksrud, & Mclaughlin, 2013; Paus-Hasebrink, Ponte, Dürager, & Bauwens, 2012).

It is crucial that children and adolescents enjoy attention and guidance from their parents, so that they gain the ability to deal with everyday life, as well as to deal with media competently. Even as children mature, they require much support from their parents on how to use the media, and especially the internet. As the outcomes of the pan-European and representative EU Kids Online-Survey show, children are not only on the internet or using smartphones at a younger age, but with increasing age, their ranging on the internet expands and they start to explore the stock of media services provided there, as well as becoming exposed to the potential risks of unpleasant and burdensome experiences (www.eukidsonline.net).

Hence, it is not only the ability to meaningfully deal with TV that is necessary, but a special "internet competence" is required (see Livingstone & Helsper, 2008). This competence describes the skills of operating the equipment, as well as different applications (for example, filter software) and using services appropriately, given their functions and risks. As an integrative part of media competence, internet competence fundamentally requires the willingness of the parents to deal with the specific media concerns of their children. These concerns are directly linked to the children's unique ways of perception and processing that correlate to their ages, genders and the highly individual interests. Further EU Kids Online-outcomes show that it is especially those children with a stable parent–child relationship shaped by closeness, trust and mutual appreciation who benefit from the internet's possibilities. In these families, the parents guide their children in everyday life, show interest in the children's issues and avoid restrictive educational measures. This longitudinal study regarding the media usage spanning the years from kindergarten to the end of adolescence shows how important an appropriate family context is, together with *doing family*, as applied to the media usage during the socialisation of the children and adolescents.

However, not all families are the same. Supportive concepts should rather focus on differentiating and shaping (media-)educational concepts for parents, basing these on every family's individual way of living and, therefore, on the specific patterns of media usage. As the outcomes of this longitudinal study show, families who suffer from a poor socio-economical and/or socio-emotional background particularly need vastly more support than concepts and projects offering media-pedagogic assistance can provide by themselves. One worthwhile approach to the competences needed in adolescents' media usage is peer-education. It is a low-threshold form of communication, which can be combined with a comparatively large range of options from other compensatory and care services (see Neumann-Braun & Kleinschnittger, 2012) and does seem particularly helpful with school-age children.

Krämer points out that "the parental impact happens rather through the actual mediation of practices by the parents and casually occurring the respective child" than through "essential media education" (Krämer, 2013, p. 431, translated by the authors). This insight claims that media-pedagogical help, on its own, has limited effect. Based on the family's individual situation, concepts are needed to direct the parents' behaviour towards their children, as well as—and this is the most important thing—reinforcing parental competences, so parents do not feel overtaxed as role models for their children. Our families suffering multiple deprivation (Type 1, see Chapter 8) are all extensively overwhelmed by difficult socio-economic situations and problematic socio-emotional relationship structures, often flanked by the parents' or children's severe health problems. These families—and this might be the painful consequence—could be supported, but only with appropriate measures. They need socio-pedagogic help based on a socio-political foundation, not only well-meant media-pedagogical concepts, as well as consistent and sustainable action from a network of relevant stakeholders. Educational concepts for the whole family are needed as well as a sustainable socio-economic basis (for example, dignified occupations). Given how the everyday life of these families was often strained and burdened. Television and the internet, or respectively the overall media usage was less a factor relevant to the problems within the families. Instead, their extensive and undifferentiated media usage has, in fact, to be seen as a consequence of their stressful living conditions. Offering appropriate media practices has to be embedded in comprehensive socio-pedagogical support. Such an approach may help to build bridges towards, for example, internships or, further, to apprenticeships: Several boys within the panel managed to gain extensive technical knowledge, because of their media usage and especially their gaming practices. This was the basis for their desire to work in IT and, in addition, to eventually enter on a suitable apprenticeship (see also Eurostat, 2017). The support concepts we advance have to be aligned and supported by different institutions—from kindergarten to school, as well as from extra-mural institutions like education and advanced education facilities and social assistance offices or child protection services. In this way, young people would not have to depend on simple lucky chances in life.

Socio-pedagogic support available over the long-term and intensively and individually tailored is sometimes needed for notably vulnerable families. This support has to assess the individual circumstances and needs, as well as cater to the perspective of every member of the family. As this longitudinal study indisputably shows, even children who suffered traumatic experiences in relationally disturbed families were able to get the chance to develop *competences for action* for a self-determined life, if adequate socio-pedagogic help was provided at the right time, specifically by child- or youth-facilities. Such possibilities for support are able to change the children's' lives for the better. Hence, this longitudinal study has to be understood as a vindication of such socio-pedagogic facilities, because where children were consistently supervised over a length of time, the facility demonstrably helped them in manifold ways. The example of one boy in the sample (see, for this example, the case of Benedikt Holzner, Chapter 8) shows starkly the positive impact thus made possible on the life of such a child. Likewise, other adolescents in the sample were able to find a personal stability and to explore their personal spaces with similar external assistance. Unfortunately, we have to stress how, in two cases (see the Landinger family and the Fein family, Chapter 8), the parents wanted to stop the professional supervision, in order have their children back at home the whole week—both times negative consequences ensued, most damagingly for the children. In contrast, for the families which were able to become stable, appropriate help would also have helped greatly. We can claim that the children would not then have suffered a developmental delay that first has to be made good. However, it is true their prevailing circumstances were burdens for the families and they were forced to deal with them. In consequence, some children indicated signs of deep uncertainty and helplessness, like, for example, two boys who, over several years, had problems with bedwetting. In another family, the daughter was able to become independent, through her good and trusting relationship with her mother. However, without the paternal care from a male, her brother displayed great problems. He started obsessively playing violent computer games and could only recover when he entered a socio-pedagogic facility.

During the last phase of the project, the young people moving towards apprenticeships or jobs was a highly important development. Most of the children did not seek higher education. Adolescents growing up in very burdened circumstances (like those in Type 1, see Chapter 8) need particular support in experiencing their individual inclinations and specific competences, with a view to finding an appropriate apprenticeship. Therefore, better measures are needed: a smoother transition from school to apprenticeships and trade schools has to be ensured. In addition, employment training facilities are needed for adolescents who develop cognitively and/or psychically more slowly and are not yet able to gain their desired job (see also the following suggestions in Hurrelmann & Quenzel, 2016). Hurrelmann and Quenzel stress the necessity of a comprehensive youth policy that aims to support activation of individual strengths and the advancement of individual skills and competences. They advocate a combined youth policy that includes education and family policy, as well as for recreational time and participative activity (Hurrelmann & Quenzel, 2016; see also Atkinson, Guio, & Marlier; Packer, 2017, pp. 510–511; Jenkins, Clinton, Purushotma, Robison, & Weigel, 2006; Rideout & Katz, 2016; UNICEF, 2016, pp. 21–22).

As our longitudinal study makes very clear, even a child with traumatic experiences within relationally disturbed families may have the chance to develop *competences for action* if there is timely help from a socio-pedagogical support network. In this way, we can minimise the danger of reproducing the structures of social inequality in social practices (see UNICEF, 2016, p. 2; Wischmann, 2010, p. 79). To achieve sustainable changes, it is vital to improve the socio-economic and, with that, also the socio-emotional circumstances of socially disadvantaged families and their children. The children have to gain the latitude to develop their *Eigensinn* (self-will). That requires the overall social and political will and effort to recognise the situation in life of socially disadvantaged families, and hence the problems burdening them, so that we can find ways to enable children thus affected to participate fully in society.

REFERENCES

Ang, I. (2006). Radikaler Konstruktivismus und Ethnografie in der Rezeptionsforschung [Radical constructivism and ethnography in reception research]. In A. Hepp & R. Winter (Eds.), *Kultur – Medien – Macht. Cultural Studies und Medienanalyse* [Culture—Media—Power: Cultural studies and the analysis of media] (3rd ed., pp. 61–79). Wiesbaden, Germany: VS Verlag für Sozialwissenschaften.

Arnett, J. J. (1995). Adolescents' uses of media for self-socialization. *Journal of Youth and Adolescence, 24*(5), 519–533.

Arnett, J. J. (2007). Emerging adulthood: What is it, and what is it good for? *Child Development Perspectives, 1*(2), 68–73.

Atkinson, A. B., Guio, A.-C., & Marlier, E. (2017). Monitoring social inclusion in Europe. In A. B. Atkinson, A.-C. Guio, & E. Marlier (Eds.), *Monitoring social inclusion in Europe—2017 edition* (pp. 33–49). City of Luxembourg, Luxembourg: Publications Office of the European Union. Retrieved from http://ec.europa.eu/eurostat/documents/3217494/8031566/KS-05-14-075-EN-N.pdf/c3a33007-6cf2-4d86-9b9e-d39fd3e5420c.

Aufenanger, S. (2004). Konzeptionelle Überlegungen zu medienpädagogischen Handreichungen für Eltern, Erzieherinnen und Grundschullehrerinnen [Conceptual thoughts on media-educational help for parents, child care workers and elementary school teachers]. In I. Paus-Hasebrink, K. Neumann-Braun, U. Hasebrink, & S. Aufenanger (Eds.), *Medienkindheit – Markenkindheit. Untersuchungen zur multimedialen Verwertung von Markenzeichen für Kinder* [Childhood with media—Childhood with brands] (pp. 265–280). München, Germany: kopaed.

Baudouin, P., Mahieu, B., Dor, T., Good, B., Milayi, J., Nakajima, S., & European Commission. (2015). *Mapping safer internet policies in the Member States: The better internet for kids (BIK) map* (Final report). Brussels, Belgium: European Commission, Directorate-General of Communications Networks, Content & Technology. Retrieved from https://publications.europa.eu/en/publication-detail/-/publication/dc57b568-c448-494a-9187-587ebf108cf7/language-en/format-PDF/source-65163455.

Bilandzic, H. (2005). Lautes Denken [Thinking aloud]. In L. Mikos & C. Wegener (Eds.), *Qualitative Medienforschung. Ein Handbuch* [Qualitative media research: A handbook] (pp. 362–370). Konstanz, Germany: UVK UTB.

Bilandzic, H. (2017). Lautes Denken [Thinking aloud]. In L. Mikos & C. Wegener (Eds.), *Qualitative Medienforschung. Ein Handbuch* [Qualitative media research: A handbook] (2nd ed., pp. 406–412). Konstanz, Germany: UVK UTB.

Bourdieu, P. F. (1977). *Outline of a theory of practice.* New York, NY: University Press.

Bourdieu, P. F. (1986). The forms of capital. In J. Richardson (Ed.), *Handbook of theory and research for the sociology of education* (pp. 241–258). New York, NY: Greenwood Publishing Group.

Bovill, M., & Livingstone, S. (2001). Bedroom culture and the privatization of media use. *LSE Research Online.* London, UK: LSE Research Online. Retrieved from http://eprints.lse.ac.uk/archive/00000672. First published in S. Livingstone & M. Bovill. (2001) (Eds.), *Children and their changing media environment: A European comparative study* (pp. 179–200). Mahwah, NJ: Lawrence Erlbaum Associates.

Carpentier, N., Schrøder, K. C., & Hallett, L. (2014). Audience/society transformations. In N. Carpentier, K. C. Schrøder, & L. Hallett (Eds.), *Audience transformations: Shifting audience positions in late modernity* (pp. 1–12). New York, NY: Routledge.

Dinh, T., Farrugia, L., O'Neill, B., Vandoninck, S., & Velicu, A. (2016). Internet safety helplines: Exploratory study first findings: Better internet for kids. *The EU Kids Online Network.* London, UK: LSE. Retrieved from http://eprints.lse.ac.uk/65358/.

Eurostat (2017). *Digital economy & society in the EU: A browse through our online world in figures—2017 edition: Profile of the digital society & businesses. 1.3 Digital skills for a digital world.* City of Luxembourg, Luxembourg: Publications Office of the European Union. Retrieved from http://ec.europa.eu/eurostat/cache/infographs/ict/images/pdf/pdf-digital-eurostat-2017.pdf.

Hepp, A., & Düvel, C. (2010). Die kommunikative Vernetzung in der Diaspora: Integrations- und Segregationspotenziale der Aneignung digitaler Medien in ethnischen Migrationsgemeinschaften [Communicative networking in the diaspora: Integration and segregation potentials of the adoption of digital media in ethnic migration communities]. In J. Röser, T. Thomas, & C. Peil (Eds.), *Alltag in den Medien – Medien im Alltag* [Everyday life and the media—Media and everyday life] (pp. 261–281). Wiesbaden, Germany: VS Verlag für Sozialwissenschaften.

Hepp, A., & Hasebrink, U. (2014). Human interaction and communication figurations. In K. Lundby (Ed.), *Mediatization of communication: Handbook of communication science* (pp. 249–271). Berlin, Germany: Walter de Gruyter.
Hradil, S. (1999). *Soziale Ungleichheit in Deutschland* [Social inequality in Germany]. Opladen, Germany: Leske und Budrich.
Hradil, S., & Masson, S. (2008). Familie und Sozialstruktur [Family and social structure]. In N. F. Schneider (Ed.), *Lehrbuch moderne Familiensoziologie: Theorien, Methoden, empirische Befunde* [Textbook of modern family sociology: Theories, research methods and empirical results] (7th Entirely Rev. ed., pp. 197–218). Opladen, Germany: Budrich, UTB.
Hurrelmann, K., & Bauer, U. (2015). Das Modell des produktiv realitätsverarbeitenden Subjekts [Model of a productive and reality-dealing subject]. In K. Hurrelmann, U. Bauer, M. Grundmann, & S. Walper (Eds.), *Handbuch Sozialisationsforschung* [Handbook of socialisation research] (8th Entirely Rev. ed., pp. 144–161). Weinheim, Germany: Beltz.
Hurrelmann, K., Grundmann, M., & Walper, S. (2008). Zum Stand der Sozialisationsforschung [Regarding the current state of socialisation research]. In K. Hurrelmann, M. Grundmann, & S. Walper (Eds.), *Handbuch Sozialisationsforschung* [Handbook of socialisation research] (pp. 14–31). Weinheim, Germany: Beltz.
Hurrelmann, K., & Quenzel, G. (2016). *Lebensphase Jugend. Eine Einführung in die sozialwissenschaftliche Jugendforschung* [Adolescent stage of life: An introduction to socio-scientific youth research] (13th ed.). Weinheim, Germany and Basel, Switzerland: Juventa.
Jenkins, H., Clinton, K., Purushotma, R., Robison, A. J., & Weigel, M. (2006). *Confronting the challenges of participatory culture: Media education for the 21st century—An occasional paper on digital media and learning*. Chicago, IL: The John D. and Catherine T. MacArthur Foundation. Retrieved from https://www.curriculum.org/secretariat/files/Sept30TLConfronting.pdf.
Jurczyk, K., Lange, A., & Thiessen, B. (2014). *Doing Family. Warum Familienleben heute nicht mehr selbstverständlich ist* [Doing family: Why family life is no longer self-evident today]. Weinheim, Germany and Basel, Switzerland: Beltz Juventa.
Krämer, B. (2013). *Mediensozialisation. Theorie und Empirie zum Erwerb medienbezogener Dispositionen* [Media socialisation: Theory and empiricism regarding the acquisition of media-related disposals]. Wiesbaden, Germany: Springer VS.
Krappmann, L. (1991). Sozialisation in der Gruppe der Gleichaltrigen [Socialisation in peer groups]. In K. Hurrelmann & D. Ulrich (Eds.), *Neues Handbuch der Sozialisationsforschung* [New handbook of socialisation research] (pp. 355–375). Weinheim, Germany and Basel, Switzerland: Beltz.
Kuntz, B., Waldhauer, J., Zeiher, J., Finger, J. D., & Lampert, T. (2018). Soziale Unterschiede im Gesundheitsverhalten von Kindern und Jugendlichen in

Deutschland – Querschnittergebnisse aus KiGGS Welle 2 [Social differences in the health behaviour of children and young people in Germany—Cross-sectional results from KiGGS wave 2]. *Journal of Health Monitoring*, 3(2), 45–63.

Lampert, C. (2013). Informationsangebote, -verhalten und -bedürfnisse von Eltern zur Medienerziehung [Information services, behaviour und needs of parents regarding media education]. In U. Wagner, C. Gebel, & C. Lampert (Eds.), *Zwischen Anspruch und Alltagsbewältigung: Medienerziehung in der Familie* [Between claim and dealing with everyday life: Media education within the family] (pp. 221–242). Berlin, Germany: Vistas.

Livingstone, S., & Helsper, E. J. (2008). Parental mediation of children's internet use. *Journal of Broadcasting & Electronic Media*, 52(4), 581–599.

Livingstone, S., Mascheroni, G., Dreier, M., Chaudron, S., & Lagae, K. (2015). How parents of little children manage digital devices at home: The role of income, education and parental style. *The EU Kids Online Network*. London, UK: LSE. Retrieved from http://www.lse.ac.uk/media@lse/research/EUKids Online/EUKidsIV/PDF/Parentalmediation.pdf.

Lobe, B., Livingstone, S., Ólafsson, K., & Simões, J. A. (2008). Best practice research guide: How to research children and online technologies in comparative perspective. *The EU Kids Online Network*. London, UK: LSE. Retrieved from http://eprints.lse.ac.uk/21658/1/Best%20practice%20research%20guide%28lsero%29.pdf.

Lundby, K. (2014). Mediatization of communication. In K. Lundby (Ed.), *Mediatization of communication: Handbook of communication science* (pp. 3–35). Berlin, Germany: Walter de Gruyter.

Morgan, D. (2011). *Rethinking family practices*. Basingstoke, UK: Palgrave Macmillan.

Neumann-Braun, K., & Kleinschnittger, V. (2012). Peer Education und Medienkompetenzförderung [Peer education and improvement of media competences]. *Soziale Sicherheit CHSS. Familie, Generationen und Gesellschaft. Medienkompetenzförderung* (4), 231–235. Retrieved from http://www.jugendundmedien.ch/fileadmin/user_upload/3_Medienkompetenz/Peer_Education/Artikel_CHSS_Peer_Education.pdf.

O'Neill, B., Staksrud, E., & Mclaughlin, S. (Eds.). (2013). *Towards a better internet for children: Policy pillars, players and paradoxes. Research Antologies*. Gothenburg, Sweden: Nordicom.

Packer, M. J. (2017). *Child development: Understanding a cultural perspective*. London, UK, Los Angeles, CA, New Dehli, India, and Singapore: Sage.

Patton, M. Q. (2002). *Qualitative research & evaluation methods* (3rd ed.). Thousand Oaks, CA, London, UK, and New Dehli, India: Sage.

Paus-Hasebrink, I., Bauwens, J., Dürager, A. E., & Ponte, C. (2013). Exploring types of parent–child relationship and internet use across Europe. *Journal of Children and Media—JOCAM, 7*(1), 114–132.
Paus-Hasebrink, I., & Bichler, M. (2008). *Mediensozialisationsforschung. Theoretische Fundierung und Fallbeispiel sozial benachteiligte Kinder* [Media socialisation research—Theoretical foundation and a case study on socially disadvantaged children]. Assisted by C. Wijnen. Innsbruck, Austria: Studienverlag.
Paus-Hasebrink, I., & Kulterer, J. (2014). *Praxeologische Mediensozialisationsforschung. Langzeitstudie zu sozial benachteiligten Heranwachsenden* [Praxeological media socialisation research: A longitudinal study regarding socially disadvantaged adolescents]. Assisted by P. Sinner. Baden-Baden, Germany: Nomos.
Paus-Hasebrink, I., Ponte, C., Dürager, A. E., & Bauwens, J. (2012). Understanding digital inequality: The interplay between parental socialization and children's development. In S. Livingstone, L. Haddon, & A. Görzig (Eds.), *Children, risk and safety on the internet: Research and policy challenges in comparative perspective* (pp. 257–271). Bristol, UK: The Policy Press.
Paus-Hasebrink, I., Prochazka, F., & Sinner, P. (2013). What constitutes a 'rich' design in qualitative methodology? In M. Barbovschi, L. Green, & S. Vandoninck (Eds.), *Innovative approaches for investigating how children understand risk in new media: Dealing with methodological and ethical challenges. The EU Kids Online Network* (pp. 23–26). London, UK: LSE. Retrieved from http://eprints.lse.ac.uk/53060/.
Prout, A. (2008). Culture-nature and the construction of childhood. In K. Drotner & S. Livingstone (Eds.), *The international handbook of children, media and culture* (pp. 21–35). Los Angeles, CA, London, UK, and New Dehli, India: Sage.
Rideout, V., & Katz, V. S. (2016). *Opportunity for all? Technology and learning in lower-income families.* A report of the families and media project. New York, NY: The Joan Ganz Cooney Center at Sesame Workshop. Retrieved from http://digitalequityforlearning.org/wp-content/uploads/2015/12/jgcc_opportunityforall.pdf.
Rothbaum, F., Martland, N., & Beswick Jannsen, J. (2008). Parents' reliance on the web to find information about children and socio-economic differences in use, skills and satisfaction. *Journal of Applied Developmental Psychology, 29*(2), 118–128.
Smetana, J. G., Robinson, J., & Rote, W. (2015). Socialization in adolescence. In J. E. Grusec & P. D. Hastings (Eds.), *Handbook of socialization* (2nd ed., pp. 60–84). New York, NY: Guilford Press.
UNICEF. (2016). *Fairness for children: A league table of inequality in child well-being in rich countries.* Innocenti report card 13. Children in the developed world. Florence, Italy: UNICEF Office of Research—Innocenti. Retrieved from https://www.unicef-irc.org/publications/pdf/RC13_eng.pdf.

Vekiri, I. (2010). Socioeconomic differences in elementary students' ICT beliefs and out-of-school experiences. *Computers & Education, 54*(4), 941–950.

Wagner, U., Gebel, C., & Lampert, C. (2013). Medienerziehung zwischen Anspruch und Alltagsbewältigung. Zusammenführung und Fazit [Media education between claim and dealing with everyday life: Consolidation and conclusion]. In U. Wagner, C. Gebel, & C. Lampert (Eds.), *Zwischen Anspruch und Alltagsbewältigung: Medienerziehung in der Familie* [Between claim and dealing with everyday life: Media education within the family] (pp. 243–273). Berlin, Germany: Vistas.

Weiß, R. (2000). Praktischer Sinn, soziale Identität und Fern-Sehen [Practical sense, social identity and tele-vision]. *Medien und Kommunikationswissenschaft, 48*(1), 42–62.

Wischmann, A. (2010). *Adoleszenz – Bildung – Anerkennung. Adoleszente Bildungsprozesse im Kontext sozialer Benachteiligung* [Adolescence—education—appreciation: Educational processes in context of social disadvantage]. Wiesbaden, Germany: VS Verlag für Sozialwissenschaften.

Open Access This chapter is licensed under the terms of the Creative Commons Attribution 4.0 International License (http://creativecommons.org/licenses/by/4.0/), which permits use, sharing, adaptation, distribution and reproduction in any medium or format, as long as you give appropriate credit to the original author(s) and the source, provide a link to the Creative Commons licence and indicate if changes were made.

The images or other third party material in this chapter are included in the chapter's Creative Commons licence, unless indicated otherwise in a credit line to the material. If material is not included in the chapter's Creative Commons licence and your intended use is not permitted by statutory regulation or exceeds the permitted use, you will need to obtain permission directly from the copyright holder.

Appendix

Standardised Questionnaire for the Parent(s)

Living and Housing Situation of the Family

Name of the family: _____

1. Gender:
   - ☐ female
   - ☐ male

2. Position in the family:
   - ☐ mother
   - ☐ stepmother
   - ☐ father
   - ☐ stepfather

3. Marital status:
   - ☐ married
   - ☐ cohabitation/relationship
     → Is your husband/wife/partner the biological father/mother of your child?
     yes ☐ no ☐
   - ☐ single
   - ☐ divorced
   - ☐ widowed

Family structure

4. How many people are permanently living in your household?
   _____

5. Apart from yourself, who else is living in this apartment/house?
   - ☐ my partner
   - ☐ my children
   - ☐ my mother
   - ☐ my father
   - ☐ my mother-in-law
   - ☐ my father-in-law
   - ☐ other relatives or friends
   - ☐ other: _____

6. How many children do you have?
   - ☐ one
   - ☐ two
   - ☐ three
   - ☐ four
   - ☐ five
   - ☐ more than five

7. Please indicate which of your children are boys and which are girls

   Girls: _____

   Boys: _____

8. How many children are currently living with you in this household?
   - ☐ one
   - ☐ two
   - ☐ three
   - ☐ four
   - ☐ five
   - ☐ more than five

9. Date of birth of the mother (month/year): _____

10. Date of birth of the biological father (month/year): _____

11. Date of birth of new partner (month/year)

12. Date of birth of the interviewed child (month/year)

    _____

13. Date of birth of other child/children (name/month/year)

    _____

14. Your nationality? _____

15. Your religious affiliation? _____

Occupation

16. Which occupation do you currently have?
    - ☐ in training/re-education
    - ☐ working full-time (more than 35 hours/week)
    - ☐ working part-time (between 10 and 35 hours/week)
    - ☐ marginally employed (less than 15 hours/week)
    - ☐ maternity/paternity leave
    - ☐ currently unemployed
    - ☐ retired
    - ☐ not pursuing any occupational activities

17. What form of education have you completed?
    - [ ] primary school
    - [ ] high school
    - [ ] apprenticeship
    - [ ] professional school without secondary school leaving examination
    - [ ] secondary school
    - [ ] institution of higher education (e.g. university)

18. What professional occupation do you have?
    - [ ] I have never worked.
    - [ ] student
    - [ ] worker
    - [ ] skilled labour
    - [ ] farmer
    - [ ] freelancer
    - [ ] self-employed
    - [ ] employee
    - [ ] civil servant
    - [ ] other: _____

    → Please describe your occupation in more detail – in case you are unemployed – which occupation have you had before?
    _____

If you are single, please continue with question 22!

19. Which occupation does your partner have?
    - [ ] in training/re-education
    - [ ] working full-time (more than 35 hours/week)
    - [ ] working part-time (between 10 and 35 hours/week)
    - [ ] marginally employed (less than 15 hours/week)
    - [ ] maternity/paternity leave
    - [ ] currently unemployed
    - [ ] retired
    - [ ] not pursuing any occupational activities

20. What form of education has your partner completed?
    - [ ] primary school
    - [ ] high school
    - [ ] apprenticeship
    - [ ] professional school without secondary school leaving examination
    - [ ] secondary school
    - [ ] institution of higher education (e.g. university)

21. Which professional occupation does your partner have?
    - [ ] S/he has never worked.
    - [ ] student
    - [ ] worker

☐ skilled labour
☐ farmer
☐ freelancer
☐ self-employed
☐ employee
☐ civil servant
☐ other: _____

22. If you consider all of the earnings within the household, how high is your monthly net income?

    ☐ up to 1,000 Euro
    ☐ 1,001 – 1,300 Euro
    ☐ 1,301 – 1,600 Euro
    ☐ 1,601 – 1,900 Euro
    ☐ 1,901 – 2,200 Euro
    ☐ 2,201 – 2,500 Euro
    ☐ 2,501 – 2,800 Euro
    ☐ 2,801 – 3,100 Euro
    ☐ more than 3,100 Euro

23. Do you receive any social welfare benefits?

    ☐ Yes, _____
    ☐ No

24. Do you have any other forms of additional income (e.g. from renting, from an inheritance, etc.?

    ☐ Yes, _____
    ☐ No

25. Do you have any other assets (freehold flat, savings, stocks etc.)? Please indicate which ones:

    ☐ Yes, _____
    ☐ No

26. How much pocket money does the interviewed child get? _____

27. Does the interviewed child have any other sources of income (work, grandparents, gifts etc.)?

    _____

Housing situation

28. Where do you live?
    - ☐ city
    - ☐ vicinity of the city
    - ☐ country side

29. Do you…?
    - ☐ subled
    - ☐ rent
    - ☐ live in an owner-occupied flat
    - ☐ live in your own house
    - ☐ other: _____

30. How big is the flat/the house (in squaremeters)? _____

31. Does your child/does each child have their own room? Zimmer?
    - ☐ Yes
    - ☐ No

32a. Have you moved since we last visited?
    - ☐ Yes
    - ☐ No

32b. If yes, how often and when? _____

33. Are you planning to move any time soon?
    - ☐ Yes, to _____
    - ☐ No

34. Finally we'd like to ask you to update your contact details

Address:_____

Phone/Mobile:_____

E-Mail:_____

Observation Protocol

Observation Criteria for Researchers in the Field

Family: ....
Date: ....

Criteria	Observation/Notes
How clean is the flat/house? How tidy is the flat/house? What condition is the furniture in? What media equipment is visible? Are there any pets? What do the family's clothes look like? How do the family members appear and behave? Other observations	

Interview Guidelines

Interview Guidelines for Interviews with the Parent(s)

Main thematic areas of the interview guideline and example questions

(1) *Social living conditions of the family/everyday world of the family/ participation of children and parents in different social areas/recreational activities of parents and children, changes in living conditions (as compared to previous interviews)*: In what social situation are the children living? How is the familial everyday life structured and how does the family climate of the children seem? Are the children integrated in society because of their own activities or the activities of their parents? What do the living conditions of the family in contrast to earlier waves of the survey look like?

Examples questions:

- Are you satisfied with your current housing situation? Is there anything you would like to change/improve?
- How does your child spend his/her leisure time?

- Do you know your child's friends? What do you know about them? Do you like them?
- What are your plans for the future?

(2) *Attitude towards media/media usage of the parents, the child and siblings/media usage within the family*: How important are different media services and contents for the parents? What status/importance do individual media devices and services have within the family (parents and siblings)? Is there any kind of collective, familial media usage and if yes, what does it look like? Who is the "media expert" within the family?

Example questions:

- What do you think about media like TV, radio and newspaper in general? What about the computer and the internet? How important or unimportant are these media for you?
- How important are media in your everyday life? Are there any media you can relinquish? If yes, which ones?
- How important are media in the everyday life of your family and of each family member?
- Which media (devices) do you own?

(3) *Media repertoire: possession of media devices in the family (child, parents, siblings)/media usage of the children/significance of media for the children/role and function of media for the children/media education and regulation*: What does the media repertoire of the family, of the parents themselves and the children look like? Which media are available to the children? How important are media in the children's everyday lives? How, when, with whom, where and why do the children use these media? How do the children deal with media? Do the parents pursue a specific way of media education? Are there any restrictions by the parents regarding the media usage of their children?

Example questions:

- Do you know which media your child uses, how s/he uses them and when? Is this important to you to know this?

- Which media does your child use for which purpose? Are media used in the context of school?
  - Which media are used most frequently?
  - How often and how long is your child using these media services?
- Which devices/services/content is your child using regularly? (e.g. TV shows)
- Does your child tell you what he or she is doing with different media devices/services?

(4) *Type and adoption of values and behavioural manners of the children/role, function and credibility of the family regarding the mediation of knowledge and values/role, function and credibility of other socialisation contexts (media, kindergarten, school, peer groups, friends) regarding the mediation of knowledge and values (and changes as opposed to previous interviews)*: How do children learn about specific values behavioural codices? Who do they learn them from? Do the children have certain role models or idols? Which role does the family play as a mediator of values and behavioural standards? Which role do other socialisation contexts like media, school and peer groups/friends play regarding the mediation of values and behavioural standards? Which changes can be observed since the last interview? (For the last interviews: what role does ongoing puberty play in this context?)

Example questions:

- How would you describe your own relationship with your child?
- How do you feel about gratification and punishment as educational instruments?
  - Which gratifications/punishments do you use?
- Does your child ask you for advice? In which matters?
- Is there anything that your child can learn from/through media (usage)?
- What can your child learn from you?

Interview Guidelines for Interviews with the Child

Main thematic areas of the interview guideline and example questions

(1) *Social living situation of the children/everyday wold of the family/ participation in different social areas/children's recreational activities:* In what social situation are the children living? How is the everyday life of the family structured and what does the family climate look like from the childrens' perspective? Are the children integrated in society because of their own activities or the activities of their parents? How do children shape their leisure time?

Example questions:

- Do you like your room? Is there anything you would like to change about it?
- Tell us something about your everyday life. What does a typical day look like for you? What are you doing, what happens throughout the day?
- How much leisure time do you have and what are you usually doing during this time? Are you member of a sports club (soccer, gymnastics, etc.). Which other activities do you pursue?
- Who can you talk to when you have problems?

(2) *Media repertoire/possession of media/media usage and practices/significance of media/role and function of media:* What does the media repertoire of the children look like, what is it made up of? Which media are available (within the family)? Which media do they own themselves? Which media are used by children? How important are different media devices/services in the everyday life of the children? How, when, with whom, where and why do they use these media? How do children deal with media?

Example questions:

- Which devices do you have at home (TV, radio, computer—with or without internet access—CD player, DVD recorder, Smartphone, Tablet, etc.)?

- Which books, newspapers and magazines do you have at home? Which do you own yourself, which belong to your parents?
- Which devices do you own yourself (Radio, TV, computer, games console, mobile phone, etc.). Is there anything with regard to media devices that you wish for, because you don't have it at the moment?
- Which media services and what content do you currently use? Which media do you like best? What do you prefer to read, to listen to, to browse? What do you like about it? How long do you usually use it?

(3) *Attitude towards media/media usage of the parents, the child and siblings/media usage within the family/media education and regulation*: How important are different media for the members of the family? Does the family use media together, what does this look like? What does the individual media usage within the family (parents and siblings) look like from the children's perspective? Who is the "media expert" within the family as perceived by the child? Do parents pursue a specific approach towards media education? Are there any restrictions by the parents regarding the media practices of their children?

Example questions:

- Are you talking to your parents about things you have seen on TV, heard on the radio, played on the computer or seen on the internet on a regular basis?
  - Do your parents discuss media in general with you?
  - Or do they discuss things you have seen on the media spontaneously? What are the issues you are talking about?
- Do your parents sometimes prohibit you to listen to the radio, to watch TV, to play on the computer or to browse the internet?
  - Are you allowed to watch TV, play games, browse and listen to the radio as extensively as you like?
  - Are there any specific rules for using the TV, the computer, the mobile phone, the internet?

- Are you allowed to watch all the shows you like? Which programmes are you not allowed to watch?
- Are there computer games you're not allowed to play?
- Has there ever been a conflicted because of the TV, the radio, the computer, a magazine, etc.? What happens during such conflicts? Do you and your parents tolerate each other later again?
- Do your parents explain to you why they prohibit certain things?
- Do you understand and accept these rules and regulations?

(4) *Type and adoption of values and behavioural manners of the children/role, function and credibility of the family regarding the mediation of knowledge and values/role, function and credibility of other socialisation contexts (media, kindergarten, school, peer groups, friends) regarding the mediation of knowledge and values:* Who do the children learn about values and manners from? Do the children have certain role models or idols? Which role does the family play as a mediator of values and behavioural standards? Which role do other socialisation contexts play like media, school and peer groups/friends play regarding the mediation of values and behavioural standards?

Example questions:

- Do you have any role models/idols? Who are your role models/idols? Earlier they were X and Y, who are they today?
  - Why is that? What do you like about them?
- Do you have a good relationship with your parents/siblings? What do you like about your parents/siblings? What don't you like about your parents/siblings?
- What happens if you do something that you are not allowed to do?
  - Are you occasionally punished at home? What is this punishment? Who punishes you? Does he or she explain why you are being punished or why you are not allowed to do certain things?
- You are stranded on a desert island and could only safe three things to bring with you, which things would that be?
- Who do you turn to for advice (on different matters)?

Complementary Methods of Data Collection
Guideline for Thinking Aloud-Method About Favourite Social Media Tools

Following the thinking aloud method (see Chapter 4) the researchers investigated the adolescent's individual social media profiles together with them at a convenient time during the interview. The children should voluntarily show and comment on what they do on social media so as to allow the interviewers to better understand the adolescent's practices.

They were asked to show their profiles and settings (for example, privacy settings, friends list, photos, groups, single chats, followed pages and channels and so on) and to talk about how they make use of the applications and features. The guideline for this method contained only a few questions and topics and more instructions for the interviewers as to what they should pay attention to. The purpose was to reveal how competent and knowledgeable the adolescents were about the social networking tools.

Example: When looking at the Facebook profile

- Landing page is shown and explained, make sure to pay attention to:
  - Which messages are displayed/How many notifications are there?
  - Which advertisements are shown?
  - Which suggestions for the child are given by the Facebook algorithms?
- Number of friends within the friends list
  - Big/mall circle of friends? Are all friends known personally? How does the child deal with friendship requests?
- In which groups is the child a member?
  - Only as a passive or also as an active member? Is the child aware of all groups he or she joined?
- Likes
  - Which persons and sites are liked by the child?
  - Which genres are included (movies, TV, books, persons, etc.)?
  - Self-presentation because of likes? [Ask specifically].
- Games used
  - Still as an active gamer or retired?

- Privacy Settings
  - Is the child's entire name shown? [Ask for explanation and reasons]
  - Which profile picture and cover picture are shown on the profile? Is the child pictured? [Let explain, why the respective pictures are chosen.]
  - Which photographs and photo albums are available online?
  - Who can see the child's photographs and postings? Are there any restrictions initiated by the child?
  - Is the child's profile easy to find—which settings?
  - Ask the child to explain how privacy settings can be adapted –> Knowledge about the function within the application? Is the child aware of the possibilities?
- How does the child use chat and message functions?
  - Regularly or just occasionally? Who are the chat partners?

[Please note: The child primarily explains what he or she is usually doing on social network sites and what central functions he or she is using.]

Example: Looking at WhatsApp

Child starts WhatsApp:

- Design and Wallpaper
  - Is the screen personalised and is the child aware of the possibility to personalise the application's design?
- Name
  - Does the child use a nickname?
- Profile picture, headline, status
  - Is there a profile picture? [Explanation of what the picture is supposed to show.]
  - Is there an individual status, what does it mean for the child? Are the suggested sentences like "Hey there, I am using WhatsApp" used?
  - How is the status configured?
  - Are these things changed and adapted regularly?
- Visibility
  - Activated/deactivated?
  - Last online?

- Does the child chat with one person or rather with groups more frequently? Which groups are open to the child and with whom is the child communicating directly; who is the child's favourite person to chat with?
- Are there more text messages or rather pictures and (audio) files being sent?

[Please note: Again, the primary question is, which are the most important functions of this service and how they were used by the children.]

Coding Schemes for Interviews

Coding Scheme for the Evaluation of the Interviews with the Parents

Living conditions
  Perceived changes
  Attitude towards the refugee issue
    Mother
      Valuation positive
      Valuation negative
      Valuation neutral
      Thematisation of this issue
      Information about this issue
      Communication about this issue
    Father/life companion of the mother
      Valuation positive
      Valuation negative
      Valuation neutral
      Thematisation of this issue
      Information about this issue
      Communication about this issue
    Child
      Communication about this issue
      Information about this issue
      Thematisation of this issue
      Valuation positive
      Valuation negative
      Valuation neutral

- Sibling
    - Communication about this issue
    - Information about this issue
    - Thematisation of this issue
    - Valuation positive
    - Valuation negative
    - Valuation neutral
- Visions and plans for the future
    - Of the child
    - For the family
    - For the child
    - Own plans and visions
- Daily routine
    - Mother
    - Father
    - Child
    - Siblings
- Valuation of the
    - Housing situation
    - Residential area
- Family climate
    - Other
    - Problems/dispute
    - Relationship between mother and father
    - Relationship between mother and her new life companion
    - Relationship between siblings
    - Relationship between mother and child
    - Relationship between father and child
    - Relationship between new life companion and child
    - Relationship between father and his new life companion
    - Relationship between all family members
- Leisure activities of the family members
    - Activities together
    - Mother's activities
    - Father's activities
    - Sibling's activities
- Leisure activities of the child
    - Alone
    - With siblings

- At school
- In a (sports)club
- With friends
- Elsewhere
- Friends/peers of the child
  - Romantic relationships/being in love
  - Knowledge about friends
  - Support
  - Elsewhere
- (Pocket) money
  - Child's access to money
  - Child's dealings with money
  - Child's wishes
- Media ownership, media practices and usage of the family
  - Media competence
    - Mother's
    - Father's
    - Child's
    - Sibling's
    - Of further family members and caregivers
  - Perceived changes
  - Attitude towards media in general
    - Valuation positive
    - Valuation negative
    - Valuation neutral
  - Significance of media for the family in general
    - For the mother
      - Valuation positive
      - Valuation negative
      - Valuation neutral
      - Ascribed chances
        - Creativity
        - Identity
        - Social relationships
        - Learning
        - Participation
      - Ascribed risks
        - Plagiarism
        - Trust in information

    Deception
    Advertising
    Exposure of personal information
    Pornographic content
    Violent content
    Online mobbing
    (Unexpected) sexual messages
    Meeting online acquaintances
    Online shopping
    Other
   Exceptional experiences
  For the father
   Valuation positive
   Valuation negative
   Valuation neutral
   Ascribed chances
    Creativity
    Identity
    Social relationships
    Learning
    Participation
   Ascribed risks
    Plagiarism
    Trust in information
    Deception
    Advertising
    Exposure of personal information
    Pornographic content
    Violent content
    Online mobbing
    (Unexpected) sexual messages
    Meeting online acquaintances
    Online shopping
    Other
   Exceptional experiences
  For the child
   Valuation positive
   Valuation negative
   Valuation neutral

    Ascribed chances
        Creativity
        Identity
        Social relationships
        Learning
        Participation
    Ascribed risks
        Plagiarism
        Trust in information
        Deception
        Advertising
        Exposure of personal information
        Pornographic content
        Violent content
        Online mobbing
        (Unexpected) sexual messages
        Meeting online acquaintances
        Online shopping
        Other
    Exceptional experiences
For the siblings
    Valuation positive
    Valuation negative
    Valuation neutral
    Ascribed chances
        Creativity
        Identity
        Social relationships
        Learning
        Participation
    Ascribed risks
        Plagiarism
        Trust in information
        Deception
        Advertising
        Exposure of personal information
        Pornographic content
        Violent content
        Online mobbing

(Unexpected) sexual messages
Meeting online acquaintances
Online shopping
Other
  Exceptional experiences
Media ownership
  Family's
  Child's
    Media devices
    Media services
    Merchandising
Used media/media services
  Mother
    TV/TV programme/TV show
    Video/DVD
    Radio/Audio cassette/CDs/MP3s
    Personal Computer/Laptop
    Computer games
    Internet
    Social Web
    Mobile phone
    Books
    Magazines
    Newspaper
    Other (for example comics)
  Father
    TV/TV programme/TV show
    Video/DVD
    Radio/Audio cassette/CDs/MP3s
    Personal Computer/Laptop
    Computer games
    Internet
    Social Web
    Mobile phone
    Books
    Magazines
    Newspaper
    Other (for example comics)
  Child

TV/TV programme/TV show
Video/DVD
Radio/Audio cassette/CDs/MP3s
Personal Computer/Laptop
Computer games
Internet
Social Web
Mobile phone
Books
Magazines
Newspaper
Other (for example comics)
  Siblings
TV/TV programme/TV show
Video/DVD
Radio/Audio cassette/CDs/MP3s
Personal Computer/Laptop
Computer games
Internet
Social Web
Mobile phone
Books
Magazines
Newspaper
Other (for example comics)
  Whole family
TV/TV programme/TV show
Video/DVD
Radio/Audio cassette/CDs/MP3s
Personal Computer/Laptop
Computer games
Internet
Social Web
Mobile phone
Books
Magazines
Newspaper
Other (for example comics)
Duration of usage

- Mother
- Father
- Child
- Siblings
- Day-time/night-time of usage
  - Mother
  - Father
  - Child
  - Siblings
- Places of usage
  - Mother
  - Father
  - Child
  - Siblings
- Motives of usage
  - Mother's
  - Father's
  - Sibling's
  - Child's
- Parental evaluation of the link between surrounding world and media practices
- Significance of media during the childhood of the parents
  - Used media
  - Mentioned characters/persons
  - Significance of media
  - Conflicts because of media practices
- Parental media education
  - Regulations
  - No regulations
  - Conflicts
  - Argument about children's media practices
  - Mediation of media competences
  - Not interested/indifferent
- Communication about media within the family
- Valuation of media/media services for children
  - Mentioned media
    - Positive
    - Negative
    - Neutral

            Not interested/indifferent
          Mentioned media services
            Positive
            Negative
            Neutral
            Not interested/indifferent
  Socialisation contexts
    Personality of the child
      Developmental characteristics (cognitive/social/emotional-affective/physical)
    Mentioned role models by the child
    Mentioned caregivers by the child
    Ways of Education
      Reward
      Punishment
      Neutral
      Not interested/indifferent
    Significance for development
      Family
        Valuation positive
        Valuation negative
        Valuation neutral
        Not interested/indifferent
      School
        Valuation positive
        Valuation negative
        Valuation neutral
        Not interested/indifferent
      Profession
        Valuation positive
        Valuation negative
        Valuation neutral
        Not interested/indifferent
      Apprenticeship
        Valuation positive
        Valuation negative
        Valuation neutral
        Not interested/indifferent

Media
  Valuation positive
  Valuation negative
  Valuation neutral
  Not interested/indifferent
Peers
  Valuation positive
  Valuation negative
  Valuation neutral
  Not interested/indifferent
Surroundings
  Valuation positive
  Valuation negative
  Valuation neutral
  Not interested/indifferent

Coding Scheme for the Evaluation of the Interviews with the Children
Living conditions
  Perceived changes
  Visions and plans for the future
  Desired career
  Daily routine
  Attitude towards the refugee issue
    Mother
      Communication about this issue
      Information about this issue
      Thematisation of this issue
      Valuation positive
      Valuation negative
      Valuation neutral
    Father
      Communication about this issue
      Information about this issue
      Thematisation of this issue
      Valuation positive
      Valuation negative
      Valuation neutral
    Child
      Communication about this issue
      Information about this issue

        Thematisation of this issue
        Valuation positive
        Valuation negative
        Valuation neutral
     Sibling
        Communication about this issue
        Information about this issue
        Thematisation of this issue
        Valuation positive
        Valuation negative
        Valuation neutral
  Valuation of the housing situation
     Room
     Flat/House
     Residential area
  Family climate
     reference person for problems
     Problems/dispute
     Relationship between all family members
     Relationship between siblings
     Relationship between mother and child
     Relationship between mother and her new life companion
     Relationship between mother and father
     Relationship between new life companion and child
     Relationship between father and child
     Relationship between father and his new life companion
  Leisure activities of the child
     Alone
     With family
        With the whole family
        With parents
        With siblings
     In school
     In a (sports)club
     With friends
     Elsewhere
  Leisure activities of the family members
     Mother's
     Father's
     Sibling's
     Other

- School
  - Status and role within the class/Relationship with class mates
  - Relationship with teachers
  - Favourite subject/Achievements in school
  - Attitude towards school
- Occupation
  - Other
  - Unemployed
  - Unlearned activities
  - Apprenticeship
- Friends/Peers
  - Romantic relationships/being in love
  - Number of friends/peers
  - Gender
  - Age
  - Familiar through
  - Best friend
- (Pocket) Money
  - Child's access to money
  - Child's dealings with money
  - Child's wishes

Media ownership, media practices and usage of the family
- Perceived changes
- Media ownership
  - Already owning
  - Wishes in the future
- Financing of Media ownership
  - Parents
  - Child
  - Other
- Used media/media services
  - TV/TV programme/TV series
    - Valuation
      - Positive
      - Negative
      - Neutral
    - Ascribed chances
      - Creativity
      - Identity

    Social Relationship
    Learning
    Participation
  Ascribed risks
    Trust in information
    Deception
    Advertising
    Exposure of personal information
    Pornographic content
    Violent content
    (Unexpected) sexual messages
    Tele-purchase
    Other
  Exceptional experiences
Video/DVD
  Valuation
    Positive
    Negative
    Neutral
  Ascribed chances
    Creativity
    Identity
    Social Relationships
    Learning
    Participation
  Ascribed risks
    Trust in information
    Deception
    Advertising
    Exposure of personal information
    Pornographic content
    Violent content
    (Unexpected) sexual messages
    Other
  Exceptional experiences
Radio/Audio cassettes/CDs/MP3s
  Valuation
    Positive
    Negative

                Neutral
            Ascribed chances
                Creativity
                Identity
                Social Relationships
                Learning
                Participation
            Ascribed risks
                Trust in information
                Deception
                Advertising
                Exposure of personal information
                Pornographic content
                Violent content
                (Unexpected) sexual messages
                Other
            Exceptional experiences
    Personal Computer/Laptop
        Valuation
            Positive
            Negative
            Neutral
        Ascribed chances
            Creativity
            Identity
            Social Relationships
            Learning
            Participation
        Ascribed risks
            Trust in information
            Deception
            Advertising
            Exposure of personal information
            Pornographic content
            Violent content
            (Unexpected) sexual messages
            Other
        Exceptional experiences
    Computer games

Handheld consoles
  Valuation
    Positive
    Negative
    Neutral
  Ascribed chances
    Creativity
    Identity
    Social Relationships
    Learning
    Participation
  Ascribed risks
    Trust in information
    Deception
    Advertising
    Exposure of personal information
    Pornographic content
    Violent content
    (Unexpected) sexual messages
    Other
  Exceptional experiences
Steady consoles
  Valuation
    Positive
    Negative
    Neutral
  Ascribed chances
    Creativity
    Identity
    Social relationships
    Learning
    Participation
  Ascribed risks
    Trust in information
    Deception
    Advertising
    Exposure of personal information
    Pornographic content
    Violent content

                (Unexpected) sexual messages
                Other
            Exceptional experiences
        Personal Computer/Laptop games
            Valuation
                Positive
                Negative
                Neutral
            Ascribed chances
                Creativity
                Identity
                Social relationships
                Learning
                Participation
            Ascribed risks
                Trust in information
                Deception
                Advertising
                Exposure of personal information
                Pornographic content
                Violent content
                (Unexpected) sexual messages
                Other
            Exceptional experiences
    Internet
        E-Mail
            Valuation
                Positive
                Negative
                Neutral
            Ascribed chances
                Creativity
                Identity
                Social relationships
                Learning
                Participation
            Ascribed risks
                Plagiarism
                Trust in information

            Deception
            Advertising
            Exposure of personal information
            Pornographic content
            Violent content
            Online mobbing
            (Unexpected) sexual messages
            Meeting online acquaintances
            Online shopping
            Other
        Exceptional experiences
Chats
    Valuation
        Positive
        Negative
        Neutral
    Ascribed chances
        Creativity
        Identity
        Social relationships
        Learning
        Participation
    Ascribed risks
        Plagiarism
        Trust in information
        Deception
        Advertising
        Exposure of personal information
        Pornographic content
        Violent content
        Online mobbing
        (Unexpected) sexual messages
        Meeting online acquaintances
        Online shopping
        Other
    Exceptional experiences
Forums/Boards
    Valuation
        Positive

                Negative
                Neutral
            Ascribed chances
                Creativity
                Identity
                Social Relationships
                Learning
                Participation
            Ascribed risks
                Plagiarism
                Trust in information
                Deception
                Advertising
                Exposure of personal information
                Pornographic content
                Violent content
                Online mobbing
                (Unexpected) sexual messages
                Meeting online acquaintances
                Online shopping
                Other
        Exceptional experiences
    Own homepage
        Valuation
            Positive
            Negative
            Neutral
        Ascribed chances
            Creativity
            Identity
            Social relationships
            Learning
            Participation
        Ascribed risks
            Plagiarism
            Trust in information
            Deception
            Advertising
            Exposure of personal information

                Pornographic content
                Violent content
                Online mobbing
                (Unexpected) sexual messages
                Meeting online acquaintances
                Online shopping
                Other
            Exceptional experiences
    Online games
        Browser games
            Valuation
                Positive
                Negative
                Neutral
            Ascribed chances
                Creativity
                Identity
                Social relationships
                Learning
                Participation
            Ascribed risks
                Plagiarism
                Trust in information
                Deception
                Advertising
                Exposure of personal information
                Pornographic content
                Violent content
                Online mobbing
                (Unexpected) sexual messages
                Meeting online acquaintances
                Online shopping
                Other
            Exceptional experiences
        Multiplayer games
            Valuation
                Positive
                Negative
                Neutral

                    Ascribed chances
                        Creativity
                        Identity
                        Social relationships
                        Learning
                        Participation
                    Ascribed risks
                        Plagiarism
                        Trust in information
                        Deception
                        Advertising
                        Exposure of personal information
                        Pornographic content
                        Violent content
                        Online mobbing
                        (Unexpected) sexual messages
                        Meeting online acquaintances
                        Online shopping
                        Other
                    Exceptional experiences
        Shopping
            Valuation
                Positive
                Negative
                Neutral
            Ascribed chances
                Creativity
                Identity
                Social relationships
                Learning
                Participation
            Ascribed risks
                Plagiarism
                Trust in information
                Deception
                Advertising
                Exposure of personal information
                Pornographic content
                Violent content

                Online mobbing
                (Unexpected) sexual messages
                Meeting online acquaintances
                Online shopping
                Other
            Exceptional experiences
    Online research/searching for information
        Valuation
            Positive
            Negative
            Neutral
        Ascribed chances
            Creativity
            Identity
            Social relationships
            Learning
            Participation
        Ascribed risks
            Plagiarism
            Trust in information
            Deception
            Advertising
            Exposure of personal information
            Pornographic content
            Violent content
            Online mobbing
            (Unexpected) sexual messages
            Meeting online acquaintances
            Online shopping
            Other
        Exceptional experiences
    Network platforms
        Valuation
            Positive
            Negative
            Neutral
        Ascribed functions
            Communication
            Participation

Entertainment/pastime
  Mood creation
  Creation of own worlds
  Making and maintaining social relationships
  Daily routines
  Information
  Opinion making
  Building and consolidating social status
  Other
Motives of active production
  Being discovered
  Curiosity/gaining new experiences
  Love of experimentation
  Self-presentation
  Being perceived as an expert
  Expression of opinion
  Evaluation through others
  Subculture/scene
  Building and consolidating social status
  other
Ascribed chances
  Creativity
  Identity
  Social relationships
  Learning
  Participation
Ascribed Risks
  Plagiarism
  Trust in information
  Deception
  Advertising
  Exposure of personal information
  Pornographic content
  Violent content
  Online mobbing
  (Unexpected) sexual messages
  Meeting online acquaintances
  Online shopping
  Other

       Exceptional experiences
    Miscellaneous Social Media Services
       Valuation
           Positive
           Negative
           Neutral
       Ascribed chances
           Creativity
           Identity
           Social relationships
           Learning
           Participation
       Ascribed risks
           Plagiarism
           Trust in information
           Deception
           Advertising
           Exposure of personal information
           Pornographic content
           Violent content
           Online mobbing
           (Unexpected) sexual messages
           Meeting online acquaintances
           Online shopping
           Other
       Exceptional experiences
Mobile phone
    Phone calls
       Valuation
           Positive
           Negative
           Neutral
       Ascribed chances
           Creativity
           Identity
           Social relationships
           Learning
           Participation
       Ascribed risks

                Trust in information
                Deception
                Advertising
                Exposure of personal information
                Violent content
                (Unexpected) sexual messages
                other
            Exceptional experiences
        Instant Messaging und SMS
            Valuation
                Positive
                Negative
                Neutral
            Ascribed chances
                Creativity
                Identity
                Social Relationships
                Learning
                Participation
            Ascribed risks
                Trust in information
                Deception
                Advertising
                Exposure of personal information
                Pornographic content
                Violent content
                Online mobbing
                (Unexpected) sexual messages
                other
            Exceptional experiences
        Mobile internet usage
            Valuation
                Positive
                Negative
                Neutral
            Ascribed chances
                Creativity
                Identity
                Social relationships

            Learning
            Participation
        Ascribed risks
            Plagiarism
            Trust in information
            Deception
            Advertising
            Exposure of personal information
            Pornographic content
            Violent content
            Online mobbing
            (Unexpected) sexual messages
            Meeting online acquaintance
            Online shopping
            other
        Exceptional experiences
    Photographs
        Valuation
            Positive
            Negative
            Neutral
        Ascribed chances
            Creativity
            Identity
            Social relationships
            Learning
            Participation
        Ascribed risks
            Trust in information
            Deception
            Advertising
            Exposure of personal information
            Pornographic content
            Violent content
            (Unexpected) sexual messages
            Other
        Exceptional experiences
    Videos/movies
        Valuation

            Positive
            Negative
            Neutral
        Ascribed chances
            Creativity
            Identity
            Social relationships
            Learning
            Participation
        Ascribed risks
            Trust in information
            Deception
            Advertising
            Exposure of personal information
            Pornographic content
            Violent content
            (Unexpected) sexual messages
            Other
        Exceptional Experiences
    Games
        Valuation
            Positive
            Negative
            Neutral
        Ascribed chances
            Creativity
            Identity
            Social relationships
            Learning
            Participation
        Ascribed risks
            Trust in information
            Deception
            Advertising
            Exposure of personal information
            Pornographic content
            Violent content
            (Unexpected) sexual messages
            Online shopping

         Other
      Exceptional experiences
Music
   Valuation
      Positive
      Negative
      Neutral
   Ascribed chances
      Creativity
      Identity
      Social relationships
      Learning
      Participation
   Ascribed risks
      Trust in information
      Deception
      Advertising
      Exposure of personal information
      Pornographic content
      Violent content
      (Unexpected) sexual messages
      Online shopping
      Other
   Exceptional experiences
Free SMS services
   Valuation
      Positive
      Negative
      Neutral
   Ascribed chances
      Creativity
      Identity
      Social relationships
      Learning
      Participation
   Ascribed risks
      Trust in information
      Deception
      Advertising

							Exposure of personal information
							Pornographic content
							Violent content
							(Unexpected) sexual messages
							Other
					Exceptional experiences
				Apps (free and fee-based)
					Valuation
						Positive
						Negative
						Neutral
					Ascribed chances
						Creativity
						Identity
						Social relationships
						Learning
						Participation
					Ascribed risks
						Trust in information
						Deception
						Advertising
						Exposure of personal information
						Pornographic content
						Violent content
						(Unexpected) sexual messages
						Online shopping
						Other
					Exceptional Experiences
				Miscellaneous
					Valuation
						Positive
						Negative
						Neutral
					Ascribed chances
						Creativity
						Identity
						Social relationships
						Learning
						Participation

            Ascribed risks
                Plagiarism
                Trust in information
                Deception
                Advertising
                Exposure of personal information
                Pornographic content
                Violent content
                Online mobbing
                (Unexpected) sexual messages
                Meeting online acquaintances
                Online shopping
                Other
            Exceptional Experiences
    Books
        Valuation
            Positive
            Negative
            Neutral
        Ascribed chances
            Creativity
            Identity
            Social relationships
            Learning
            Participation
        Ascribed risks
            Plagiarism
            Trust in information
            Deception
            Advertising
            Exposure of personal information
            Pornographic content
            Violent content
            (Unexpected) sexual messages
            Other
        Exceptional experiences
    Magazines
        Valuation
            Positive

            Negative
            Neutral
        Ascribed chances
            Creativity
            Identity
            Social relationships
            Learning
            Participation
        Ascribed risks
            Plagiarism
            Trust in information
            Deception
            Advertising
            Exposure of personal information
            Pornographic content
            Violent content
            (Unexpected) sexual messages
            Other
        Exceptional experiences
    Newspaper
        Valuation
            Positive
            Negative
            Neutral
        Ascribed chances
            Creativity
            Identity
            Social relationships
            Learning
            Participation
        Ascribed risks
            Plagiarism
            Trust in information
            Deception
            Advertising
            Exposure of personal information
            Pornographic content
            Violent content
            (Unexpected) sexual messages

      Other
     Exceptional experiences
  Miscellaneous
    Valuation
      Positive
      Negative
      Neutral
    Ascribed chances
      Creativity
      Identity
      Social relationships
      Learning
      Participation
    Ascribed risks
      Plagiarism
      Trust in information
      Deception
      Advertising
      Exposure of personal information
      Pornographic content
      Violent content
      (Unexpected) sexual messages
      Other
    Exceptional experiences
Mentioned figures
  Valuation positive
  Valuation negative
  Valuation neutral
Mentioned persons (stars and so on)
  Valuation positive
  Valuation negative
  Valuation neutral
  Exceptional experiences
Identification/para-social interaction in general
  To be like them
  To act like them
  Solidarisation
  Wish for interaction
  Other

Way of usage
  With friends
  Alone
  With parents
  With siblings
  With others
  Under ward of caregivers
  Concentration on the medium
  Secondary reception
Duration of usage
  TV
  Video/DVD
  Radio/Audio cassettes/CDs/MP3s
  Personal Computer/Laptop
  Computer games
  Internet
  Social Web
  Mobile phone
  Books
  Magazines
  Newspaper
  Other
Places of usage
  TV
  Video/DVD
  Radio/Audio cassettes/CDs/MP3s
  Personal Computer/Laptop
  Computer games
  Internet
  Social Web
  Mobile phone
  Books
  Magazines
  Newspaper
  Other
Times of usage
  TV
  Video/DVD
  Radio/Audio cassettes/CDs/MP3s

- Personal Computer/Laptop
- Computer games
- Internet
- Social Web
- Mobile phone
- Books
- Magazines
- Newspaper
- Other
- Motives of usage
  - TV
  - Video/DVD
  - Radio/Audio cassettes/CDs/MP3s
  - Personal Computer/Laptop
  - Computer games
  - Internet
  - Social Web
  - Mobile phone
  - Books
  - Magazines
  - Newspaper
  - Other
- Link to the lifeworld
- Media ownership, media practices and usage of the family
  - Media ownership
  - Used media
    - Mother
    - Father
    - Siblings
    - Whole family
  - Times of usage
  - Duration of usage
  - Communication via media
  - Parental media education
    - Media regulation
      - Temporal restriction
      - Restriction on content
      - Other
    - No regulations
    - Conflicts

Role, function and credibility of socialisation contexts
  Mentioned role models
  Meaning of
    Family
      Valuation positive
      Valuation negative
      Valuation neutral
    Peers
      Valuation positive
      Valuation negative
      Valuation neutral
    Media/media figures
      Valuation positive
      Valuation negative
      Valuation neutral
    Other
  Experienced educational measures
    By parents
    By teachers/school
    With friends
    Other
  Knowledge transfer via
    Parents
    Siblings
    Friends
    Teachers/school
    Media
  Competences of
    Parents
    Siblings
    Friends
    Teachers/school
    Media
  Competences of the child

Index

A
active subject, 47, 48
ADHD, 177, 188
adolescence, 4, 13, 24, 52–55, 57, 83, 90, 127, 128, 133, 134, 139, 164, 215, 231, 233, 234, 239, 241, 245
adolescent(s), 1–6, 11, 12, 16–18, 20–23, 25–32, 45, 46, 50–52, 54–56, 58, 59, 66, 77, 81, 82, 85, 86, 88–94, 97, 98, 121–123, 125–130, 132, 133, 135, 136, 138, 141–146, 148, 150, 168, 174, 189, 225, 227, 228, 231–233, 235–237, 239–247
adulthood, 17, 32, 53–55, 141, 143, 231, 233
AfD, 15
affair, 108, 207
Africa, 13
age, 7, 12, 21, 24, 25, 27, 29, 52–54, 81, 110, 123, 124, 128, 134, 146, 149, 150, 157, 159, 165, 167, 177, 179, 182–184, 186, 192, 195, 203, 231, 238, 244, 245
agency, 47, 48, 52, 110, 202
aggression, 133, 134, 141, 179, 193
alcoholic, 196, 202
alimony, 109, 195, 207, 218
analytical concepts
  competences for action, 5, 7, 61, 64–66, 85, 96, 97, 122, 134, 135, 143, 149, 157, 162, 165–167, 173, 175, 177, 185, 186, 195, 205, 209, 212, 224–227, 234, 236, 239, 240, 246, 247
  options for action, 7, 63, 64, 66, 85, 96, 97, 122, 134, 149, 161, 162, 165–167, 173, 175, 177, 186, 188, 194, 198, 207, 209, 211, 218, 220, 222, 224–227, 235, 236, 239
  outlines for action, 7, 63, 64, 85, 96, 97, 122, 134, 135, 149, 157, 161, 162, 164–167, 173, 175, 178, 184, 185, 188, 190,

192, 194–198, 201, 205, 206, 208–210, 212, 214, 217, 222, 224–227, 235, 236, 239
anonymisation, 6, 93, 95, 242
apprenticeship, 86, 93, 113, 118, 123, 131, 133, 142–144, 149, 246, 247
approval, 82, 132
arbitrary, 7, 162, 164, 165, 181, 197
Asia, 13
assisted living community, 138
asylum seeker, 182, 195
attention, 6, 24, 25, 27, 29, 31, 32, 46, 78, 88, 107, 135, 137, 141, 144, 159, 185, 212, 214, 221, 228, 233, 234, 236, 241, 244
audio-cassettes, 124
aunt(s), 138, 139, 220, 222, 238
Austria, 2, 3, 8, 11–18, 20, 21, 23, 29, 31, 77, 79, 82, 108, 113, 116, 117, 125, 126, 145, 147, 149, 176, 199, 200, 207, 215, 218, 228, 231, 232, 236
axial coding, 95

B
bedroom culture, 92, 240
behavioural problem, 135, 184
Belgium, 13, 15
Bertelsmann Stiftung, 8, 12, 13, 16
biography, 52, 63
biological father, 107, 111, 114, 116, 117, 175, 189, 194, 195, 197, 214, 218, 223, 224
bloggers(s), 148
boarding school, 113, 189, 195
book(s), 2, 3, 13, 18, 21, 30, 32, 123, 124, 128, 157, 159, 180, 201, 202, 205, 216, 217, 222, 231, 234, 236, 242
Brazil, 27–29

bullying, 30, 218
burdened, 144, 146, 174, 196, 246, 247

C
call-back interview, 93, 119
cancer, 108, 207
capital
    cultural capital, 62
    economic capital, 61, 62
    material capital, 2
    social capital, 25, 61
    symbolic capital, 62
caregiver, 138, 144
case study, 16, 31, 97
category, 96
CD, 191
challenges, 5, 11, 16, 23, 26, 32, 52–54, 56, 58, 63, 77, 82, 86, 99, 132, 134, 135, 141, 158, 160–163, 167, 172–175, 180, 192, 193, 198, 200, 211, 212, 214, 219, 221, 224–227, 231, 233–235, 237, 240–243
chat, 130, 141
childhood, 2–4, 13, 17, 20, 45, 50, 52–54, 57, 62, 65, 82, 121, 123, 133, 134, 138, 139, 146, 164, 178, 226, 236, 238
child poverty rate, 17
child support, 195
citizen, 79
citizenship, 87, 88
city, 108, 110, 116–118, 140, 189, 195, 206, 218
classifying practices, 61
coding
    axial coding, 95
    open coding, 95
    selective coding, 95
coding scheme, 95

communication, 1, 19, 22, 24, 25, 27, 30, 32, 45, 58, 87–89, 91, 92, 141, 163, 192, 207, 209, 211, 224, 226, 231, 233, 240, 245
communication and media studies, 19
communicative practices, 3, 49, 56, 130
companionship, 132
comparison group, 233
competences for action, 5, 7, 61, 63–66, 85, 96, 97, 122, 134, 135, 143, 149, 157, 162, 165–167, 173, 177, 208, 209, 212, 224–227, 234–236, 239, 240, 246, 247
computer, 21, 25, 95, 124, 125, 128, 130–133, 140–142, 144, 150, 160, 165, 177, 179, 180, 184, 192, 201, 208–210, 227, 247
computer games/video games
   Jump and Run; Animal Crossing, 125; Mario Kart, 125; Naruto, 125; Super Mario, 125; Super Mario Galaxy, 125
   simulation games, 125
   violent computer games/ego-shooter/battle games; Age of War, 192; Call of Duty 3, 125; Call of Duty 4, 125; Grand Theft Auto(GTA), 130; League of Legends, 130; Skyrim, 217; World of Warcraft, 130
conflict, 139, 175, 215, 220
constructivist theories, 47
consumer society, 2
consumption, 15, 139, 179, 185, 206, 234
contexts of socialisation, 7, 51, 87, 89, 123, 148, 171, 194
contextual in-depth analysis, 96
contextualism, 51, 121, 232
convergence, 3, 7
coping, 7, 54, 56, 58, 66, 77, 97, 134, 135, 161, 163, 165–167, 172, 187, 193, 195, 198, 224, 225, 227, 228, 235–237
counselling, 201
countryside, 116, 196, 199, 206, 221
crisis/crises, 15, 16, 54, 56, 108, 139, 147–149, 176, 195, 216, 218, 219
cross-media, 21, 32
cross-media distribution, 124
cultural studies, 59, 60
cultural values, 15, 31
cyber-bullying, 29, 30
Cyprus, 27, 30
Czech Republic, 14

D

data collection, 5, 77, 81–84, 87, 90, 93, 94, 96, 97, 100, 119, 122, 126, 172, 173, 176, 183, 184, 186, 189
data processing, 22, 93, 94, 98
dedicated social research, 2
Denmark, 15, 17
depression, 30, 114, 141, 143, 182, 184, 185
deprivation, 8, 13, 171, 174, 175, 192, 224, 226, 245
developmental phase, 54
developmental tasks, 4, 51–58, 61, 63, 66, 123, 127, 132–135, 149, 173, 209, 219, 225, 226, 232, 236–238
digitalisation, 7, 19, 22
digital skills, 24, 29
divorce, 8, 109, 112, 134, 207, 210, 237
documentation, 242
doing family, 4, 8, 58, 59, 63, 65, 66, 78, 85, 90, 123, 137, 141, 164,

166, 167, 171, 187, 198, 225, 227, 236, 239, 240, 245
drop-out quota, 82
Dutch, 28
DVD, 191
DVD player, 191
dynamic process, 49, 53
dysfunctional, 165

E
Eastern Europe, 13, 183, 199, 200, 202
eating disorder, 135
ecological model, 47
ecological theory, 47
ecology, 47
economic circumstances, 17
economic development, 15
economic disadvantage, 17
economic migrant(s), 15
education, 4, 12, 18, 20, 22, 24, 25, 27, 31, 53, 54, 57, 58, 62, 85–87, 89, 93, 111, 116, 124, 128, 140, 145, 150, 163, 174, 175, 180, 182, 183, 189, 190, 193, 214, 219, 220, 226, 231, 244–247
educational achievement, 12
educational background, 26
educational institutions, 46, 60, 121
educational level, 26, 239
EFTA, 17, 79
emotional-affective development, 177
empirical data, 56
empirical research, 56
entertainment, 27, 125, 128, 166, 180, 197, 207, 216
Estonia, 23
ethical challenges, 5, 97
ethical guideline, 99
EU-28, 17, 23
EU candidate, 17

EuRegio, 14
Europe, 16, 25, 28, 31
European Union, 14–17, 23, 116, 118
everyday life, 2–5, 14, 45, 48, 50–52, 56, 59–63, 65, 66, 78, 85, 87, 88, 93, 123–125, 130, 133, 135, 138, 149, 157, 161–163, 167, 171, 174, 179, 180, 192, 198, 200, 209, 211, 212, 219, 225, 227, 228, 232, 233, 235, 236, 240, 241, 244–246
expense allowance, 81
expertise, 52, 87
extra-familial socialisation contexts, 123, 138

F
Facebook, 83, 91, 125, 130, 141, 161, 165, 185, 186, 192, 196, 202, 216
family allowance, 15
family climate, 85, 113, 137, 150, 172, 184, 238
family communication, 57, 59, 167
family constellation
    large family, 86, 114, 175, 182, 206, 207
    migration background, 6, 16, 30, 107, 132, 140, 146, 148, 149, 188
    nuclear family, 6, 107, 109, 187, 226
    patchwork family, 6, 107, 111
    single-parent family, 6, 79, 80, 163, 174
family life, 16, 58, 88, 93, 158, 226, 228, 239
family structures, 16, 17, 135, 243
family system, 58
family ties, 210, 220
family types, 97, 173, 174
father

biological father, 107, 111, 114, 116, 117, 175, 189, 194, 195, 197, 214, 218, 223, 224
step father, 167, 213, 214, 216, 217, 219, 223, 233
father role, 213
filter software, 211, 217, 244
final secondary school examination, 112
financial situation, 109–112, 114, 115, 117, 138, 171, 172, 174, 176, 182, 187, 194, 197, 200, 213, 218, 220–222, 225, 237
financial stability, 184, 185, 223
Finland, 17
flat, 86, 90, 93, 111, 113–117, 137, 210
flat screen TV, 215, 224
focused analysis, 96, 122, 157
formal education, 2, 5, 6, 12, 16, 18, 22, 26, 30, 31, 50, 60, 63, 79, 80, 107, 150, 244
foster child, 117, 194
FPÖ, 15
France, 13
friend(s), 7, 12, 13, 21, 50, 56, 77, 88, 89, 91–93, 95, 96, 123, 125, 127, 130, 132, 133, 138–142, 147–149, 177, 181, 183, 186, 192, 194, 196–198, 201, 202, 204, 205, 207, 209–211, 214–216, 218, 219, 221, 222, 224, 225, 227, 238
friendship, 127, 140, 147
frustration, 55, 133

G

game console
  PlayStation (2, 3, 4), 179, 215
  PlayStation Portable (PSP), 179
gender, 52, 63, 126, 128, 134, 149, 238

general qualification for university entrance, 108, 116, 118
German Länder (Federal States), 18
Germany, 3, 11–18, 20–23, 31, 109, 116, 125, 145, 150, 207, 208, 218
gifts, 81
globalisation, 19
government, 24, 81, 149
grandparent(s), 115, 138, 139, 210, 220, 222, 238
Greece, 15

H

habitus, 62, 63
hard-core media content, 126
health, 12, 16, 17, 24, 112–114, 118, 139, 144, 158, 176, 182, 185, 210, 212, 213, 225, 231, 245
home, 7, 25, 27, 30, 45, 108, 109, 111, 113–116, 142–144, 147, 148, 163, 165, 175, 177, 179–182, 185, 190, 191, 193, 196, 198, 207, 210, 218, 224, 226, 246
house, 13, 82, 86, 90, 93, 108–110, 112, 113, 115–118, 166, 176, 177, 180, 188, 194, 199, 207, 208, 214, 220
household, 17, 20, 47, 86, 110, 115, 118, 165, 180
housing benefits, 186, 205
housing conditions, 79, 86, 90
humiliation, 165, 176
Hungary, 23

I

identification, 50, 172
identity, 3, 23, 24, 51–56, 59, 62, 63, 66, 127, 139, 141, 142, 179, 237, 240

identity construction, 49–51
identity management, 127
idol, 126
immigrants, 140, 150, 183, 184, 188, 218
inclusive workshop, 113
income, 2, 5, 6, 12, 13, 15, 17, 18, 24–29, 31, 60, 63, 79–81, 86, 107–110, 112–118, 138, 166, 206, 207, 211, 213, 214, 216, 220, 237, 239
income gap, 15, 18
independence, 55, 57, 129, 187, 204, 205, 208, 210, 214, 218, 219, 226
individualisation, 19
individuality, 57
inequality gap, 1, 11, 15, 16
Information and Communication Technologies (ICT), 22, 23, 28, 150
information management, 127
information society, 19
infrastructure, 24, 28, 31, 79, 108, 174, 183, 237
insecurity, 185
Instagram, 130, 185, 191, 192, 202
integrative approach, 32, 46, 121, 232
internet access, 28, 31, 124, 192
internet risks
    conduct-related risks, 23
    contact-related risks, 23
    content-related risks, 23
    health-related risks, 24
    lack of internet safety in general, 24
intersubjective traceability, 241
intersubjectivity, 5
intervention, 98, 110, 190, 191, 243
isolation, 2, 17, 108
IT(s), 112, 114, 131, 143
Italy, 15, 28

J
JIM, 20, 23
job training, 49, 51, 56, 110, 111, 114, 115, 174, 177, 180, 184, 189, 190, 194, 195, 198, 210, 214, 216–218, 221, 223

K
KIM, 20–22, 125
kindergarten, 4, 7, 49, 51, 56, 66, 79, 81, 82, 85, 86, 88, 89, 108, 123, 126, 138, 140, 142, 159, 161, 191, 192, 218, 220, 233, 239, 245, 246

L
labour market, 12, 15, 31, 60, 237
laptop, 201
lebenswelt, 61, 234
leisure opportunities, 12, 145
leisure time, 29, 45, 55, 131, 142, 145, 161, 178, 179, 191, 195, 211–215, 217, 218, 221
Let's play-videos, 128
life prospects, 12
life satisfaction, 12
life span, 47, 49
lifestyle, 238
life tasks, 52, 58, 61, 173, 175, 237, 238
lifeworld, 3, 29, 32, 60, 61, 64, 131, 174, 234, 236
literacy, 28, 30, 50
literary transcription, 95
literature review, 4, 27, 31, 80, 234
living conditions, 2, 12, 13, 29, 80, 84, 86–88, 231, 246
Lombardy, 28
longitudinal design, 79

long-term research, 82
loss, 186, 201, 214
Luxembourg, 15
luxury, 206

M
macro-level, 77, 237
Malta, 23
marginalisation, 1, 12, 17
masculinity, 213
mass communication, 24
material deprivation, 11–13, 17
material world, 52
maternity leave, 112, 237
matrix/matrices, 96, 122, 173, 242
maturationist theory, 47
media activities, 45
media application, 5, 127, 130
media-based practices, 49, 58
media behaviour, 89, 91, 92
media brand(s), 21
media content, 7, 20, 45, 46, 125, 126, 133, 134, 149, 158, 179, 193, 201, 203, 217, 221, 222
media device, 192, 196, 202
media environment, 6, 20, 22, 123, 239
media expertise, 89
media hardware, 90
media literacy, 7, 157, 159, 161, 180, 181, 195, 217, 228
media processing, 89
media repertoire(s), 6, 7, 21, 32, 87–89, 92, 100, 123–125, 128, 148, 160, 171, 233, 235
media service(s), 20, 21, 32, 92, 96, 125, 128, 130, 134, 141, 149, 150, 232–235, 238, 240, 241, 244
mediation, 3, 7, 19, 24, 26, 85, 87, 89, 149, 157–159, 161, 162, 164–168, 171, 179, 181, 184, 186, 191, 199, 203, 204, 209, 212, 217, 222, 226–228, 244, 245
mediation practices
 amicability, 7, 162, 166, 204, 206
 arbitrary control and exploitation of dominance, 7, 162, 164, 181, 197
 child-centred, 162, 166, 227
 laissez-faire, 7, 162, 164, 191, 198, 206, 208, 217, 227
 unmethodological restriction, 7, 162, 181, 183, 184
mediation strategies
 active mediation, 26, 158
 coviewing/co-use, 158
 restrictive mediation, 26, 158, 159
mediatised socialisation, 3, 51, 123
mediatization, 1–4, 11, 19, 20, 22, 23, 31, 32, 45, 46, 50, 158, 234
media usage, 7, 12, 20, 21, 23, 26, 32, 59, 77, 78, 83, 85, 87–89, 92, 96, 123, 126, 134–137, 149, 157–159, 161, 162, 164, 166, 180, 181, 185, 186, 207, 214–217, 224, 227, 234–236, 238, 241, 245, 246
meso-level, 77, 238
messenger(s)
 Facebook messenger, 125, 165, 186
 MSN, 141
meta process, 1, 19
methodological approach, 5, 8, 32, 77, 78, 81, 239, 240
methods, 5, 66, 83–85, 90, 91, 94, 96, 99, 100, 123
micro-level, 77, 238
mid childhood, 24
migrant, 16, 79, 80, 116, 140, 183, 184
milieu, 62, 233, 237
Millennium Development Goals, 14
mobile phone(s), 128, 168, 179

movies
  Jungle Book, 201
  Spiderman, 201

N
national research, 30
neighbourhood, 47, 58, 79, 86, 108, 110, 111, 140, 146, 161, 183, 188, 197, 212, 214, 218
The Netherlands, 30
network map, 177, 178, 190, 204, 208, 213, 215, 222, 223, 228
news, 192, 193, 202
Norway, 14, 17, 30

O
objective factors, 4, 49
observation protocol, 90
OECD, 1, 16
Ofcom, 20, 122, 126, 128–130
online-banking, 204
online computer games, 124
online-dating platform, 202
open coding, 95
options for action, 7, 64–66, 85, 96, 97, 122, 134, 149, 161, 162, 165–167, 173, 224–227, 235, 236, 239, 240
orientation, 29, 50, 56, 59, 62, 65, 66, 81, 118, 124, 126, 133, 141, 142, 148, 195, 222, 228, 233, 234, 236
outlines for action, 7, 63–66, 85, 96, 97, 122, 134, 135, 149, 157, 161, 162, 164–167, 173, 224–227, 235, 236, 239
overextension, 187, 188, 225, 226, 228
overwhelmed, 135, 174, 182, 187, 192, 193, 224, 245

P
panel, 5–7, 32, 56, 77, 79, 81, 82, 95, 96, 99, 107, 112, 115, 121, 122, 124, 127–130, 133, 141, 142, 145, 147, 157, 160, 166, 171, 179, 191, 204, 221, 222, 233, 242, 243, 246
panel maintenance, 100
parental media guidance, 134
parent-child relationship, 57, 167
parentification, 135
parenting, 7, 28, 57, 150, 157, 159, 162, 165, 167, 173, 175, 181, 188, 192, 193, 199, 203, 209, 212, 217, 218, 222, 225–228
parenting practices, 157
parenting style, 181, 192, 203
participation, 1–4, 12, 13, 16, 19, 24, 25, 30, 31, 81, 87, 88, 144, 145, 207, 231
participation divide, 25, 158
participation gap, 25
participatory observation, 90
paternity leave, 221
pay television
  Sky, 128
  Sky Go, 128
peer-group, 56, 86, 161
peers, 4, 12, 21, 24, 46, 49–52, 55, 58, 59, 66, 77, 88, 89, 93, 95, 96, 116, 121, 123, 130, 132, 133, 139–141, 149, 183, 215, 221, 225, 238
person of reference, 197, 209, 219
pet(s), 90, 95, 203, 217
pew report, 21
physical health, 12
pocket money, 86, 110, 138
politics, 63, 123, 146, 149, 183, 193
popular culture, 50
pornography, 126, 217
Portugal, 27

poverty, 1, 2, 8, 11–14, 16–19, 23, 29–31, 79, 80, 109–111, 113, 115, 118, 145, 228
praxeological approach, 51, 59, 60, 66, 77
preschool, 123
primary school, 81, 177, 222
print media
   magazine, 128, 141, 180, 202
   newspaper, 32, 81, 128, 129, 180; tabloid, 129
privacy setting(s), 28, 91, 202, 211
private bankruptcy, 114
private sphere, 63, 197
private television channel(s), 124
professional re-training, 110
psychiatric clinic, 177
psychodynamic theories, 47
psychologically impaired, 176, 177
psychological problems, 110, 144, 184, 210
psychological wellbeing, 113
psycho-social development, 46, 51, 121
puberty, 53, 85, 129, 138, 165, 211, 219
public discourse, 12, 126
public transport, 79, 109, 182
purposeful sampling, 79
push-services, 192

Q
qualitative data analysis software (MAXQDA), 95, 96
qualitative longitudinal study, 5, 99
qualitative long-term study, 32, 97, 99
qualitative research paradigm, 78
qualitative types, 171

R
radio, 32, 141, 159, 192, 216
real estate, 117, 138, 187, 194, 206
recruitment, 5, 79, 81, 111
refugee crisis, 15, 16, 147–149, 195, 216, 218
refugees, 15, 31, 147, 148, 182, 193, 197
relationship management, 127
resilience, 144, 194, 206, 226
resources, 2–4, 12–14, 16, 26, 28, 50, 55, 57, 61, 64, 80, 81, 85, 96, 97, 99, 139, 146, 158, 160, 162, 164, 166, 167, 171, 182, 183, 207, 212, 220, 225–227, 234–236, 238
rich country, 11, 231
rich design, 5, 83, 84, 99, 237
role model, 136, 209
role of media, 1, 11, 27, 31, 46, 51, 59, 65, 66, 77, 89, 98, 123, 127, 231, 232
role-playing questions
   100 Euro-question/500 Euro-question, 89
   island question, 89
romantic partners, 56, 66, 123, 149
romantic relationship(s), 55, 59, 139, 142, 225, 238
room, 88, 92, 93, 131, 137, 150, 165, 176, 179, 180, 199, 215, 224
rural, 28, 79, 81, 108, 110, 174, 176
Russia, 27–29

S
school, 4, 8, 13, 14, 28, 45, 51, 56, 79, 81, 85, 86, 88, 89, 93, 96, 108–110, 113–116, 123, 124, 126, 133, 138, 140–143, 148, 160, 163, 165, 175, 177, 179,

183, 186, 189–194, 196, 201, 202, 204, 205, 207, 214–220, 238, 245–247
secondary medium, 128
secondary school, 109, 112, 116–118, 190, 201, 219, 222
second level digital divide, 158
selection criteria, 6, 79
selective coding, 95
self-efficacy, 132, 143, 179, 216
self-esteem, 143, 176, 179, 183, 212, 216
selfie, 192
self-perception, 140
self-presentation, 50
sensitive data, 6
separation, 111, 187, 195, 196, 223
sexual abuse, 185
siblings, 81, 87, 89, 90, 107, 112, 123, 135–137, 140, 148, 150, 175, 182, 183, 188, 189, 191, 194, 199, 205–207, 218, 235, 237, 238
simulation, 125
Sky, 128
Sky Go, 128
Skype, 141
smartphone(s), 21–23, 25, 29, 124, 127, 128, 138, 160, 192, 195, 196, 202, 209, 215, 216, 219, 221, 222, 224, 244
smoking, 90, 215
Snapchat, 130, 192, 196, 202
social climber, 211, 227
social desirability, 159, 180
social disadvantage, 1–3, 11–14, 16, 19, 22, 23, 25, 30, 31, 79, 80, 157, 172, 201, 221, 231, 239, 244
social exclusion, 16, 186
social fields, 61
social housing, 15
social inclusion, 14, 27, 91

social inequality, 2, 3, 16, 27, 60, 79, 121, 158, 239, 247
socialisation, 1–6, 8, 11, 15, 24, 26, 27, 32, 45–51, 53, 56–60, 62–66, 77–79, 85, 98, 121, 123, 134, 135, 138, 145, 146, 149, 157, 167, 171, 173, 174, 181, 193, 204, 227, 228, 231–239, 241, 245
socialisation context(s), 4, 7, 56, 134, 142, 181, 192, 193, 203, 217, 232, 237
socially disadvantaged, 1–4, 11, 13, 16, 20–27, 31, 32, 55, 66, 77, 79–81, 98, 122, 158, 159, 231–233, 236, 241, 242, 244, 248
Social Media, 5, 91, 127, 129, 130, 148, 160, 161, 185, 186, 191, 196, 202, 207, 211, 216, 219
social milieu, 5, 62–64, 66, 234–237, 239
Social Networking Sites
    Facebook, 91, 125, 130, 196, 202, 216
    Instagram, 130, 185, 192, 202
    Snapchat, 130
    WhatsApp, 83, 91, 92, 128, 130, 166, 186, 197
    YouTube, 91, 125, 128, 129, 148, 192, 202
social order, 48, 63
social place, 46
social practices, 49, 247
social sphere, 63
social welfare, 15, 31, 108, 110–112, 114, 116, 182, 188, 192, 205
society, 1–4, 7, 11–13, 16, 19, 20, 26, 31, 32, 46, 48, 49, 52, 54, 55, 59, 60, 62, 64, 77, 87, 88, 123, 127, 129, 146, 149, 158, 231, 235, 239, 248
socio-economic, 2, 3, 6, 7, 16, 25, 26, 28, 29, 31, 32, 59, 60, 86, 97,

107, 111, 113, 116, 118, 122, 123, 139, 141, 143–146, 159, 163, 167, 172, 174, 184–187, 196, 198, 205, 208, 209, 211, 223–227, 236, 240, 245, 247
socio-emotional, 3, 6, 7, 16, 26, 32, 97, 130, 137, 141, 158, 163, 167, 172, 185, 187, 188, 196, 198, 199, 209, 211, 220, 223, 225–227, 237, 240, 245, 248
socio-structural, 5, 26, 46, 53, 57, 59, 64–66, 78, 167, 235–239
South America, 13, 28
Southern Europe, 27
Spain, 15
sport events, 216
sports, 12, 123, 144–146, 149, 192, 221
sports activities, 144, 146
sports clubs, 123, 144–146, 149, 221
stakeholder(s), 8, 24, 245
State of Bavaria, 14
State of Salzburg, 14
study grant, 15
subjective factors, 49
subjective sense, 32, 60
subordination, 177
success, 52, 116, 129, 147, 176
suicide, 184
supervised living facility, 110, 112, 113, 184, 185, 189, 191, 193, 200
survey, 4, 13, 21, 80, 82, 90, 123–125, 133, 137–142, 145–147, 150, 160, 233, 239, 240, 243, 244
Sweden, 13, 15
Switzerland, 15
symbolic world, 52

T
tablet, 29, 124
technological innovation, 19
television, 21, 25, 32, 124–126, 128, 134, 141, 159, 160, 162–165, 179, 180, 192, 193, 196, 197, 201, 206, 210, 216, 219, 221–223, 246
television series
  cartoon/anime series, 125, 126; Benjamin Blümchen, 125; Bibi Blocksberg, 125; Disney's Adventures of the Gummi Bears, 141; Dragonball (Z), 125; Herkules, 125; Kim Possible, 125; Lilo and Stitch, 140; One Piece, 125; Pokémon, 125, 133, 179; Pumba Bear, 140; Spongebob, 125; Superman, 126; Tarzan, 125; Tom and Jerry, 125; Yu-Gi-Oh!, 125
  crime series, 126, 201, 216
  daily soaps, 125, 126
  Reality TV & casting shows, 126; Deutschland sucht den Superstar (DSDS), 126; Shopping Queen, 206
  sitcom, 201; Charmed, 125; Hannah Montana, 125, 185, 201; How I met your mother, 126; Sabrina, 125; Scrubs, 126; Sex and the City, 206; Two and a half men, 126
trash TV, 196
thinking aloud, 6, 83, 91, 240
third digital divide, 158
training programme, 114, 116
transcription, 6, 93, 95, 242

transparency, 243
Trentino, 28
triangulation, 5, 84, 98, 99, 237, 242
Turkey, 28, 29
tutoring (professional), 143
typology, 7, 8, 171–173, 224, 227, 228, 240

U

uncle(s), 138, 139, 195, 222, 238
unemployment, 16, 18, 58, 79, 80, 86, 93, 117, 158, 161, 174, 237
unemployment benefits, 15
unemployment rates, 15, 16, 23, 31
UNICEF, 1, 12, 14–18, 23, 247
United Kingdom (UK), 15, 20, 25
United Nations (UN), 14
United States of America (USA), 20, 29
Upper Austria, 20, 22, 81
urban, 24, 79, 81

V

values, 3, 48, 55, 61, 87, 89, 203
video games, 124, 128, 131, 132, 165, 179, 180, 183, 191, 198, 203, 210, 211, 214–216, 224
video platform

Burning Series, 128
kinox.to, 128
Naruto-Tube, 128
Sky Go, 128
YouTube, 91, 125, 128, 129, 192, 202
violence, 98, 144, 164, 165, 175–177, 179, 181, 188, 216, 217

W

wage, 2, 80
welfare state, 15
well-being, 12, 18, 22, 136
Western societies, 3, 4, 11, 13, 16, 31, 45, 53, 55
WhatsApp, 83, 91, 92, 128, 130, 166, 186, 191, 197
Wikipedia, 127
working poor, 15

Y

youth, 16, 20, 24, 25, 29, 45, 46, 54, 81, 82, 85, 127, 159, 215, 217, 238, 244, 246, 247
YouTube, 91, 125, 128, 129, 148–150, 191, 202
YouTuber, 129

The manufacturer's authorised representative in the EU is Springer Nature Customer Service Centre GmbH, Europaplatz 3, 69115 Heidelberg, Germany. If you have any concerns regarding our products, please contact ProductSafety@springernature.com

Printed and bound by CPI Group (UK) Ltd, Croydon, CR0 4YY

23/03/2026

02076663-0010